"'R. C. Sproul,' someone said to me in the 1970s, 'is the finest communicator in the Reformed world.' Now, three decades later, his skills honed by long practice, his understanding deepened by years of prayer, meditation, and testing (as Martin Luther counseled), R. C. shares the fruit of what has become perhaps his greatest love: feeding and nourishing his own congregation at St. Andrew's from the Word of God and building them up in faith and fellowship and in Christian living and serving. The St. Andrew's Expositional Commentary will be welcomed throughout the world. It promises to have all R. C.'s hallmarks: clarity and liveliness, humor and pathos, always expressed in application to the mind, will, and affections. R. C.'s ability to focus on 'the big picture,' his genius of never saying too much, leaving his hearers satisfied yet wanting more, never making the Word dull, are all present in these expositions. They are his gift to the wider church. May they nourish God's people well and serve as models of the kind of ministry for which we continue to hunger."

—**Sinclair B. Ferguson**, Senior Minister,
First Presbyterian Church, Columbia, South Carolina

"R. C. Sproul, well known as a master theologian and extraordinary communicator, now shows that he is a powerful, insightful, helpful expository preacher. This collection of sermons is of great value for churches and Christians everywhere."

—**W. Robert Godfrey**, President, Westminster Seminary California

"I tell my students again and again, 'You need to buy good commentaries and do so with some discernment.' Among them there must be preacher's commentaries, for not all commentaries are the same. Some may tell you what the text means but provide little help in answering the question, 'How do I preach this text?' R. C. Sproul is a legend in our time. His preaching has held us in awe for half a century, and these pages represent the fruit of his latest exposition, coming as they do at the very peak of his abilities and insights. I am ecstatic at the prospect of reading the St. Andrew's Expositional Commentary series. It represents Reformed theology on fire, delivered from a pastor's heart in a vibrant congregation of our time. Essential reading."

—**Derek W. H. Thomas**,
John E. Richards Professor of Systematic and Practical Theology,
Reformed Theological Seminary;
Minister of Teaching, First Presbyterian Church, Jackson, Mississippi

"R.C. Sproul is the premier theologian of our day, an extraordinary instrument in the hand of the Lord. Possessed with penetrating insight into the text of Scripture, Dr. Sproul is a gifted expositor and world-class teacher, endowed with a strategic grasp and command of the inspired Word. Since stepping into the pulpit of St. Andrew's and committing himself to the weekly discipline of biblical exposition, this noted preacher has demonstrated a rare ability to explicate and apply God's Word. I wholeheartedly recommend the St. Andrew's Expositional Commentary to all who long to know the truth better and experience it more deeply in a life-changing fashion. Here is an indispensable tool for digging deeper into God's Word. This is a must-read for every Christian."

—**Steven J. Lawson**, Senior Pastor, Christ Fellowship Baptist Church, Mobile, Alabama

"How exciting! Thousands of us have long been indebted to R. C. Sproul the teacher, and now, through the St. Andrew's Expositional Commentary, we are indebted to Sproul the preacher, whose sermons are thoroughly biblical, soundly doctrinal, warmly practical, and wonderfully readable. Sproul masterfully presents us with the 'big picture' of each pericope in a dignified yet conversational style that accentuates the glory of God and meets the real needs of sinful people like us. This series of volumes is an absolute must for every Reformed preacher and church member who yearns to grow in the grace and knowledge of Christ Jesus. I predict that Sproul's pulpit ministry in written form will do for Christians in the twenty-first century what Martyn Lloyd-Jones's sermonic commentaries did for us last century. *Tolle lege,* and buy these volumes for your friends."

—**Joel R. Beeke**, President, Puritan Reformed Theological Seminary

ST. ANDREW'S EXPOSITIONAL COMMENTARY

1–2 PETER

1–2 Peter
Copyright © 2011 by R. C. Sproul
Published by Crossway
      1300 Crescent Street
      Wheaton, Illinois 60187

Cover design:
Cover illustration:
Typesetting: Lakeside Design Plus
First printing 2011
Printed in the United States of America

Scripture quotations are taken from *The New King James Version*. Copyright © 1982, Thomas Nelson, Inc. Used by permission.

Hardcover ISBN:	978-1-4335-2289-5
PDF ISBN:	978-1-4335-2290-1
Mobipocket ISBN:	978-1-4335-2291-8
ePub ISBN:	978-1-4335-2292-5

Library of Congress Cataloging-in-Publication Data
Sproul, R. C. (Robert Charles), 1939–
    1–2 Peter / R. C. Sproul.
        p. cm.—(St. Andrew's expositional commentary)
    ISBN 978-1-4335-2289-5 (hc)
    1. Bible. N.T. Peter—Sermons. 2. Bible. N.T. Peter—Commentaries. 3. Sermons, American—20th century. I. Title.
BS2795.54.S67 2011
227'.92077—dc22

                                                          2010036243

Crossway is a publishing ministry of Good News Publishers.

SH		22	21	20	19	18	17	16	15	14	13		12	11
14	13	12	11	10	9	8	7	6	5	4	3	2	1	

To the Ligonier Ministry board members:
Faithful witnesses in Christ's kingdom and godly support to me.

CONTENTS

I knew that I was responsible as a preacher to clearly explain God's Word *and* to show how we ought to live in light of it. I sought to fulfill both tasks as I ascended the St. Andrew's pulpit each week.

What you hold in your hand, then, is a written record of my preaching labors amidst my beloved Sanford congregation. The dear saints who sit under my preaching encouraged me to give my sermons a broader hearing. To that end, the chapters that follow were adapted from a sermon series I preached at St. Andrew's.

Please be aware that this book is part of a broader series of books containing adaptations of my St. Andrew's sermons. The title of this series is *St. Andrew's Expositional Commentary*. As you can see, this is more than a convenient title—it is a description. This book, like all the others in the series, will not give you the fullest possible insight into each and every verse in this biblical book. Though I sought to at least touch on each verse, I focused on the key themes and ideas that comprised the "big picture" of each passage I covered. Therefore, I urge you to use this book as an overview and introduction, but if you desire to enhance your knowledge of this book of Scripture, you should turn to one or more of the many excellent exegetical commentaries (see my recommendations in the back).

I pray that you will be as blessed in reading this material as I was in preaching it.

R. C. Sproul
Lake Mary, Florida
April 2009

PREFACE

Imagine what it would be like to receive a letter from someone who was a personal friend of Jesus' during his earthly ministry. Beyond that, imagine receiving two letters from such a person. That's exactly what we have in the New Testament correspondence known as 1 and 2 Peter. Peter is known as a thundering paradox of a man. On the one hand he is known for his impetuosity, for his vacillating between faith and doubt, for his treachery of public denial of Jesus at the time of Jesus' greatest peril. On the other hand he is known for his magnificent confession of faith at Caesarea Philippi where, without hesitation, he declared his confidence that Jesus was the Christ, the Son of the living God.

He is known also for his heroic acts of sacrifice and of suffering for the faith after the ascension of Jesus, even to the point of his martyrdom in Rome. When Peter writes to the church about faith and trust in the providence of God in the midst of suffering, he is speaking not in abstract terms but from the vantage point of one who has been called personally to endure such sufferings himself. He is one who testifies beyond speculation, as one who was an eyewitness, testifying not to cleverly devised myths or fables but to what he had seen with his eyes and heard with his ears. This is the testimony of a man who not only was part of the entourage of Jesus during his earthly ministry but was an eyewitness of the resurrection and part of the inner circle of disciples in the great triad of Peter, James, and John. These three were present on the Mount of Transfiguration and were able to see with their own eyes the glory of the transfigured Christ.

A letter from a man such as this is a treasure for the church. His letter, beyond the value of his own eyewitness testimony and his intimate friendship with Jesus, carries with it the weight of the divine inspiration of God the Holy Spirit. What Peter says to the church is merely an extension of what his Lord and Master, Christ, says to the church, so that we receive his apostolic testimony as from the Lord Himself. It is an enormous privilege and blessing for us to take the time to consider line upon line and percept upon percept the teaching set forth in these two majestic epistles, 1 and 2 Peter. I commend to the reader a careful and devout reading of these letters.

R. C. Sproul
Orlando, 2010

1 PETER

native language of Peter's. Even though he had no formal schooling under Gamaliel, Hillel, or any rabbi in Jerusalem, he was certainly not unintelligent, and he was articulate, as we see in the record of his speeches, particularly on the day of Pentecost. The role of Silvanus in the production of this letter was, in all probability, that of an amanuensis or secretary. The Apostle Paul customarily had a secretary to whom he dictated the substance of his message. We do not know what language he used to dictate it, but it was inscribed by the amanuensis in Greek. If Silvanus was Silas, he would have been capable of writing at a high level of the Greek language, and if he wrote the epistle under the supervision and even the dictation of the Apostle Peter, that would account for the eloquence of the Greek without denying Petrine authorship.

The final greetings of 1 Peter 5 were written from Babylon, which was biblical code in that day for Rome or Jerusalem, in this case almost certainly Rome, and the one giving greetings along with Silvanus is Mark. Mark was not an Apostle. He was part of the apostolic entourage. He had traveled with Paul on a missionary journey but was sent home following a dispute between Paul and Barnabas. We know from church history that John Mark became Peter's spokesman, and the apostolic authority that stands behind the Gospel of Mark is the authority of the Apostle Peter. So, the fact that Mark sends greetings here in this epistle is further evidence that the book was authored by Mark's principal mentor, the Apostle Peter.

To the best of our knowledge, the imperial persecutions against Christianity did not reach the outer parts of the Empire until late in the first century and early into the second century, long after Peter was martyred by being crucified upside down in Rome. However, local persecutions were constant in every decade and in every place, such as Paul suffered while on his missionary journeys in Asia Minor. People converted to Christianity in those areas constantly faced local hostility and persecution, which were keenly felt, even though not delivered by the sword of Rome.

As we noted, this epistle matches marvelously with the content of some of Paul's epistles, even though at one point Paul had opposed Peter over an issue concerning the Judaizers. That debate had been so significant that the Council of Jerusalem was called to settle the problem. The Apostle Paul had rebuked Peter publicly for falling away from the purity of the gospel by being seduced by the Judaizing heretics, but the issue was resolved long before the middle of the sixties. There is no reason to think that any ongoing dispute in perspective continued between Peter and Paul. Although Paul and Peter were separate men and had separate emphases in their ministries, they both wrote under the inspiration of the Holy Spirit, and the message they communicated was the same gospel, the same ethic, the same truth. Therefore, to see striking similarities in their teaching content is exactly what we would expect from men writing under the inspiration of the Holy Spirit.

Recipients of 1 Peter

Concerning the issue of the epistle being written to a Gentile audience, we can assume that Peter was not writing to Gentiles but to Jewish converts numbered among the Diaspora. Those were Jews who had fled from Jerusalem, expelled under the Emperor Claudius, and they had settled in little communities in Asia Minor. On Paul's missionary journeys he went to the synagogue in places such as Ephesus or the Galatian territories. Often the first converts were from the Jewish community. These Jewish Christians, members of the Diaspora, are addressed here as pilgrims or sojourners, a common label for Jews expelled from Israel, from the holy city, and living in a pagan environment that was not their sacred heritage. Jewish Christians living in a pagan community were pilgrims and sojourners in a foreign land. Therefore, the fact that this letter is addressed "to the pilgrims of the Dispersion in Pontus, Galatia, Cappadocia, Asia, and Bithynia" does not necessarily mean that it was addressed to Gentile converts in Asia Minor.

My wife, Vesta, and I were traveling from Hungary into Romania right after the breakup of the Soviet Union. We were warned about the great dangers of going across the border, as the border guards tended to be overtly hostile toward Americans. We were riding in an old train from Budapest to Cluj-Napoca in Romania, and we came to the border between Hungary and Romania. Two burly border guards got on the train where there were four of us: Vesta, me, and another couple. In gruff and broken English, the guard told us to empty our suitcases. Just as we were about to follow his command, their leader looked at our friend, who had her Bible in a brown paper bag on her lap. He grabbed the Bible from the bag and said in broken English, "You no Americans." We had our passports that identified us as Americans, but he questioned us about our citizenship. He pointed his finger at the Bible text and said, "Look what it say." *We are pilgrims and citizens of heaven.* He was a Christian. He turned to the other guards and said, "These people okay. Leave them alone." We made it through the checkpoint, but we experienced what it means to be pilgrims, sojourners, in a foreign land yet members of the kingdom of God and citizens of heaven.

The Gnostic Heresy

Finally, there is the argument that 1 Peter was written in the second century under the impetus of the Gnostic heresy. Although the concepts of Gnosticism are not found in the letter, the fact that it was written in the second century and named Peter as its author were grounds to consider that it was originally composed by one of the Gnostic heretics. We have seen products of ancient Gnosticism in recent years such as *The Da Vinci Code*, which features an ossuary that supposedly contains the bones of Jesus. Scholars appeal to the *Gospel of Peter*, the *Gospel of Thomas*, and the *Gospel of Judas*, claiming these as extrabiblical proof of gnostic teachings.

The Gnostics took a variety of religions and philosophies and sought to blend them to produce a new religion or philosophy. There was Oriental dualism, Platonism, and elements of Neoplatonism, and they tried to bring in elements of Christianity. In their zeal to win converts, they targeted the early Christian community. The word *gnostic* comes from the Greek word *gnosis*, which is Greek for "knowledge." When you get sick and go to the doctor, you are seeking a *diagnosis*. When the doctor explains that you will recover from the illness, he is giving you a *prognosis*. Prognosticators are those who think that they have knowledge of future events. The term *Gnosticism* is rooted in the Greek word for knowledge. Gnostics believed that truth was not discovered by reason, sense perception, or scientific inquiry, but only through direct mystical apprehension, and then only by an elite few.

The only way the Gnostics could seduce Christians to believe their heresy was to undermine the authority of the Apostles, so they suggested that the Apostles lacked the higher knowledge that only Gnostic practitioners could achieve. Many books have been written in the last several years about neo-Gnosticism, or New Age thinking, but there is nothing new about it.

Their strategy to undermine apostolic authority was somewhat ironic. They wrote their fanciful literature and tried to pass it off as apostolic by giving it titles such as the *Gospel of Thomas*, the *Gospel of Peter*, and the *Gospel of Judas*, but this literature denied the content of apostolic Christianity. This is why some critics say that, if 1 Peter was written later, Peter's name was attached to it as a Gnostic ploy to undermine the actual New Testament canon.

I have no doubt that this letter was written by the Apostle Peter, one of the most fascinating characters of the New Testament. Peter the impetuous; Peter the bold; the one at Caesarea Philippi who made the great confession, "You are the Christ, the Son of the living God" (Matt. 16:16); the big fisherman who gave his life being a fisher for men; the one who paradoxically refused to acquiesce to Jesus' teaching immediately after the Caesarea Philippi confession, saying, "This shall not happen to You!" (v. 22). In a matter of minutes, Peter went from being the rock to being the spokesman of Satan; from the blessing that Jesus gave him, saying, "Blessed are you, Simon Bar-Jonah, for flesh and blood has not revealed this to you, but My Father who is in heaven" (v. 17) to a dreadful rebuke from the lips of Jesus (v. 23). This is the same Peter who said he would follow Jesus to the death, and when Jesus told him that he would deny Him three times, Peter protested with all his might, only to prove Jesus' prophecy accurately. This was the one who vacillated but nevertheless, over the course of the early church history, did become the rock, a leader who remained faithful to Jesus until his death.

It is ironic that Peter writes to those suffering persecution and tells them, as we will see, that they ought not to think it strange that they should have to suffer. He once had thought it impossible that this would be the course of Christianity, but as the years passed, he understood what Jesus had said about the cost of discipleship. Peter's intimate knowledge of persecution for the gospel comes across with a pastor's heart in this epistle.

Sprinkling of the Blood
Elect according to the foreknowledge of God the Father, in sanctification of the Spirit, for obedience and sprinkling of the blood of Jesus Christ (v. 2). We do not have to wait to get to the doctrine of election; it is at the beginning of the epistle. He reminds his readers that, even though they are pilgrims and exposed to suffering, pain, and persecution, they ought not to forget who they are. They are the elect by the providence and eternal appointment of God.

When we talk about the work of redemption, we talk about it as a triune activity. There is the Father's work in election and His sovereign plan to save His people. That redemption is accomplished by Christ and applied to people's lives by the Holy Spirit. The Father sends the Son, the Son accomplishes the work, and that work is brought home to the lives of individuals through the intervention and the power of the Holy Spirit. When the Holy Spirit brings us to faith in Christ, He does not stop with the initial work of regeneration or rebirth; He is also the chief architect of our sanctification, of our being brought into conformity to Christ. All that is contained in this verse of introduction.

Peter uses an interesting image in verse 2 to speak of the work that Christ has accomplished for us: the sprinkling of His blood. We see in the New Testament that we are purchased by the blood of Christ and that Christ's blood has been poured out, but the *sprinkling* of Christ's blood is clearly a reference to the Old Testament. On the Day of Atonement, when reconciliation was made for the people of God, the blood of slain animals was taken by the high priest into the Holy of Holies and sprinkled on the mercy seat. That sprinkling of the blood of the sacrifices served as a blood covering on the throne of God. It was a symbol of the covering of our sins by the blood of the sacrifice. All the symbolism carried out on the Day of Atonement pointed beyond the Old Testament to the sacrifice that was made once for all in the atoning death of Jesus Christ, who effects our reconciliation by shedding His blood. When Jesus was on the cross, His blood was not sprinkled but poured out, yet the same principle is in view here. What took place on the Day of Atonement in the Old Testament points to the accomplishment of our redemption by Jesus with the pouring out of His blood on the cross.

Grace to you and peace be multiplied (v. 2). "Grace and peace" was the usual greeting, and here Peter is asking that such grace and peace be multiplied to his readers, elect, sanctified, and reconciled by the grace of God, and who therefore have peace with God as a result of that reconciliation won for them by Jesus Christ. Peter is asking that this grace and peace would be multiplied—not just multiplied to other people, but in them—as the Apostle Paul said in Romans, from life to life, faith to faith, and grace to grace. We do not believe that the grace of justification can be augmented or diminished, but the grace of sanctification can be augmented or diminished, so the prayer of this Apostle with the heart of a pastor is that the grace of God would increase and multiply in their lives.

It is important to know, before we get to the body of the epistle, the heart's desire of the author, the Apostle Peter, the one chosen by Christ to be an Apostle, who now bears witness to the ministry of Jesus in this epistle.

2

HEAVENLY INHERITANCE, PART 1

1 Peter 1:3–5

Blessed be the God and Father of our Lord Jesus Christ, who according to His abundant mercy has begotten us again to a living hope through the resurrection of Jesus Christ from the dead, to an inheritance incorruptible and undefiled and that does not fade away, reserved in heaven for you, who are kept by the power of God through faith for salvation ready to be revealed in the last time.

During the first lecture I attended in the Netherlands at the Free University of Amsterdam, Professor G. C. Berkouwer made a comment that I have never forgotten: "Gentlemen, all sound theology must begin and end with doxology." When theology does not begin and end with doxology, it becomes merely an abstract intellectual exercise in which the heart is not engaged and the soul is not properly moved. The Apostle Paul, in the middle of his teaching of the weightiest theological matters, breaks spontaneously into doxology: "Oh, the depth of the riches both of the wisdom and knowledge of God! How unsearchable are His judgments and His ways past finding out!" (Rom. 11:33).

of God and the universal brotherhood of man. In biblical categories God, naturally speaking, is the Father of One. He is the Father of the Son, the only begotten Son.

Christ is the Son of God by nature. Scripture tells us that by nature we are children of wrath, children of Satan, so we must never take for granted the privilege of speaking of God as "Father." In the first instance He is the Father only of Christ and, by extension, of us only when we are adopted into His family. We are not by nature the children of God. Jesus is by nature the child of God; we are by super nature the children of God.

The object of the benediction and of the doxology is the first person of the Trinity, who is called "the God and Father of our Lord Jesus Christ." There is supreme irony in Peter's saying that God is "the God and Father of our Lord Jesus Christ." The title "Lord," the Greek word *kyrios*, is the translation of the Old Testament title *Adonai*, which was reserved for God alone. It is the supreme title of God that calls attention to His sovereignty. Elsewhere Paul writes:

> Let this mind be in you which was also in Christ Jesus, who, being in the form of God, did not consider it robbery to be equal with God, but made Himself of no reputation, taking the form of a bondservant, and coming in the likeness of men. And being found in appearance as a man, He humbled Himself and became obedient to the point of death, even the death of the cross. Therefore God also has highly exalted Him and given Him the name which is above every name. (Phil. 2:5–9)

The name above every name in that text is not "Jesus." People often jump to that conclusion because the next name mentioned is the name of Jesus, but when the Father bestows the name that is above every name upon Jesus, the name He bestows is "Lord." He bestows upon Jesus this title, that at the name of Jesus every knee would bow.

The bowing of the knee means to the Jew not just submission to an earthly king but an act of worship. In the New Testament, people are rebuked for bowing to angels and offering them adoration, because, as high as the angels may be, they are not divine or worthy of worship. At the name of Jesus every knee shall bow and every tongue confess that He is *Adonai*, Lord. This does not detract from the glory of the Father but, as the Apostle says, is unto the glory of the Father. The first confession of faith in biblical days was the shortest and simple creed that simply declared, *Jesus ho Kyrios*, "Jesus is Lord," which means that Jesus is sovereign—our sovereign. He shares with the Father the fullness of deity and sovereignty, and it is the Father Himself who is pleased to bestow the title *Kyrios* upon His only begotten Son.

Regeneration

We find in the opening statements of this epistle not only a reference to election but also a specific reference to regeneration or rebirth. This is commonly distorted in our culture by the idea that we have to have faith in order to be reborn or elect, but the sovereign God, from all eternity, decrees those to whom He will give the gift of faith, which is the fruit of regeneration, not the cause of it. The Reformation church declared that regeneration precedes faith, which is a distinguishing article of Reformed theology. We tend to get that backwards and think that our faith is what causes us to be reborn. Unless we are born of the Spirit, as Jesus said to Nicodemus, we cannot see the kingdom of God, let alone enter it. Regeneration is what provokes and plants faith in our souls. The very condition that God requires for justification is by His grace sovereignly supplied.

If we try to place faith before regeneration, we expect the impossible: the natural to rise up to the supernatural. We expect those who are dead in sin and trespasses to exercise spiritual life. The Apostle Paul wrote to the Ephesians that God "even when we were dead in trespasses, made us alive together with Christ (by grace you have been saved)" (Eph. 2:5). Every pregnant woman knows the human experience called "quickening," which happens when she first feels life in her womb. That is the metaphor Paul gives to the Ephesians of what the Holy Spirit does to people while they are dead. We are as passive in our rebirth as we were in our natural birth. We had nothing to do with causing the conception in our mother's womb.

Even Jesus was generated supernaturally in His humanity. When the angel Gabriel came to the young maiden Mary and announced that she would have a baby who would save people from their sins, she said to the angel, "How can this be, since I do not know a man?" (Luke 1:34). She understood the basic biology that virgins do not have babies, so she questioned the announcement of the angel, and the angel explained it to her: the Holy Spirit would come upon her and overshadow her, so that the baby generated in her womb would be holy and of God.

The language in the annunciation is the same that we find in Genesis 1: "In the beginning God created the heavens and the earth. The earth was without form, and void; and darkness was on the face of the deep" (vv. 1–2). The deep was powerless to conquer the darkness until the Spirit of God hovered over the waters. "Then God said, 'Let there be light,' and there was from our regular classes to gather in the school auditorium and listen to him. During the speech he said, "Old soldiers never die; they just fade away." Yet Douglas MacArthur did fade away and die. The inheritance secured and reserved for us in heaven is incorruptible. It is undefiled and does not fade away because it cannot fade away.

This inheritance is reserved in heaven for you **who are kept by the power of God through faith for salvation ready to be revealed in the last time** (v. 5). Here Peter speaks of salvation in the future. In Christian jargon we talk about "being saved." I received a letter from someone who told me, "I was saved five years ago." He meant that he had come to faith, that he had been justified and had entered into his salvation. In a certain sense he was saved, because the Bible uses the verb *to save* in every tense of the Greek language. There is a sense in which we were saved from the foundation of the world. We *were being* saved, we *are* saved, and we *are being* saved, but ultimately we *shall be* saved when we enter into the fullness of the inheritance that is being reserved.

While it is being kept for eternity, the same power that keeps the inheritance reserved for us is the power that keeps us reserved for the inheritance. It is the power of God that keeps us to receive the full and final measure of salvation. Do you see why Peter gives a doxology? Peter could have given the benediction after this opening statement, because in these few lines he communicates to these Christians of the Diaspora the heart and soul of the Christian faith.

3

HEAVENLY INHERITANCE, PART 2

1 Peter 1:6–12

In this you greatly rejoice, though now for a little while, if need be, you have been grieved by various trials, that the genuineness of your faith, being much more precious than gold that perishes, though it is tested by fire, may be found to praise, honor, and glory at the revelation of Jesus Christ, whom having not seen you love. Though now you do not see Him, yet believing, you rejoice with joy inexpressible and full of glory, receiving the end of your faith—the salvation of your souls. Of this salvation the prophets have inquired and searched carefully, who prophesied of the grace that would come to you, searching what, or what manner of time, the Spirit of Christ who was in them was indicating when He testified beforehand the sufferings of Christ and the glories that would follow. To them it was revealed that, not to themselves, but to us they were ministering the things which now have been reported to you through those who have preached the gospel to you by the Holy Spirit sent from heaven—things which angels desire to look into.

In this you greatly rejoice, though now for a little while, if need be, you have been grieved by various trials** (v. 6). The first question we face is, what is the antecedent of "this"? In other words, what does the word "this" refer back to? I think it is clear that the antecedent is the work of God in His grace by which we have been begotten again to a living hope through the resurrection of Christ to that inheritance that Peter described as incorruptible and undefiled, that does not fade away and that is reserved for us in heaven. We rejoice in that promised inheritance that shall be ours in glory.

Peter tells his readers that the inheritance and the news of their having been begotten to an eternal reward provoke within them right now exceeding joy. The Christian life in all circumstances is to manifest that fruit of the Spirit, joy. The joy that has been given to us by the Holy Spirit is not a mere fleeting sense of happiness; it is something that provokes within us an abundance of rejoicing. In this promise we greatly rejoice, the Apostle says, however, "for a little while, if need be, you have been grieved by various trials."

Notice in verse 6 that Peter says, "*You* greatly rejoice" and "if need be, *you* have been grieved by various trials." In verse 3 Peter used the word "us" rather than "you": ". . . who according to His abundant mercy has begotten *us* again to a living hope." In the beginning Peter included himself in the content, but now he speaks to his readers as "you" rather than as "us." That will become somewhat significant when he makes a distinction between those who love and trust in Christ although they have never seen Him, and those who have seen Him. Peter is writing this epistle as one who did see and know Him, which is the principal difference between the author of the letter and its recipients. Although all experience the promise of the inheritance in the future, there are those incorporated here who were eyewitnesses of the resurrection and those who were not.

Purifying Trials

Peter says that "for a little while, if need be, you have been grieved by various trials." A central motif of this letter is the suffering and affliction that the Christians of the Diaspora were enduring at that time. The epistle is a letter of consolation and comfort, reminding them of the future hope that awaits them. Peter mentions that their trials are temporary, and also that they have a purpose: **that the genuineness of your faith, being much more precious than gold that perishes, though it is tested by fire, may be found to praise, honor, and glory at the revelation of Jesus Christ** (v. 7). Their trials and afflictions are not without a reason. There is a purpose clause here, namely, that the genuineness of their faith may be proved. On an earthly level, the afflictions endured by the recipients of the letter were foisted upon them by those in Asia Minor who were hostile to the gospel, hostile to Christ, and therefore hostile to Christians.

In a real sense, their sufferings and afflictions were unjust—they were victims of persecution—but we have to see beyond the human dimension, the proximate cause of the suffering, and look to the remote or ultimate cause. These afflictions were sent upon the believers by God. God uses the iniquitous afflictions wrought by human hostility for the ultimate well-being of His children. In this text here we see a marvelous reaffirmation of the doctrine of the providence of God.

The classic teaching of divine providence is found at the end of the book of Genesis. Joseph, who had been viciously betrayed by his brothers and sold into slavery, was held in prison for many years and separated from his family and homeland. He endured great suffering at the hands of his brothers. When Joseph was reunited with his brothers years later, they were terrified that he would exact revenge against them. Instead, Joseph said, "As for you, you meant evil against me; but God meant it for good, in order to bring it about as it is this day, to save many people alive" (Gen. 50:20). Their intentions were wicked, and they were responsible for that, but over and above their actions, God intended good. "All things work together for good to those who love God, to those who are the called according to His purpose," Paul wrote (Rom. 8:28). God's hand is in earthly trials that are unjustly foisted upon us by wicked people. The hand of God trumps the evil intent of those who wound us, and He uses, in His gracious providence, those various experiences of affliction and pain for His glory and for our ultimate edification.

That is a difficult thing, and Christians struggle with it. I recall watching an episode of *The 700 Club* in which the host was interviewing a young woman who had lost two children in tragic accidents. She was grief stricken about it, and she asked the host, "How could God allow that to happen?" How many times have you asked that question or heard it asked? How can God allow all the suffering, pain, and affliction that occurs? The host responded to the woman, saying, "You have to understand that God had nothing to do with it. That was the work of Satan, not of God." I understood his motives. Certainly he was trying not only to comfort this woman but also to exonerate any blame that might be given to God, which could cause this woman to stagger in unbelief. However, if God has nothing to do with death or our afflictions, we of all people are the most to be pitied. The comfort we receive from the Word of God is that God is involved with our sufferings even to the extent that He ordains them, but the purpose of that ordination is always good and righteous.

People attempt to avoid that truth by saying that God does not ordain such things but merely permits them. However, whatever God permits, He must choose to permit, and what He chooses to permit, He thereby ordains. That should not discourage us but encourage us, so that when we are falsely accused, slandered, or have our reputation injured, we can get on our knees and say, "God, please, vindicate me against these wicked people." We can ask for vindication. At the same time, we have to ask Him, "What did you have in mind in this trouble?" Even though we suffer unjustly at the hands of men, we never suffer unjustly at the hands of God.

So, Peter says, we are grieved by the trials that come upon us, but in the midst of them we can rejoice exceedingly, not only because of the inheritance laid up for us but also because we can be sure that through these trials, the genuineness of our faith, being much more precious than gold that perishes, though it is tested by fire may be found to praise, honor, and glory at the revelation of Jesus Christ.

The Value of Faith

I notice that when Peter provides a comparison or contrast between the value of faith and the value of some material substance, he chooses gold as the standard for that comparison. We may take that for granted because, throughout the Bible, we read that gold is precious and by comparison how much more precious is our faith. It is interesting that throughout the history of civilization, human beings have always found some medium of exchange to use as currency in commercial transactions, from bartering to buying and selling. All kinds of things have been used, such as beans or seashells, even tobacco, but far and away the primary medium of exchange throughout history has been gold. We speak of the "golden age" or the "gold standard" of a particular enterprise because gold has existed in a more stable environment than any other medium of exchange throughout human history. The value of gold is not denigrated by the Bible.

One of the most volatile political issues of the twentieth century was the gold standard. Our nation debated whether to back its currency with a commodity of value or to substitute the commodity for paper, which has very little value. Paper was used initially as a receipt for the real value of metals such as silver and gold, but people got so used to simply trading paper that government decided to make it legal tender and not worry about whether it was backed by anything except the power or integrity of the government. That provoked a major crisis in our country in the 1930s.

At that time, someone wrote a penetrating satire in an attempt to expose the folly of removing our currency from an objective standard, which, from a biblical standard, meant a debasing of our currency, which God prohibits. In 1939 Hollywood made a movie of this satire, *The Wizard of Oz*. "Oz" is the abbreviation for the standard quantity of gold—it is measured commercially in terms of ounces. The munchkins, the yellow brick road, and the wicked witch of the East were all part of the satire, but the ultimate point was that when the pilgrims finally reached the wizard, they discovered that his power was all smoke and mirrors behind the shield. The movie was really about gold and the gold standard.

There is a widespread economic theory called the "subjective theory of value," which holds that there is no such thing as an objective value of anything. Value is something that we deem individually or that we assign. We speak of the "market value" of something, but that only describes the value people have assigned to it. There is no such thing as an objective value for water, gasoline, or gold.

Several years ago I went to trade in a car, and I did not agree with the dealer's estimate of what he wanted to give me for it. He pulled out the Blue Book and said, "This is the objective value of your car." I replied, "No. That's the value of my car to you. It is not the value of my car to me." We failed to make a deal, so I went down the street to another dealer and found that the objective value of my car was one thousand dollars higher.

Values are subjective. We talk publicly about values, when we really mean ethics. Ethics are objective, established according to objective norms. Values are subjective. God is the supreme evaluator of everything, and as Christians we want to bring our values into conformity with the values of God. The problem is that there are certain things God values highly that we do not, and, conversely, certain things we value highly that God considers as so much rubbish.

I have taken time to discuss gold and value in order to get to the heart of the text. God says that our faith has a much greater value than gold. This is the economy of God, and it was the economy of Jesus when He said, "For what profit is it to a man if he gains the whole world, and loses his own soul? Or what will a man give in exchange for his soul?" (Matt. 16:26). In other words, how much gold is your soul worth? Our faith is valuable not only to us, but also to God, who wants to refine it. Just as gold is refined by fire, by a crucible that burns away impurities, so the crucible of suffering and affliction refines our faith, which is far more precious than gold.

The Purpose of Testing

Our faith is tested by the fire for a purpose—that it may be found to praise, honor, and glory at the revelation of Jesus Christ, **whom having not seen you love. Though now you do not see Him, yet believing, you rejoice with joy inexpressible and full of glory** (v. 8). Faith is refined so that at the last day, at the final consummation of the kingdom of Christ, it will be the occasion for praise, honor, and glory. God values your faith more than He values your gold or your present comfort. Peter is moved by the fact that the readers of his epistle love Christ, despite never having seen Him. Our Lord Himself said, "Blessed are those who have not seen and yet have believed" (John 20:29). After the resurrection when Jesus appeared to the eleven in the upper room, He rebuked them for their unbelief, for their hardheartedness. They had not believed the testimony of the angel and the women who were at the tomb. God places a premium on faith that is the substance of things not seen, as the author of Hebrews indicates (Heb. 11:1).

Inexpressible joy is a reality that human words can never adequately describe. That joy, which is a fruit of the Holy Spirit, is ineffable. It defies description. One commentator on this text likened it to the glory of the Son. He said, "A blind man who has been blind from birth cannot understand the noonday sun. No matter how many times you try to explain it to him, he has no reference point by which to understand its magnitude." The author went on to say that someone who can see may not be able to express adequately the reality of the brightness of the sun to someone who is blind, but the person who can see knows the sun the moment it shines upon him. We perceive the light. We do not have to reason about it; we see it for what it is. So it is with the Word of God. Many people are blind to the truth of God, but when the scales fall from their eyes and the Spirit of God opens their eyes to His Word, they see the truth of it immediately. We certainly have sound, objective reasons to believe the Word of God, but those reasons are about as necessary as arguments for light to people who can see the sun. Our joy is inexpressible. It is a glorious joy, a weighty joy, not a superficial joy.

Glorious Future

. . . receiving the end of your faith—the salvation of your souls (v. 9). The "end of your faith" does not mean the termination of faith. The word "end" here does not mean the final point of a journey, a destination; it means a goal, aim, or purpose, and the ultimate purpose of our faith, Peter says, is the salvation of our souls. That can be taken two ways. It can be the salvation of our personhood or, more specifically, the salvation of our soul as distinguished from our body. We, indeed, are promised in Scripture that the final consummation of our salvation will include the redemption of the body, but the first experience when we enter heaven occurs when our souls fly to the presence of Christ.

Peter is saying that the present we endure must be understood in light of the glorious future that God has raised for us. Secular cynics see this as a pie-in-the-sky theology. The term *secularism* means that the *hic et nunc*, the "here and now," is all there is. There is no eternal dimension, and the sacred is swallowed up by the secular. We have heard so much skepticism about our future hope of glory that we hardly know what it tastes like anymore.

One of the greatest testimonies in American history to Christian joy in the midst of suffering was that expressed by slaves in earlier days. The slaves had a subsistent existence. They were sold on the block, husbands separated from wives, mothers separated from children. They were bought and sold and put in chains, and they lived in subhuman conditions. There were Christians among them, and they would sing their faith. The slave would look to heaven, beyond his immediate circumstances, and sing about it:

> Swing low, sweet chariot,
> Coming for to carry me home.
>
> I looked over Jordan, and what did I see?
> Coming for to carry me home,
> A band of angels coming after me,
> Coming for to carry me home.

That is the sentiment about which Peter is telling people in the midst of trial and suffering.

Of this salvation the prophets have inquired and searched carefully, who prophesied of the grace that would come to you, searching what, or what manner of time, the Spirit of Christ who was in them was indicating when He testified beforehand the sufferings of Christ and the glories that would follow (vv. 10–11). Peter is saying that this is not a novel idea. He did not make it up, nor did it appear on the scene *de nova*, like Athena out of the head of Zeus. This teaching of Jesus' is what the prophets of old spoke of. When God put in their mouths the promises of future redemption, they looked into it. They searched carefully and made inquiries. They knew that these things were going to happen, but they did not know when. They knew that Christ would suffer, and out of that suffering, glories would follow.

To them it was revealed that, not to themselves, but to us they were ministering the things which now have been reported to you through those who have preached the gospel to you by the Holy Spirit sent from heaven—things which angels desire to look into (v. 12). The prophets did not always understand the things they taught. They were the mouthpieces of the Holy Spirit. Not until the fullness of time came and the prophetic word of God came to pass could people grasp what Joel, Isaiah, and Jeremiah had spoken of. The prophets themselves, who were faithful to those promises, inquired and searched for meaning, but they did not always know it: they had to wait to see. When Peter writes about the things that "have been reported to you through those who have preached the gospel to you by the Holy Spirit sent from heaven," his reference is to the ministry of the Apostles, who carried the gospel to Asia Minor by the Holy Spirit sent from heaven.

Not only did the prophets inquire about the marvels of these things, but also the angels in heaven have desired to look into the depths and the riches of the gospel. We are told that when one person repents, there is joy in heaven among the angels (Luke 15:10). The angels delight to watch the ministry of Christ unfold in history. They delight in observing the proving of our faith in the progress of our sanctification. Our faith, which is more precious than gold, means much to God, so He will put us in a fire to make it pure.

4

LIVING BEFORE GOD OUR FATHER

1 Peter 1:13–19

Therefore gird up the loins of your mind, be sober, and rest your hope fully upon the grace that is to be brought to you at the revelation of Jesus Christ; as obedient children, not conforming yourselves to the former lusts, as in your ignorance; but as He who called you is holy, you also be holy in all your conduct, because it is written, "Be holy, for I am holy." And if you call on the Father, who without partiality judges according to each one's work, conduct yourselves throughout the time of your stay here in fear; knowing that you were not redeemed with corruptible things, like silver or gold, from your aimless conduct received by tradition from your fathers, but with the precious blood of Christ, as of a lamb without blemish and without spot.

As I have pointed out frequently, the word *therefore* signals a conclusion that is about to be reached based upon a previous premise or argument. The "therefore" that begins the text before us now introduces us to the conclusion Peter sets forth to his exposition of our salvation, which includes a precious inheritance laid up for us in heaven as the adopted children of God. In light of the marvelous salvation that has been prepared for us, we come to the conclusion that is to be drawn from it.

Thoughtful Faith

Therefore gird up the loins of your mind, be sober, and rest your hope fully upon the grace that is to be brought to you at the revelation of Jesus Christ (v. 13). To people of the first century, a call to gird up their loins did not typically involve a mental activity or process. The metaphor is based on the customary garments of first-century people. Both men and women tended to wear long, flowing robes. Even soldiers were commonly adorned with such robes. When it came time to go into battle, however, the soldiers were hindered by the robes from moving with agility, so they girded up their robes. They hitched them above the knee and then secured them in place with a belt, which left their legs free to run into battle. Peter uses this simple metaphor to challenge his readers to prepare their minds for deep thinking.

We are living in a period of church history that may be classified as mindless. It is an anti-intellectual period of Christian history—not anti-scientific, or anti-technological, or even anti-educational, but anti-mind. While teaching in a seminary classroom I would sometimes ask a student what he thought about a particular proposition. The student would sometimes respond, "I feel that the statement is incorrect." I would stop him and say, "I didn't ask you how you felt. I wasn't inquiring into your emotional response. I was asking you what you think about it."

Thinking is done by the mind, and Christians are called repeatedly in sacred Scripture not to leave their minds in the parking lot when they enter into church but to awaken their minds so that they may think clearly and deeply about the things of God. Some people say that God does not care about the mind but only the heart and that an emphasis on the mind leads to rationalism, and from there to modernism, postmodernism, and all else that stands in antithesis to biblical Christianity. It is true that what you think in your mind will never get you into the kingdom of God until it reaches your heart, but we have been created by God in such a way that the pathway to the heart is through the mind. We cannot love with passion that which we know nothing about. The book that contains the sacred revelation of Almighty God, His Word, is addressed in the first instance to our minds. Therefore, the more we understand the truth of God, the more we will be gripped by it in our hearts and changed by it.

Rest in Hope

Gird up the loins of your mind, Peter says, and be sober; in other words, do not be intoxicated with mind-numbing drugs. For the mind to function with clarity, it must function in a state of sobriety, so we are called to be sober and to rest our hope fully upon the grace that is to be brought to us at the revelation of Jesus Christ. The biblical word for *hope* is different from our normal English use of the term. When we say in English that we hope something will happen, we are expressing our desire for a particular outcome about which we cannot be sure. In the biblical usage, hope is not an uncertainty but a certainty, which is why it is called "an anchor of the soul" (Heb. 6:19). It is that which brings stability to us. It is faith looking to the future with the full assurance that God will do what He promises He will do.

Peter reminds us of that, and he tells us where we are to put our hope—fully upon the grace of God—because that is where our hope finds its anchor. The ship is moored by grace, in grace, and to grace. We can be confident of our future with God because our future, even as our present, rests fully not on our righteousness or on God's justice, but on God's grace, which by definition is something that we do not and cannot deserve. We need to think about these things soberly so that our minds might come into action and realize that our resting place is on that grace. This is Peter's way of directing our thoughts to what the church calls her "blessed hope," the final appearance of Jesus in His return at the end of the age, when He will come in glory and manifest His majesty for every eye to see. Let your mind's activity rest upon the confidence of that future promise.

You are to rest your mind in hope **as obedient children, not conforming yourselves to the former lusts, as in your ignorance** (v. 14). Already, in just the first few verses of the first letter of Peter, we have seen passages with similarity to themes expounded by Paul in his epistles. Here Peter talks about not being conformed, and Paul did the same at the conclusion of his exposition of the doctrines of grace in Romans: "I beseech you therefore, brethren, by the mercies of God, that you present your bodies a living sacrifice, holy, acceptable to God, which is your reasonable service. And do not be conformed to this world, but be transformed by the renewing of your mind" (Rom. 12:1–2). Paul saw our sanctification as taking place as a result of a mind-set that is different from the mind-set of this world. Paul was writing of a mind-set of nonconformity, and Peter is saying the same thing here in the first chapter of his epistle. In Paul's letter to the Ephesians he writes:

> You He made alive, who were dead in trespasses and sins, in which you once walked according to the course of this world, according to the prince of the power of the air, the spirit who now works in the sons of disobedience, among whom also we all once conducted ourselves in the lusts of our flesh, fulfilling

the desires of the flesh and of the mind, and were by nature children of wrath, just as the others. (Eph. 2:1–3)

Nonconformists

The common theme in Romans 12, Ephesians 2, and 1 Peter is that of nonconformity to the patterns and the customs of fallen humanity. We are to be nonconformists.

Such nonconformity can be achieved in a superficial way. There are religious sects that want to do everything in their power to avoid any indication of worldliness. I went to college in a small town in northwestern Pennsylvania that contained the central settlement of the western Pennsylvanian Amish. We had to drive carefully through the streets at night because of the omnipresent buggies drawn by horse and illuminated only by a candle in a glass lamp. The Amish wore identical clothing containing no zippers or buttons but only hooks and eyes. The Amish farms had no electricity; they farmed by horse or hand-drawn plows. Their homes were adorned with sheets rather than curtains. All that is nonconformity. They had made a religious commitment to separate themselves from the world. Electricity and cars were considered bad because everyone else used them. As noble as such a venture may be, it misses the point of nonconformity.

The nonconformity we are called to practice is an ethical nonconformity. We are to practice the ethic of God rather than the ethic of this world. I used to teach ethics in the seminary, and one of the lectures I gave was on statistical morality. The distinction between ethics and morals has been obscured in our day so that people use the terms *morals* and *ethics* interchangeably. Historically those two words were not understood as synonyms; they had a vastly different meaning. The term *morals* comes from the concept of mores. Sociologists and historians examine the behavioral patterns of a given culture and describe how people act, which are the mores of a given society. The study of ethics, however, is the study of normative principles of behavior that tell us how people should behave. Yet we all know—and the Bible says—that there is a great chasm between how we ought to behave and how we, in fact, do behave.

Psychologists observe human behavior and discover that 90 percent of young people are involved in premarital sex. Since such a high percentage do this, we call it normal human behavior, which is only a short step from saying that it is normative. People say it is good to be normal, and to deviate from the normal is to fall into the ditch of abnormality. On the one hand, there are also sociologists and psychologists saying that it is perfectly normal and common for teens under the pressures of erotic propaganda to fall into related patterns of behavior. On the other hand, the Bible says we are not to let fornication even once be named among us, as befits saints (Eph. 5:3). The oldest argument in the world for defending behavior is that everybody else is doing it, but God does not care what everybody else is doing. God knows what everybody else is doing; He is concerned about what we are doing, and He tells us not to be conformed to those patterns. Before God raised us from the dead spiritually, we walked according to the course of this world, according to the prince of the power of the air, the spirit who even now works in the sons of disobedience (Eph. 2:2). Here in his epistle, Peter is making a sharp contrast between the sons of disobedience and the children of God.

A recent poll that measured the sexual behavior of Americans indicated that premarital sex is more prevalent among young people who claim to be born again than among young people who do not. How is that possible? It is possible because Christians confuse ethics and morality. They assume that what the group is doing (mores) is what they ought to be doing (ethics). I call this "statistical morality," following the customs of a culture. If we are to gird up the loins of our minds, we need to be able to discern the difference between the patterns of this world and the patterns to which we are called as Christians.

The only way you can be in Christ is if the Holy Spirit has regenerated you. The term "born-again Christian" is a redundancy. You cannot be a Christian without being reborn, and if you are reborn by the Holy Spirit, you cannot be anything but a Christian. If you are a Christian, you have been born anew by the power of the Holy Spirit, which means that your constituent nature as a human being has been changed by God. Once we have been changed, God expects our behavior to manifest that change. We ought no longer to be conformed to this world. Instead, from the day of our rebirth to the end of our pilgrimage in this world, we are called to go through the process of ongoing sanctification by which we gain the mind of Christ and show our love for Him by keeping His commandments.

It is terrible that the civil magistrate, government, sanctions abortion on demand, but it does not matter what the civil magistrate says about it. What the civil magistrate allows has nothing to do with what God allows. We are called to obey God, not taboos, customs, or what our peers do and expect us to do in this world. The hardest thing in the Christian life is to remember to whom we belong and what it means to say *Jesus ho Kyrios*, "Jesus is Lord." If

He is our Lord and Master, then we are to obey Him rather than the impulses of the flesh or the patterns of the pagan world around us.

When Justin Martyr addressed his *apologia*, his defense of Christianity, to Emperor Antoninus Pius, he sought to defend the truth claims of Christianity. Not only did he give the normal arguments for the truth claims of Christianity, but he also challenged the emperor to examine the lives of Christians and to observe their purity. No apologist would use that as an argument for Christianity in our culture today. We cannot.

Be Holy

But as He who called you is holy, you also be holy in all your conduct, because it is written, "Be holy, for I am holy" (vv. 15–16). The character of God is holy. The concept of holiness refers to purity. God's holiness involves His purity, but the dimension of purity is the secondary meaning of the term *holy*. The first and primary meaning of the term *holy* refers to God's transcendent majesty, His otherness, the sense in which God is different from anything in the created order. The term *holy* in the Old Testament was used when God consecrated a people or a place or a time and set it apart because it was different. The idea here in Peter's epistle is that the basis for the call to nonconformity is that we are to be imitators of God in His difference. Just as God is different from the world, so are we as His children and heirs of the inheritance set before us in heaven, to be different from the world.

Of all the things I have done, the one that has brought me the most enjoyment is my ministry at St. Andrew's Church. I find great satisfaction doing expositional preaching to the same people week after week and in not traveling to speak here and there, never knowing what the impact will be. To have a congregation is wonderful but also a sober responsibility. Sometimes I think, *What would happen if God erased St. Andrew's Church from Sanford, Florida, and pushed it into nonexistence? What difference would it make?* I am too much of a Calvinist to think that it would make no difference; I have to be optimistic and say that the church of Christ makes a difference. If the New Testament church had been erased, what difference would that have made to the world? We probably would not be in our churches today. Those people heard the Word of God and decided they were not going to behave like the rest of the world but as children and heirs of God, joint heirs with Christ. That is our destiny.

And if you call on the Father, who without partiality judges according to each one's work, conduct yourselves throughout the

time of your stay here in fear (v. 17). We are justified by faith, but we are rewarded according to our works. The Father, who rewards His children according to their obedience, does so impartially, so we are to conduct ourselves throughout the time of our stay on earth in fear—not the servile fear that the prisoner has for his torturer, but the filial fear that a child has for his parents, whom he respects. This is a fear of offending, disappointing, or misrepresenting, a fear born in reverence in a spirit of adoration.

When the Apostle Paul gave a similar admonition and called us not to be conformed to this world, he said we are to present our bodies as living sacrifices, holy, acceptable to God, which is our reasonable service, or otherwise translated, our spiritual worship (Rom. 12:2). Worship is not just something we do on Sunday mornings; we worship God when we obey Him. No one said it more simply than Jesus Himself: "If you love Me, keep my commandments" (John 14:15). That is Peter's meaning here.

So, conduct yourself throughout the time of your stay here in fear; **knowing that you were not redeemed with corruptible things, like silver or gold, from your aimless conduct received by tradition from your fathers** (v. 18). You were purchased, which is what redemption means here. Supermarkets used to give out S&H green stamps, and most communities housed a redemption center where the booklets of stamps were taken and exchanged for a television set, a barbecue grill, or another premium. That is probably the deepest understanding of redemption that we have in American culture, but in biblical terms, to redeem something is to buy it back, to purchase it from slavery.

Lamb without Blemish

Peter speaks of our redemption as having been bought with a price. We were not redeemed with corruptible things, like silver and gold (notice again here the reference to gold) **but with the precious blood of Christ, as of a lamb without blemish and without spot** (v. 19). There is an adjective in verse 19 that we dare not pass over too quickly. We are redeemed not just by the blood of Christ but by the *precious* blood of Christ. We talk about gems as being precious stones; that is, they are ascribed the highest possible value. Something you regard as precious is what you hold in the highest possible esteem, and the Apostle is telling us here that precious things go beyond silver and gold. The most precious thing that has ever been on this earth is the blood of Christ. When His blood was shed, it was human blood, but it was holy blood—the most valuable blood that has ever been spilled.

In referring to Christ as a lamb without blemish and without spot, Peter is taking his readers back to the Old Testament celebrations of the Passover and Yom Kippur, the Day of Atonement. Commemorated at Passover is the occasion when the angel of death passed over homes on which the doorposts were marked with the blood of the lamb. When God saw the mark of the blood upon a doorpost, His judgment passed by. God told the Israelites never to forget what He had done. That very celebration reached its fulfillment in the celebration of the Lord's Supper, in which we remember the shedding of the blood of Christ for our salvation. On the Day of Atonement, the blood of an animal was taken by the high priest into the Holy of Holies and sprinkled on the mercy seat, on the throne of God, as a covering for the sins of the people. That pointed to the One whose blood was precious, not because of a divinely commanded ritual but because the blood had inherent value.

So let us gird up the loins of our minds and think about the call of God to His children, whom He has redeemed by the precious blood of Christ, that they may walk not as the world walks but as redeemed children of God.

5

THE ENDURING WORD

1 Peter 1:22–25

Since you have purified your souls in obeying the truth through the Spirit in sincere love of the brethren, love one another fervently with a pure heart, having been born again, not of corruptible seed but incorruptible, through the word of God which lives and abides forever, because

> "All flesh is as grass,
> And all the glory of man as the flower of the grass.
> The grass withers,
> And its flower falls away,
> But the word of the LORD endures forever."

Now this is the word which by the gospel was preached to you.

*C*oram Deo was one of the rallying cries of the sixteenth-century Protestant Reformation. The two-word phrase means literally "before the face of God." The idea is that even though God's face is not visible to us, every second of our lives is lived before His face. We cannot see Him, but He can see us. We need to cultivate a kind of God-consciousness in which we realize that everything we do is done before the face of God.

The first time I had to preach in the presence of my mentor John Gerstner, I was quite intimidated. I was exceedingly nervous about his presence among the congregation. I told him so, and when he asked why, I said, "I'm afraid I'm going to make a theological blunder or an exegetical error and bring shame and embarrassment to myself and to the church." He replied, "Why should you find it daunting to preach in the presence of men, when God listens to every word you say?"

Peter has been calling us to be aware of living our life before the face of God. *Coram Deo* includes within it not only the idea of living before the face of God but also living under the sovereignty of God and to the glory of God—before His face, under His authority, and to His glory. That captures the essence of the Christian life.

Obedience to the Truth

Since you have purified your souls in obeying the truth through the Spirit in sincere love of the brethren, love one another fervently with a pure heart (v. 22). There is much written here for our consideration. Peter indicates that our souls are purified through obedience, yet the reason we fail to give God due obedience is that our souls are not yet purified. We usually think that purification of the soul takes place so that we will obey God, yet here, strikingly, the Apostle tells us that purification is not only *unto* obedience but also *by* obedience. The more our souls are involved in obedience, the greater the purification that occurs, and the more our souls are purified, the greater our obedience will be. This is not a vicious circle but a glorious circle by which obedience feeds purification and, symbiotically, purification feeds obedience.

The concept of obedience is exceedingly important to the message of the New Testament. At St. Andrew's, after I read Scripture, I quote words that Jesus often used: "He who has ears to hear, let him hear." Elsewhere the New Testament tells us that we are to be doers of the Word and not hearers only (James 1:22). There is something of a play on words in the Greek between the verb *to hear* and the verb *to obey*. The verb *to hear* in Greek is *akouō* from which we get the English word *acoustics*. The verb that means "to obey" is the Greek word *hupoakouō*. There is a similar root in both Greek words. The second word, *to obey*, simply repeats the verb *to hear* and attaches to it the preparatory word *hupo*, which comes into the English language by the prefix *hyper*. Children might be hyperactive, which means that they are active to a higher degree than others. So, in Greek the word *to obey* simply means "hyper hearing," that is, hearing beyond the simple sensory experience of sound striking our auditory nerves and being processed by the brain in such a way that we hear something. The hearing that God wants from His people means hearing not only in the eardrum but in the ears of the soul. Such hearing brings change to our lives, which is manifested in obedience.

The obeying of which Peter speaks is obedience to the truth. Our culture is against the idea of objective truth, and this antipathy is rooted and grounded in fallen humanity's fundamental hostility to truth itself. People do not want truth to be objective. We do not want truth to be binding upon our consciences, because by nature truth is our enemy and we do not want to submit to it, or, as Peter says here, we do not want to obey it. The tragedy of fallen humanity is that we tend to give ourselves in obedience to the lie, to that which is false, but the purification of our souls comes in obeying the truth.

It is not enough simply to hear the truth. It is not enough even to recite the truth of the creeds. It is not enough to affirm our agreement with the propositions of the truth. Peter says there is a deeper step, which is to obey the truth. Such obedience happens through the Spirit. Peter is speaking here of that process of growth and development in the Christian life that we call "sanctification," which is dependent on the operation and energizing influence of the Holy Spirit. I will never obey the truth of God apart from the power, grace, and assistance of the Spirit.

We are living in strange times in terms of how the church functions. We have been caught up with a fierce desire to find a way to relate to a culture that has been immunized to Christianity. We try to find new methods to reach the lost. The motivation is righteous, because we should have compassion for the lost. The danger comes when we ask the lost how they want to come into the kingdom of God, how they want to worship God, and how they want to hear God's Word, and then tailor our method to their tastes and preferences. That is fatal. Sooner or later the church must come back to confidence in God's way of doing God's work, because the Bible does give us a blueprint for evangelism. It gives us a blueprint for reaching the lost and for generating spiritual growth among the people of God. The blueprint is not a matter of rocket science or Madison Avenue technology; it is a blueprint that God guarantees will not be fruitless. It is accomplished by the method of proclaiming the Word of God, which, as Peter says here, changes lives and purifies souls through the power of the Holy Spirit.

God has established a church, a fellowship and communion of believers, to gather for mutual support, edification, and encouragement. The church is to be a group which, when assembled, experiences an extraordinary kind of love. The grace that comes through the preaching of the Word is confirmed

by the sacraments that Christ has given to His church and strengthened by
the discipline of prayer, both personal and corporate. Whatever we try to
do to make the message attractive to a fallen world, we must never negotiate those fundamental, biblical methods of worship, preaching, evangelism,
and spiritual growth.

The constituent nature of human beings did not change with Generation
X, nor did it change with the Baby Boomers. Television changes culture, and
technology changes the way we do things, but the fundamental nature of
our humanity remains the same as when God created Adam and Eve. The
way to the heart is through the mind, so mindless Christianity never really
produces purification of the soul. The purification of the soul comes through
obeying the truth of the Word of God through the Spirit of God. There are
no substitutes or shortcuts for that. There is no such thing as sanctification
in three easy lessons.

Love Thy Neighbor

The love of which Peter speaks is also fervent and accompanied by a pure
heart. The Apostle is speaking of an extraordinary kind of love. The Great
Commandment says that we are to love the Lord our God with all our mind
and strength and soul, and the second is added to it, that we must love our
neighbors as much as we love ourselves (Matt. 22:37–39). Our neighbor is
not simply someone who lives next door or someone in our class, group, or
community.

Some Pharisees came to Jesus, and one asked, "Who is my neighbor?"
(Luke 10:29). Jesus then told them a story about a man who went down
from Jericho and fell among thieves. He was robbed, beaten, and left by the
roadside for dead. Then some clergy came along and noticed the plight of
the poor man. Maybe they whispered a prayer for him before hurrying on
their way, but they did not cross the street to offer assistance. It was one from
the despised Samaritans, with whom Jews had no dealings, who stopped to
care for the injured man. "So which of these three do you think was neighbor
to him who fell among the thieves?" Jesus asked, and the Pharisees replied,
"He who showed mercy on him." Then Jesus said, "Go and do likewise"
(vv. 36–37). Everyone we meet is our neighbor.

Loving our neighbor means treating him with care, kindness, and patience,
as the good Samaritan did. It has very little to do with feelings of great warmth
and affection. We can love our neighbor actively apart from any personal
affection, but when we get beyond the neighborhood to the brotherhood,
everything changes. Love of the brethren is to be done fervently with a pure

heart. I once heard a pastor in Mississippi say, "We stick with the stuck," by which he meant that family trumps everything. We stick together because we are family. We are to have that kind of fervent love not only for our biological families but also for our family in the Spirit, our brothers and sisters in Christ. "By this all will know that you are My disciples, if you have love for one another" (John 13:35).

That is the impression we should make on a watching world. Those outside the church should look at Christians and note that we do not backbite or fault-find and that we protect one another with fervent love, the love that comes from a pure heart. This is not natural, which Peter reminds us when he adds, **having been born again, not of corruptible seed but incorruptible, through the word of God which lives and abides forever** (v. 23). The reason we have the capacity for this kind of brotherly and sisterly love in the body of Christ is that God has changed our hearts. He has caused us to be born anew so that what is not natural can be accomplished by the supernatural work that God performs upon our hearts.

Reborn

Regeneration or *rebirth* is the result of the immediate work of the Holy Spirit upon the human soul, once dead to the things of God but now quickened to new life. You are in Christ because the Spirit has raised you from spiritual death, quickened your soul, and given you an affection for God that you did not have naturally. You were not given simply the potential for change; you have become a changed person. Regeneration is the beginning of the Christian life. It is a *monergistic* work, which means that only one person is involved in it. The only one who does the work of regeneration is God. You have no activity in it. You cannot make yourself born again. You cannot choose to be born again. You can do nothing to affect your regeneration, but from the instant of your regeneration, for the rest of your Christian life, that process is *synergistic*. It is a joint venture between you and God. "Therefore, my beloved, as you have always obeyed, not as in my presence only, but now much more in my absence, work out your own salvation with fear and trembling; for it is God who works in you both to will and to do for His good pleasure" (Phil. 2:12–13).

Peter reminds us what is involved in having been reborn. We have been born again of a different kind of seed from that which customarily produces life, whether in humans, animals, or plants. Whether a seed that is thrown into the ground actually dies is a moot question that we will allow botanists to argue, but to grow a lawn, the soil is first prepared before the seed is sown. Afterward, the sown seed is covered with straw to keep the birds from eating it, and the ground must be watered regularly. We assume that we are trying to bring forth life in this process, but we are actually trying to kill those seeds, to rot them so that the shells will decay and germinate and bring forth life. That is the biblical metaphor of a seed dying before it can come to life, just as we must die before we can enter into our resurrected state.

For human conception to occur, an egg must be fertilized by a seed. God is so concerned for our reproducing the species that in every act of joining between the male and the female, millions of seeds are released, even though it takes only one to fertilize an egg. It may seem like a waste, but in the economy of God it is not, because God knows how weak the human seed is. It is corruptible and perishable. It does not last forever. Yet the seed by which we have been reborn is not from corruptible seed, the Apostle tells us, but from incorruptible seed. When God generates a soul to life and the Holy Spirit quickens that seed, it cannot perish. This is not a comparison; it is a contrast.

Peter goes on to say that all this occurs through the Spirit, "having been born again, not of corruptible seed but incorruptible, through the word of God which lives and abides forever." The word "through" or "by means of" is emphasized. The Word of God is alive. It pulsates with life. It is the very power of God, because that Word is energized by God Himself. We read in Romans that the gospel is the power of God to salvation (Rom. 1:16).

In Martin Luther's final sermon he said, "If you do not want God to speak to you every day in your house and in your parish church, then be wise. Look for something else. In Trier is our Lord God's coat; in Aachen are Joseph's britches and our Blessed Lady's chemise. Go there and squander your money; buy indulgences and the pope's second-hand junk." Peasants were making pilgrimages to these places because they thought there was power in Joseph's pants or in Mary's milk. That is not where God has put the power. The power is not in the eloquence of a preacher or in the novelty of a program. The power is in the Word of God. "For the word of God is living and powerful, and sharper than any two-edged sword, piercing even to the division of soul and spirit, and of joints and marrow, and is a discerner of the thoughts and intents of the heart" (Heb. 4:12). It is a living Word.

An Abiding Word

Peter says also that it is an abiding Word. Nothing is more worthless than yesterday's newspaper. A candy bar machine deposits only one candy bar with the insertion of a coin, but when you put a coin into a newspaper dispenser and open the slot, there are ten or fifteen newspapers available for the taking. Newspaper publishers are not concerned about theft because they understand the economic rule of marginal utility. Who needs yesterday's newspaper? Yesterday's candy bar may still be succulent, but not yesterday's newspaper. Books have a longer shelf life than magazines, but even books come and go. One of the hardest things to do is to get people to read the classics of the giants that God has given to the church. If people would read Luther and Calvin they could take my books and burn them, because all I try to do is direct people back to the giants. All Luther and all Calvin wanted to do was direct people back to the Word of God, because that Word is not only living but also abiding—forever.

"All flesh is as grass, and all the glory of man as the flower of the grass. The grass withers, and its flower falls away, but the word of the LORD endures forever" (vv. 24–25). I love football, and I continually read about it, for all its uselessness. I find testimonies of men who have labored hard to win a Super Bowl, and almost all say that once they have celebrated such a victory, the thrill of it wears out quickly. They feel let down and want to say, "Is this all that there is?" Is that not true for every ambition and achievement known to the flesh? We are like the grass that, when the arid weather comes, withers. We are like the flower that blooms with its glory and beauty but wilts and withers away. How unlike the Word of the Lord, which endures forever.

Now this is the word which by the gospel was preached to you (v. 25). I once read an obscure essay of Augustine's on the philosophical foundation of language. In the middle of that essay, to illustrate a point, Augustine made reference to a passage in Romans: "The righteousness of God is revealed from faith to faith; as it is written, 'The just shall live by faith'" (1:17). Augustine said that this passage, which speaks of the righteousness of God, is not defining or describing the righteousness by which God Himself is righteous but the righteousness that God makes available to unrighteous people by faith. As I read this essay, which was written in the fourth century, I realized that it contained the text from Romans that Luther's eyes had fallen upon when he was preparing his lectures on Romans, and it became the text that started the Reformation. Luther said, "When I understood that, the doors of paradise swung open, and I went through." We do that every time we open the Bible.

Peter says that "the word of the LORD endures forever." Two thousand years after he wrote those words, we assemble to study the Word that endures through all the criticism and hostility launched against it, proving thereby the poet's expression:

Hammer away, ye hostile hands;
your hammers break; God's anvil stands.

6

A LIVING STONE

1 Peter 2:1–8a

Therefore, laying aside all malice, all deceit, hypocrisy, envy, and all evil speaking, as newborn babes, desire the pure milk of the word, that you may grow thereby, if indeed you have tasted that the Lord is gracious. Coming to Him as to a living stone, rejected indeed by men, but chosen by God and precious, you also, as living stones, are being built up a spiritual house, a holy priesthood, to offer up spiritual sacrifices acceptable to God through Jesus Christ. Therefore it is also contained in the Scripture,

"Behold, I lay in Zion
A chief cornerstone, elect, precious,
And he who believes on Him will by no means be put to shame."

Therefore, to you who believe, He is precious; but to those who are
disobedient,
"The stone which the builders rejected
Has become the chief cornerstone,"
and
"A stone of stumbling,
and a rock of offense."

Since 1 Peter 2 begins with the word "therefore," I would like to spend a few moments reviewing what precedes it. Peter said, "Since you have purified your souls in obeying the truth through the Spirit in sincere love of the brethren, love one another fervently with a pure heart, having been born again, not of corruptible seed but of incorruptible" (1:22–23). In our last study, we looked at what it means to be born again from a seed that cannot and will not perish.

I said earlier that the term "born again Christian" is a redundancy. If you are not reborn by the power of the Holy Spirit, you are not truly a Christian, and if you are reborn by the power of the Holy Spirit, you are a Christian. We talk about rebirth in terms of the doctrine of regeneration, which refers to a genesis or a new beginning. We know that rebirth is necessary, because the Scriptures tell us that, by nature, we are dead in our sin. This description of our condition is not biological but spiritual. We are born in this world DOA, dead on arrival. We may be alive biologically, but we are dead spiritually. We have within us a heart of stone, to use a biblical metaphor. It has no pulse, no flesh of life. It is calcified. Therefore, in our fallen condition we have no inclination or desire for the things of God. That is why Jesus said to Nicodemus, "Unless one is born of water and the Spirit, he cannot enter the kingdom of God. That which is born of the flesh is flesh, and that which is born of the Spirit is spirit" (John 3:5).

In order to embrace the things of God—spiritual things—a new birth is required, a birth wrought in our souls by the supernatural power of the Holy Spirit. Paul speaks of this experience as being quickened, or made alive, by the Holy Spirit (Eph. 2:1). The Apostles' Creed in its more archaic form says that Jesus will come to judge "the quick and the dead," meaning not only those who have died but also those who are alive. The language of the New Testament is that of new life wrought in our souls. Whereas before we had no inclination or desire for the things of God, God has quickened our souls and created in us a desire for Him and for His Son. Peter makes mention of our having been born again and then goes into chapter 2 with the consequences and implications of that.

Some hold to the doctrine of the carnal Christian. It has permeated the evangelical Christian world today. The doctrine teaches that regeneration does not necessarily change the disposition of the believer's will or soul. Someone can be a believer in Christ and indwelt by the Holy Spirit yet remain completely unchanged. However, that doctrine is on a collision course with orthodox Christianity and certainly with the biblical understanding of regeneration. No one can be brought to spiritual life without also being fundamentally changed.

Laying Aside

We see that implication when Peter says, **Therefore, laying aside all malice, all deceit, hypocrisy, envy, and all evil speaking** (v. 1). Because we have been born anew by a seed that cannot and will not perish, we ought therefore to lay aside all malice. Malice is the first thing that should disappear from the heart of a Christian.

Our legal system describes certain actions as being done "with malice aforethought." Malice does not necessarily describe an action by which one person is injured by another. An injurious action might be a malicious action, but the term *malicious* indicates a desire to harm or injure. When someone tells us that we have done something to hurt him or her, we typically respond, "I surely didn't mean to do that." We may have done it and admit to it, but we are saying that we did not plan to bring pain or harm. Malice has to do with a desire in the heart, a purposeful desire to wound or hurt another person. Peter says that we have to put that aside. The language he uses is that which describes a person undressing and putting his garments to the side. From a spiritual standpoint, Peter says we are to take the clothes of malice out of our soul, put them in the closet, and leave them there.

He said we are also to put away all deceit, hypocrisy, envy, and evil speaking, or slander. I believe he gives us the whole followed by its parts. All that Peter lists here are examples of malice. Deceitfulness is borne of malice. Deceit involves a definite attempt to distort, hide, or undermine the truth. It is done intentionally.

We are also to lay aside all hypocrisy. Jesus often described the Pharisees in terms of hypocrisy, which was in antiquity a kind of play acting or pretense. A hypocrite tries to deceive other people about his spiritual state. He pretends to be more righteous than he actually is. So, along with malice and deceitfulness, hypocrisy has to go.

Several years ago, the Evangelism Explosion team in Fort Lauderdale kept a record of answers that people gave to certain diagnostic questions such as, "Have you come to the place in your thinking where you know for sure that when you die you will go to heaven?" and "If you were to die tonight and God were to ask 'Why should I let you into my heaven?' what would you say?" The majority gave some kind of works-righteousness answer: "I tried to be good," or "I went to church." The team also kept a record of the top ten objections raised against the Christian faith, and the primary objection was the charge that the church is full of hypocrites.

The reason that charge is brought so often is that we call ourselves Christians but we do not always act in a Christian manner. However, if we were hypocrites, we would claim to be without sin—a claim that born-again Christians do not make. Only if we claim to be sinless are we guilty of the charge of hypocrisy. The church is the only institution I know of in which being a sinner is mandatory for membership. The church is a communion of sinners, but among our sins is not to be listed hypocrisy, because hypocrisy is a kind of deceit, and deceit is a kind of malice.

Peter goes on to say that we ought to lay aside all envy and slander. Just as deceit and hypocrisy are twins, so also envy and slander are twins. The primary motivation for slandering people is jealousy or envy toward them. When we envy people, we tend to speak badly about them, and in doing that, we fail to love our neighbor. So, Peter says, if you have been born of the Spirit of God, then get rid of malice. Do not let deceitfulness be a part of your character or behavior. Put aside all forms of hypocrisy. Christians must not be envious, because when we envy, we not only do violence to our neighbor, but we also do insult to God, who has given us the pearl of great price. It is tragic that some Christians are envious of unbelievers. No matter what an unbeliever has—wealth, fame, position, status—it is not comparable to the unspeakable gift that God has given to us. We have no right to envy anyone. Setting aside envy goes a long way toward curing our lips from slandering others.

Slander is incompatible with the new birth. Paul writes:

> You He made alive, who were dead in trespasses and sins, in which you once walked according to the course of this world, according to the prince of the power of the air, the spirit who now works in the sons of disobedience, among whom also we all once conducted ourselves in the lusts of our flesh, fulfilling the desires of the flesh and of the mind, and were by nature children of wrath, just as the others. (Eph. 2:1–3)

In our natural condition, the Bible says, we were followers of Satan, and Satan's name means "slanderer." The vocation of Satan is to slander Christ, His church, and His people. We certainly do not want to imitate the father of lies and join him in this destructive activity. If you are a Christian, put the slander aside and never pick it up again.

Pure Milk

As newborn babes, desire the pure milk of the word, that you may grow thereby (v. 2). Peter is not so much assuming that his audience is comprised of recent converts, who are, therefore, merely babes in Christ. The Bible does speak of new converts as being babes in terms of their spiritual progress, and there are other occasions when the Bible rebukes people who have been Christians for some time yet are still on a milk diet, not interested in chewing on the meat and the substance of the weightier things of God. The point Peter is making is that just as infants have a strong desire for milk, so the Christian, who is born of God, should have a similar thirst for the Word of God. When it is time for a baby to be fed, he will protest vociferously if the meal is even a few minutes delayed. The baby's desire for his next bottle becomes a great passion. Peter says that we ought to desire the pure milk of the Word just like a baby does his bottle. You will not grow as a Christian unless you are nurtured by the Word of God. There is no substitute for that. We are to be people who, having been changed by the power of the Holy Spirit, have a desire within our soul, a hunger and thirst, for the pure milk of the Word. No one has a great desire to drink spoiled milk; nothing is spit out of the mouth faster than a taste of milk that has become impure. We are to desire to be fed by a substance without impurities, which Peter describes in metaphorical terms as the Word of God.

If indeed you have tasted that the Lord is gracious (v. 3). If indeed you have been born of God's Spirit, if indeed the Spirit has put a taste in your mouth for the things of God—apart from that, you can have no taste for spiritual things. The world around you does not care about spiritual things. Spiritual milk is not high on the world's list of dietary pleasures, but if you have tasted it, if you have tasted of the Lord, as the psalmist said, and know that He is good (Ps. 44:8), how can you taste of Christ and not want more? That is why, in the Sermon on the Mount, Jesus said, "Blessed are those who hunger and thirst for righteousness, for they shall be filled" (Matt. 5:6).

What motivates you to go to church to hear the Word of God? Most likely, your purpose is not to be seen by other people. Very few will give up a Sunday just to be seen in church by others. The people who are drawn are the hungry, those who have a desire for the things of God because they have tasted them. It tastes so good that you want to have more. I cannot get enough of it. I am fed by studying the text as I prepare to preach, and it tastes fantastic. It makes me want more.

A Living Stone

Coming to Him as to a living stone, rejected indeed by men, but chosen by God and precious (v. 4). Peter uses many metaphors here, and "a living stone" is an important one. In high school I studied biology, which comes from the Greek word *bios*, meaning "life." I also studied zoology, which is the study of animal life, but I never had a course that included the study of stones. We think of stones as being inert, as having no vitality flowing through them. Yet when Peter speaks of coming to Jesus, he says it is like coming to a living stone. When the disciples were rebuked for praising Christ, He responded, "I tell you that if these should keep silent, the stones would immediately cry out" (Luke 19:40). What could be more impossible than that? Stones do not speak, because they are not alive, but here Peter says that when we come to Christ, we come to a stone that is alive.

I find it interesting that here Peter did not use the word *rock* (Greek *petros*), which is the name Jesus gave him, saying, "You are Peter, and on this rock I will build My church" (Matt. 16:18). Here Peter uses the word translated "stone." This is the stone that the people despised. We have come to a living stone that other people flee from. They have rejected Him, but this stone, in the language of Peter, is the elect stone, the One whom the Father has elected, and the One that in God's eyes is considered precious. What is odious to us in our fallen condition is considered precious by God Himself.

Living Stones

Peter then speaks of our participation: **You also, as living stones, are being built up a spiritual house, a holy priesthood, to offer up spiritual sacrifices acceptable to God through Jesus Christ** (v. 5). Not only is Christ the stone that is living, elect, and precious in the sight of God, but also all who belong to Christ participate in His life as being ourselves living stones, chosen of God. This epistle of Peter's is shot full of the doctrine of election. He uses a metaphor rarely applied to the church. The church is described in a variety of ways in the New Testament. Perhaps most frequently it is likened to a body; the church is the body of Christ. It is also called the *laos tou theou*, "the people of God." In every one of those metaphors, the church is made up of people. The church, the *ecclesia*, in the New Testament is comprised of the "called out ones." The church is the communion of saints, not a building. Now, all of a sudden, Peter gives a metaphor of the church as a building, but this building is made up not of brick and mortar but of living stones, of people. We are the church, because the church is made up of stones that are alive.

We are not just a spiritual house; we are a priesthood. This passage was very dear to Martin Luther. When he spoke about the priesthood of all believers, he was not saying that there is no distinction in the church between clergy and laity; the New Testament lays the foundation for those distinctions. Luther was saying that the priesthood of the New Testament is given to the whole Christian community.

In the Old Testament, the basic function of the priest was to offer up sacrifices to God in keeping with the sacrificial system of the old covenant. The sacrifices that the priests offered were physical sacrifices, animals and grain offerings. We are a different kind of priesthood, a spiritual priesthood, in which each believer is called to offer up spiritual sacrifices to God. At the very heart of worship is the concept of the offering of sacrifices. From the very beginning, with Cain and Abel, God's people brought their offerings to God as a sacrifice.

Paul wrote in Romans that we are to present ourselves as living sacrifices to God, which is our spiritual worship, or reasonable service (12:1). So, the first way in which we function as spiritual priests is by offering the sacrifice of praise to God, which is what worship is. Worship is not entertainment. Worship is when the people of God lift up their praises, adoration, and affection to God. Just as the priests lifted up the blood offering in the Old Testament, we lift up our reverence and adoration to God in praise. We do not come to church to watch the minister do that. We are all to do it.

If we were to offer our sacrifices to God on the basis of our own merit, God's response to our sacrifices would be the same as it was to Israel when Israel had violated the terms of its covenant. At that time God said that He hated their feasts. "Bring no more futile sacrifices; incense is an abomination to Me. The New Moons, the Sabbaths, and the calling of assemblies—I cannot endure iniquity and the sacred meeting" (Isa. 1:13). Trying to offer up spiritual sacrifices to God on our own merit is just as repugnant to Him as those sacrifices were in the Old Testament. What makes them precious to God and a sweet aroma to Him is that they are offered through Jesus Christ. Our sacrifice of praise, our spiritual sacrifice, is carried to the Father through our great High Priest, who sanctifies our worship. Apart from Christ, our worship would not be acceptable to God. It is Christ who makes our worship acceptable and pleasing to Him.

The Chief Cornerstone
Therefore it is also contained in the Scripture, "Behold, I lay in Zion a chief cornerstone, elect, precious, and he who believes on

**Him will by no means be put to shame." Therefore, to you who
believe, He is precious; but to those who are disobedient, "The
stone which the builders rejected has become the chief cornerstone," and "A stone of stumbling and a rock of offense"** (vv. 6–8a).
Peter carries the metaphor to its conclusion by saying that this living stone
to which we come has been the occasion for unbelievers to stumble. They
trip over Christ. In their rejection of Christ, they miss the kingdom of God.
The stone which they reject God has declared as the chief cornerstone of
His church.

The image here is again one of the church's being built upon a foundation. The hymn "The Church's One Foundation" contains the lyrics, "The
church's one foundation is Jesus Christ our Lord." I do not like the language
used in that line of the hymn because, in the New Testament, the primary
sense of the role of Jesus in the building is not that of the foundation. The
New Testament says that no foundation can be laid except that which is
laid in Christ Jesus, but He is not the foundation. When the New Testament
speaks of the building, it speaks of the foundation as being the Prophets and
the Apostles. They gave us the Word of God, which is established as the
foundation of the whole edifice. As the psalmist said in the Old Testament,
"If the foundations are destroyed, what can the righteous do?" (Ps. 11:3).

A friend of mine was the minister of a large Presbyterian church in the
Los Angeles area. Years ago, while he was en route to Los Angeles on a
plane, a terrible earthquake shattered the portion of Los Angeles where
his church was situated. When he heard the news, he was fearful that the
church had been destroyed, and he was relieved to find not a pane of glass
broken or a tile moved from the roof and no apparent damage to the church
building. However, within two weeks the building was posted as unsafe for
human assembly because, in the earthquake, the foundation had moved. It
had shifted.

It is not by accident that the greatest attack on the church in our day is
that against the trustworthiness of sacred Scripture. It is therefore important
that we hold fast to the Word of God; it is the foundation of the church, and
if the foundation is shaken, the church cannot endure. The Prophets and
the Apostles are the foundation of the church, and that foundation was laid
with the chief cornerstone, Christ Himself. This stumbling block, this stone
that the builders rejected and is despised by men, is precious to God.

7

A ROYAL PRIESTHOOD

1 Peter 2:8b–10

They stumble, being disobedient to the word, to which they also were appointed. But you are a chosen generation, a royal priesthood, a holy nation, His own special people, that you may proclaim the praises of Him who called you out of darkness into His marvelous light; who once were not a people but are now the people of God, who had not obtained mercy but now have obtained mercy.

I n our last study we considered the metaphor of the living stone, Jesus, who assembles to Himself a people who also are living stones, and through this group of living stones Christ's church is built. This stone, the foundation of the church, is at the same time a stone of stumbling by which many find their ruin. It is called a rock of offense. **They stumble, being disobedient to the word, to which they also were appointed** (v. 8b).

This stumbling is occasioned by the rock that is Christ. People who are disobedient to the Word of God are tripped up by Jesus, this rock of offense. We hear from Peter the grim message that to this they were appointed or destined, as some translations read. We find here, as we have already in Peter's writing, reference to predestination, to the sovereign election by which God pours His grace on those whom He has chosen from the foundation of the world. We understand also that the doctrine of predestination is double; that is, it involves not only election but also reprobation. This is clearly set forth in Romans 9, where Paul contrasts the destiny of Jacob to that of Esau. There are some who clearly understand that the Bible teaches election in the positive sense, but the idea that there is another side to it seems to be a horrible decree from which they shrink.

There is a theory set forth called in Latin *destinare ad pecatum.* The idea is that God from all eternity has predestined people to sin, that He set forth their destiny as sinners in order that they may be damned. This is exactly what the Reformed doctrine of predestination does not teach. Rather, the doctrine teaches that God's decrees of election and reprobation were given in light of the fall. God did not before time began consider an unfallen, innocent humanity out of which He destined some for salvation and others to damnation. Rather, as Augustine pointed out, when God was considering the human race, He knew them prior to the fall as a mass of perdition, and out of this mass of fallen, unbelieving, disobedient humans, God chose sovereignly to bestow His saving grace on some but to allow others to do what they pleased. God simply passed them over. No one in this equation is subjected to divine injustice, but the redeemed receive grace and the unredeemed receive justice. People complain against this, saying that God is unfair to give His mercy to some and not to all. However, when we complain about God's sovereign grace in salvation, we see how gracious that salvation really is, because our complaining reveals how obstinate our hearts are toward the majesty and sovereignty of God.

They were appointed to a destiny of judgment on the basis of their unbelief—their disobedience—because that is the inevitable conclusion for all who refuse to bow before Christ. All who reject the cornerstone find that very stone to be that which will trip them up forever. As one commentator mentioned, you cannot trip across a stone unless at least your toe touches it. Peter is describing those who had encountered the living Christ and stumbled over Him. In stark contrast, Peter speaks comfort to those to whom he addressed the epistle: **But you are a chosen generation, a royal priesthood, a holy nation, His own special people** (v. 9).

Royal Priesthood

I frequently have breakfast at a restaurant. One of the assistant managers regularly greets me and asks, "How are you?" I reply, "I am fine. How are you?" When he answers me, he does not say, "I am fine" but rather "I am blessed." As we exchange greetings I am reminded of his belief in the Savior and his understanding of the grace of God. That is who we are—a blessed people who have received the riches of God's grace in our lives, "a chosen generation, a royal priesthood."

This is the second time in the epistle that Peter has made reference to our being involved in a priesthood. In the first instance he called it a "holy priesthood" (v. 5). We looked at that in light of Luther's understanding of the priesthood of all believers. Here, Peter qualifies the priesthood in a different way. He says that we are chosen and that we are royal, that is, we serve in the presence of and under the aegis of a king. Christ is not only our King, but He is also our great High Priest, an affirmation with which people in the Jewish community struggled.

In the Old Testament, the priesthood was given to the tribe of Levi. In order to be ordained as a priest, one had to be from that tribe. Jesus was not a Levite; He was from the tribe of Judah, and it was to Judah that the kingdom was given. In the blessing Jacob gave to his sons, he said:

> Judah is a lion's whelp;
> > From the prey, my son, you have gone up.
> > He bows down, he lies down as a lion;
> > And as a lion, who shall rouse him?
> The scepter shall not depart from Judah,
> > Nor a lawgiver from between his feet,
> > Until Shiloh comes;
> > And to Him shall be the obedience of the people. (Gen. 49:9–10)

The lion of Judah became a title for the king who came out of Judah. Jesus is that King.

If Jesus is the king, how can He be the priest? This was the question considered by the author of Hebrews. He argued that Jesus was a priest from a different order of priesthood. He was not a Levitical priest, a descendant of Aaron. Rather, He was of the order of Melchizedek. The author recounts the incident from the book of Genesis in which Abraham met Melchizedek (14:18–24). Melchizedek pronounced his blessing on Abraham, and in turn Abraham paid a tithe to Melchizedek. The point is, according to Hebrews, that the superior blesses the subordinate, and the subordinate gives tithes to the superior. Abraham was subordinating himself to the authority of this enigmatic character Melchizedek. The author of Hebrews goes on to say that if Melchizedek is greater than Abraham, and Abraham is greater than Isaac, and Isaac is greater than Jacob, and Jacob is greater than Levi, then Melchizedek is greater than Levi.

Melchizedek is given a name and a title (see Heb. 7:1–3). He is called Melchizedek the king of Salem. The meaning of the name Melchizedek is based upon two Hebrew words: *melek,* which means "king," and *tsaddiyq,* which means "righteousness." Melchizedek means "king of righteousness." He was the king of Salem, or king of peace. There is some evidence that prior to Jerusalem's being called Jerusalem, it was called Salem. Many think that the appearance of Melchizedek in the Old Testament was a Christophany, a pre-incarnation appearance of Christ Himself. The point, however, is that Melchizedek was a priest and a king, and Christ receives His priesthood from that order and His kingship from the ancestry of Judah. Therefore, Jesus supremely is the king-priest.

In the Old Testament, apart from Melchizedek, there was a sharp line of division between the function of the king and the function of the priest. King Uzziah reigned faithfully for decades until he took to himself the role of priest and came into the Holy Place to offer sacrifices. The priests were aghast, and they rebuked him. Uzziah exercised his wrath on the priests whereupon God struck him with leprosy and removed him from the throne, and he died in shame (2 Chronicles 26). That union of priesthood and kingship was reserved for Christ, our King and our great High Priest who intercedes for us daily at the right hand of God. The One whom God anointed King of kings is at the same time our priest.

However, this conjunction of kingship and priesthood does not finish with Jesus. Peter gives us the astonishing affirmation that in Christ we are a chosen generation and a royal priesthood. By virtue of our being in Christ, we participate in His kingdom. We participate in His priesthood as those who make intercession for the lost as well as for the people of God. We are a nation that is holy, sacred, consecrated, and transcendent. We are a nation that is different from any nation that has ever appeared on this planet.

Pilgrims

In at least two earlier occasions and again soon to follow, Peter addresses his readership as pilgrims or sojourners, drawing attention to the past of the people of Israel. They had been semi-nomadic people who rarely had a place to call home. At the heart of the promises God had made to Abraham was that the people would become a nation and have a homeland; they would have a permanent place that would give them stability. The history of Israel is the history of instability. If you read the newspaper today, you will see how many nations have their weapons of destruction aimed at Israel. Since the destruction of Jerusalem in A.D. 70, the Jewish people have been dispersed.

They have been a people without a home, a people without a country, until the Balfour Declaration in 1948.

We as Christians are a people without a country. There is never an equation in the Bible between the people of God and a peculiar nationalism. The kingdom of God is not limited to the borders of the United States of America. It transcends every human border. The kingdom of God is spread throughout the whole world, and the reason is that citizens in that kingdom belong to a different kind of country, a holy nation—as the Scriptures define it, a heavenly nation. Our citizenship really cannot be defined by our passports, because in this world we remain pilgrims. In the words of the old gospel hymn, "This world is not my own; I'm only passing through," but that does not mean that we are a people without a country. We are citizens of a holy nation created by God, His own special people.

The reason that we are a chosen generation and a royal priesthood and that God has conferred upon us citizenship in a heavenly, holy country is, according to Peter, this: **that you may proclaim the praises of Him who called you out of darkness into His marvelous light** (v. 9). We have received our citizenship for the purpose of proclaiming God's praises. To worship God is to offer Him not an animal sacrifice or a cereal offering but the sacrifice of praise. The praise of God should be on our lips every moment because citizens of this heavenly kingdom spend eternity praising the King of that heavenly nation, singing with the angels, "Worthy is the Lamb who was slain to receive power and riches and wisdom, and strength and honor and glory and blessing!" (Rev. 5:12).

Light and Darkness

The contrast between light and darkness is a common metaphor in the New Testament. Darkness is a place where no light intrudes, where deeds of evil are conceived and carried out. The Bible tells us that we are by nature the children of darkness. Darkness is our natural habitat. In our fallen condition, we feared more than anything else that a searchlight would be placed on our souls and that our sins would be made manifest to the world. We read in John's Gospel:

> For God so loved the world that He gave His only begotten Son, that whoever believes in Him should not perish but have everlasting life. For God did not send His Son into the world to condemn the world, but that the world through Him might be saved. He who believes in Him is not condemned; but he who does not believe is condemned already, because he has not believed in the name of the only begotten Son of God. And this is the condemnation, that

the light has come into the world, and men loved darkness rather than light, because their deeds were evil. For everyone practicing evil hates the light and does not come to the light, lest his deeds should be exposed. But he who does the truth comes to the light, that his deeds may be clearly seen, that they have been done in God. (John 3:16–21)

We tend to stop at John 3:16. We do not consider that the flipside to that wonderful message is judgment—men love darkness. The reason they love the darkness is that their deeds are evil. When our deeds are placed in the light, they are exposed for the wickedness that motivates them, which is lived out in darkness, our natural habitat. Our natural disposition toward God is indisposition. We have a built-in allergy to the things of God. Our natural disposition is not to seek Him but to flee from Him. From the commission of the first sin by Adam and Eve in the garden, the activity of fallen creatures is to hide from the face of God.

Peter says, however, that God has called us out of the darkness into the light. We greatly distort Peter's words in our evangelism if we interpret him as saying that we were groping in the dark as blind men until God appealed to us to come out of the cave and into the light of day, and then we exercised our wills and came into the light. No human being left to himself will do that. We come out of darkness only when God effectually calls us out, when God brings His light to us, as He did at the dawn of creation when darkness was upon the face of the deep. The lights came on by the effectual call of God, who said, "Let there be light" (Gen. 1:3), and the darkness could not overcome the light that God called into being.

If you go into your bedroom tonight and turn out all the lights and shut the shades so that the slightest inkling of light cannot enter the room, you will feel the intensity of the darkness. Then throw the light switch and count the seconds it takes for the darkness to vanish. Darkness has no power to extinguish light. When the light comes on, the darkness vanishes. God, in His effectual call by the power of the Holy Spirit, changed your heart. He changed the desire you were born with, to seek and cleave to the darkness, and gave you a taste of joy and a love for the light, so that you willingly, gladly came and basked in the light of His presence if you are a Christian.

The motto of the sixteenth-century Reformation was *ex tenebras lux*, "out of the darkness, light." The glorious light of the gospel had been eclipsed by and substituted with a false gospel. When the light of the true gospel shone once more, the face of the world was changed. The darkness fled before the light.

There is an expression that some use in a rather pejorative manner when describing someone who claims to have been converted to Christ: "He saw the light." If someone were to say that of me, I would reply, "Yes, I have seen the light, and it is glorious. It dispels the darkness of my soul." Only God can do that. He has called us out of darkness not simply into light but into *His* light, and even beyond that, into His *marvelous* light. It is a marvel when God displays His light into the darkness of a human soul. Words cannot express the wonder of being brought out of the darkness into His light.

Then Peter calls attention back to the Old Testament: **. . . who once were not a people but are now the people of God, who had not obtained mercy but now have obtained mercy** (v. 10). Peter must have in mind the story of the prophet Hosea, who was called of God to marry a woman of harlotry. The children she bore were given names significant of God's judgment on His people.

> So he went and took Gomer the daughter of Diblaim, and she conceived and bore him a son. Then the LORD said to him:
>
> > "Call his name Jezreel,
> > For in a little while
> > I will avenge the bloodshed of Jezreel on the house of Jehu,
> > And bring an end to the kingdom of the house of Israel.
> > It shall come to pass in that day
> > That I will break the bow of Israel in the Valley of Jezreel."
>
> And she conceived again and bore a daughter. Then God said to him:
>
> > "Call her name Lo-Ruhamah,
> > For I will no longer have mercy on the house of Israel,
> > But I will utterly take them away.
> > Yet I will have mercy on the house of Judah,
> > Will save them by the LORD their God,
> > And will not save them by bow,
> > Nor by sword or battle,
> > By horses or horsemen."
>
> Now when she had weaned Lo-Ruhamah, she conceived and bore a son. Then God said:
>
> > "Call his name Lo-Ammi,
> > For you are not My people,
> > And I will not be your God." (Hos. 1:3–9)

Every Jew knew that story, so when Peter tells them, "You are a chosen generation, a royal priesthood, a holy nation, His own special people," they would have understood that they, a people who once were Lo-Ammi, not a people, had become the people of God. Those who were Lo-Ruhamah, who had not obtained mercy, have now obtained mercy. That is what God has done for us. He has called us out of darkness to be His people and the vessels of His mercy. What a destiny.

8

HONORABLE CONDUCT

1 Peter 2:11–17

Beloved, I beg you as sojourners and pilgrims, abstain from fleshly lusts which war against the soul, having your conduct honorable among the Gentiles, that when they speak against you as evildoers, they may, by your good works which they observe, glorify God in the day of visitation. Therefore submit yourselves to every ordinance of man for the Lord's sake, whether to the king as supreme, or to governors, as to those who are sent by him for the punishment of evildoers and for the praise of those who do good. For this is the will of God, that by doing good you may put to silence the ignorance of foolish men—as free, yet not using liberty as a cloak for vice, but as bondservants of God. Honor all people. Love the brotherhood. Fear God. Honor the king.

Peter begins this section by addressing his readers as **Beloved** (v. 11). The NIV translates this as "friends," which I think is a weak translation because the idea goes far beyond the level of human friendship to a higher dimension of affection. There are two aspects to Peter's term of address.

First, the term has reference to the people's standing before God. Peter has just shown us that as Christ is the chief cornerstone and the living stone, so by the birth of the Holy Spirit we have been made living stones in Him. Throughout the teaching of the New Testament, we see that Christ is the

Beloved, and we are the beloved by extension. Insofar as we are in Christ and participate in the inheritance that the Father gives to Him, we also participate in this special level of affection that the Father has for the Son. So, the first import of this greeting is Peter's reminding his readers, and by extension us, that we are God's beloved.

Second, in the greeting there is an element of the Apostle's personal affection for the people of God. Sometimes I refer to those in my congregation as "friends," but my favorite form of addressing the congregation is as "beloved." The term is used richly in the biblical witness.

We see in the book of Acts some of the conflict in the early church that focused on how the Gentiles were to be received among Jewish Christian believers. The debate over this question escalated to serious measures, particularly between the leading Apostle to the Jews, Peter; and the Apostle to the Gentiles, Paul. The debate even provoked the calling of the Council of Jerusalem in Acts 15. Paul had to call out Peter for his tendency to be weak at times and to capitulate to the negative influence of the Judaizers. Yet, when we read Peter's epistle, we find that there are many parallels between how Paul and Peter approached the Christian life. One reason for the similarity is that they were both inspired by the same Holy Spirit. Whatever differences they may have had in the flesh, those differences were overruled when it came to the penning of sacred Scripture.

Souls at War

At the end of his doctrinal teaching in Romans, Paul writes, "I beseech you therefore, brethren, by the mercies of God, that you present your bodies a living sacrifice, holy, acceptable to God, which is your reasonable service" (Rom. 12:1). Similarly here, Peter writes, **I beg you as sojourners and pilgrims, abstain from fleshly lusts which war against the soul** (v. 11). Peter used the term "pilgrims" earlier (1:1). In the Old Testament, one of the most important duties that God imposed upon the Jewish people was the practice of hospitality. That practice, which became high on the list of cultural imperatives for the Jews, was grounded in the fact that they had once been pilgrims, sojourners who possessed no land. They had wandered as strangers. Since they had experienced the kindness and graciousness of other people, they were to dispense that grace in turn in the form of hospitality. Peter will not allow the Jewish people to forget that they are sojourners on earth, because their real citizenship is in heaven. Peter stresses this because one's citizenship is where one learns his customs and mores.

The behavior of fallen people should never become the standard of right and wrong. A big problem in the church today is that even after people are converted to Christ, they still take their marching orders from what is acceptable and expected in the culture. We must remember that we do not belong to the culture. As Paul wrote, "Do not be conformed to this world, but be transformed by the renewing of your mind" (Rom. 12:2). The way to get a new mind is not by paying attention to Gallup polls but by paying attention to the mind of Christ, so that we begin to think like Jesus. No matter what everyone else does or approves, if Jesus does not approve, then we cannot. We need to remember who we are—citizens of heaven—and our lives are supposed to demonstrate that as we take our cue not from this world but from heaven itself.

A quick glance at verse 11 might lead a person to think that Christians are called to behave with respect to sexual matters in a manner completely different from how pagans behave. That is true and also emphasized by the Apostle Paul, but the fleshly lusts of which Peter speaks here include far more than sexual behavior. Fleshly lusts have to do with the desires of the *sarx*, which is the Greek term translated "flesh," in its entirety. To abstain from fleshly lusts is basically to abstain from the desires of this world, in keeping with the One from whom we receive our marching orders. These fleshly lusts, which place success above obedience, have everything to do with the corrupt nature. Paul describes it this way: "The flesh lusts against the Spirit, and the Spirit against the flesh; and these are contrary to one another" (Gal. 5:17). Peter says that these fleshly lusts—desires, passions, or ambitions—war against the soul. They do not simply present stumbling blocks to the soul or set up rival interests, but they are at war with the soul.

I get a bit impatient when I hear television preachers say, "Come to Jesus, and all your problems will be over." My life did not get complicated until I became a Christian. Before I was a Christian, I did whatever I wanted; I went along with the group and the world. When I became a Christian, I knew the war between flesh and spirit in a new way. Satan has declared war on our souls, and we are engaged every day in a spiritual battle to maintain our integrity and our obedience to Christ. What things war against your soul? Where is the battle in your life? Is it with your ambition? Do you have to compromise your integrity to get what you want or to achieve what you want to achieve? There is a unique battle for each person. My struggles might be different from yours, and yours might be different from mine. Each of us comes into the Christian life from a different background and with different scars and deeply ingrained habits, so that one man's struggle is another man's ease. Nevertheless, each of us has a battle, so every now and then we need to ask, "What is churning up that conflict in my soul?"

Jesus expressed a rudimentary principle when He asked, "What will it profit a man if he gains the whole world, and loses his own soul?" (Mark 8:36). Jesus was uttering the calculus of economics. He measured the benefits this world offers against the value of the soul. If you were to gain the whole world at the cost of your soul, would it be worth it? He also put it this way: "What will a man give in exchange for his soul?" (Matt. 16:26). He was using the language of barter. Literary masterpieces have been written in which someone with a great desire for something is met by Mephistopheles or some other Satan figure who offers to give him his desire in exchange for his soul. How much value do we attribute to our souls? What price tag do we place on our integrity? If we do not own anything—if our bank account is zero, if we are jobless and homeless—we still have our integrity. How much is it worth? We have to deal with that question in the conflicts with the world every day. Integrity is priceless.

Day of Visitation

At this point, the Apostle is reduced to begging for an abstinence from not just sexual temptation but all that wars against our souls. Then he says something somewhat strange, although it is similar to what Paul says elsewhere: **having your conduct honorable among the Gentiles, that when they speak against you as evildoers, they may, by your good works which they observe, glorify God in the day of visitation** (v. 12).

A metaphor used to describe people's pet peeves is that of land mines, which are dangerous and incendiary. The personality of some people renders land mines few and far between. You have to walk a long way with such a person to find something that upsets him. Some personalities, however, produce wall-to-wall land mines. Whatever you say is likely to provoke them to rage. Our conduct is to be honorable so that people's speaking evil against us will not be a land mine. It does not matter how others behave; it matters how we as Christians behave. We cannot control what other people do, but we can control what we ourselves do, and God holds us responsible for that.

Throughout this passage Peter uses some form of the word *honor*. I remember several years ago speaking with a group of Christian men. They referred to one of their colleagues as an "honorable man." My ears perked up because it is rare to hear people talk in terms of honor. Judges are still addressed as "Your Honor," and long ago General Douglas MacArthur said in a speech, "Duty, honor, country: those three hallowed words reverently dictate what you ought to be, what you can be, what you will be." Nevertheless, the word *honor* has all but disappeared from our vocabulary; it belongs to a former era. However, if you look up the word *honor* in a Bible concordance, you may be surprised how frequently the word is used, even in the Ten Commandments: "Honor your father and your mother" (Ex. 20:12). Honor goes beyond respect; to honor is to bend over backwards to show respect for other people.

As a result of your good works, people may say something that, in spite of their hostility toward you and their lack of devotion toward God, in the final analysis gives glory to God. There are many religious institutions in America, one being the Salvation Army. Salvation Army volunteers, with their kettles and bells at Christmastime, are the object of ridicule until a natural disaster occurs and those volunteers are the first ones on scene. During the first week I was in Amsterdam, some of my American colleagues wanted to drive me around downtown Amsterdam, the prostitution capital of Europe. Prostitutes stand before picture windows scantily attired and try to attract tourists. The practice is wide open and protected by the government. The first time I witnessed it, I thought, *Does anyone minister to these people?* I saw prostitutes standing in front of a church door and considered that the minister would have to walk past them to go inside to his office. As I stood there pondering that, I saw a young woman cross a canal to speak to one of the girls. She was from the *Leger des Heils*, the Army of Salvation. The only people I knew who ministered good works were the women of the Salvation Army, and those prostitutes always spoke with respect for that organization.

The prostitutes' glowing appreciation of the Salvation Army women is a backhanded expression of the glory of God, who will be glorified in what Peter calls "the day of visitation." This is a lengthy expression of a phrase found throughout the Old Testament, "the day of the Lord," which referred to the day when God would come. Early on in Jewish prophetic history, the day of God's coming—the day of His visitation—was anticipated with great joy. Later, however, Israel fell into such corruption that the prophet Amos said to the people, "Woe to you who desire the day of the LORD! For what good is the day of the LORD to you? It will be darkness, and not light" (Amos 5:18).

In the New Testament the word *visit* is formed from the root of the word *bishop*. The concept of the bishop in the New Testament is that of a visitor. It comes from the Greek military community where, from time to time, the general would drop in unannounced and review the troops. If the troops were battle-ready, they received the praise of the general. If the troops were ill-prepared, they would receive the judgment of the general. That metaphor is used to describe the day of visitation, the day when our heavenly Bishop comes. When He arrives what will He find?

The parable of the persistent widow begins, "He spoke a parable to them, that men always ought to pray and not lose heart" (Luke 18:1). In the parable Jesus tells a story of a poor woman who was treated unjustly. She goes to a judge to have her case heard, but the judge does not care about her. He ignores her plaintive cries time after time until finally she wears him down by her importunity. To stop her nagging, the judge hears her case and vindicates her. Afterward Jesus said, "Hear what the unjust judge said. And shall God not avenge His own elect who cry out day and night to Him, though He bears long with them? I tell you that He will avenge them speedily. Nevertheless, when the Son of Man comes, will He really find faith on the earth?" (vv. 6–8). If He comes to us tonight, He will find faith, because we have been visited by the Bishop of our souls, who keeps us prepared for that day of visitation.

Submission

Then we come to a link signaling a conclusion: **Therefore submit yourselves to every ordinance of man for the Lord's sake** (v. 13). Peter transitions here into a large section about submission to kings, governors, and civil magistrates, and the submission that slaves are to give to their masters, and wives to their husbands. We will come back to that section as a whole, but here we will focus on Peter's introductory comment, "Therefore submit yourselves."

First, we must not wait to be coerced into submission. Submission is something we are to initiate and are responsible to do. We are to submit ourselves to every ordinance of man. In my neighborhood there are stop signs on every corner. Somebody spent a lot of money for nothing, because at least eight in ten people give a hint of slowing down but never come to a direct stop. They do not submit to the ordinance. A friend of mine—a Christian—ran a stop sign while I was riding with him, and I asked, "Didn't you see that stop sign?" He replied, "Yes, but I'm not going to let a bit of tin and red paint control my behavior."

Peter says that we are to submit to every ordinance of man, but that has to be qualified. We are to do so unless those ordinances prohibit us from doing what God commands or command us to do what God forbids. Then not only may we not be submissive, but we must not submit. Peter is speaking in general terms here. What is important to note is why Peter comes to this conclusion. He tells us to submit to authorities for the Lord's sake—not for your sake or my sake, but for the Lord's sake.

To understand this, we have to see the scope of the biblical concept of obedience, submission, and authority. The universe in which we live is not a democracy; God does not rule by referendum. It has been said many times that the Ten Commandments are not ten suggestions. There is a hierarchical structure of authority in the universe, and at the top of that structure is the sovereign God, who reigns and rules. He has delegated all authority in heaven and earth to His Son, the King of kings and the Lord of lords. So, at the top of this hierarchical structure of the universe is Christ. Nero, who was king when this epistle was written, was under the authority of Jesus, but he would not submit because his was a spirit of lawlessness, the spirit that now works in the sons of disobedience.

Satan is intimately identified with lawlessness. The plunge of the human race into disaster came as a result of our original parents' act of lawlessness—the refusal of Adam and Eve to submit to the Creator. Therefore, every time we do not submit to the rules that plague us all, we are casting our vote with lawlessness, and every time we go out of our way to submit, we bear witness to the One whose law stands above every law. Every time we obey our employer, our schoolteacher, and our parents, we give honor to Christ, who reigns over the whole universe. This is where the word *honor* comes into play.

When we were strangers to the kingdom of God, we walked according to the course of this world. We walked according to the power of the prince of the air, according to the lusts of our flesh, just as the rest of the world. While we were in that state, the Holy Spirit quickened us, made us new creatures, and called us out of the land of darkness into the land of life. He put within our souls a new inclination, a desire to please God rather than to disobey Him. So, when we offer submission, we are not acting like Casper Milquetoast and offering a doormat-like weakness; we are showing our commitment to the King.

9

SERVANTS AND MASTERS

1 Peter 2:18–25

Servants, be submissive to your masters with all fear, not only to the good and gentle, but also to the harsh. For this is commendable, if because of conscience toward God one endures grief, suffering wrongfully. For what credit is it if, when you are beaten for your faults, you take it patiently? But when you do good and suffer, if you take it patiently, this is commendable before God. For to this you were called, because Christ also suffered for us, leaving us an example, that you should follow His steps:

"Who committed no sin,

Nor was deceit found in His mouth";

who, when He was reviled, did not revile in return; when He suffered, He did not threaten, but committed Himself to Him who judges righteously; who Himself bore our sins in His own body on the tree, that we, having died to sins, might live for righteousness—by whose stripes you were healed. For you were like sheep going astray, but have now returned to the Shepherd and Overseer of your souls.

In our last study, we spent some time on the principle that we are to give obedience and submission to those in a position of authority over us, and we are to do that unto the Lord. Since all authority ultimately rests with God and those to whom He delegates it, all unjust disobedience to authority is an insult to the One who is the ground of all authority. Having given us that general principle, the Apostle Peter applies it to specific life situations, beginning with one that deals with the obligation of slaves or bondservants to their masters.

Before we look at this, let us acknowledge that the institution of slavery is repugnant to us, as well it should be. Some people are overwhelmed by finding slavery in Scripture, particularly in the New Testament. The late theologian John Murray said that the New Testament thereby does not endorse slavery, and yet at the same time it did not forbid it, but, as Murray said, all the seeds for the dissolution of slavery were sown in the New Testament. So, with that in mind, let us look at this first application of the general principle of submission.

Bondservants

Servants [or slaves], be submissive to your masters with all fear, not only to the good and gentle, but also to the harsh (v. 18). Peter has just declared that we have freedom in Christ, yet we have been set free to a new kind of bondage—not to sin and Satan but as bondservants of God. The Apostle Paul defined himself as a servant of Christ. The paradoxical truth is that we are never free until we become servants of God.

The application here is to those who were living as bondservants. Peter admonishes them to be submissive to their masters with all fear, that is, with all reverence, not only to the good and gentle master but also to the harsh one. We could add other qualifiers. The slave was called not only to be submissive to the harsh master but also to the unjust, the unfair, and the cruel master. Does it not jolt your sensibilities to hear the New Testament saying that this is the way it should be done? Peter said, **For this is commendable, if because of conscience toward God one endures grief, suffering wrongfully** (v. 19). Enduring cruelty and harshness from fear or cowardice is not necessarily commendable. That kind of submission does not get us a commendation from God. His commendation comes when we do it for conscience's sake. If we submit because we are trying to honor the lordship of God, then such submission, even in times of harshness and cruelty, is commendable.

For what credit is it if, when you are beaten for your faults, you take it patiently? (v. 20). When we suffer for doing wrong, we rarely do so patiently and quietly. Even when we know that our punishment is deserved, we protest against it and find a way to describe it as unjust. However, the Word of God says that there is no credit if we are beaten for our faults and take it patiently. We ought to do it, so it should not require any particular virtue or progress in sanctification. **But when you do good and suffer, if you take it patiently, this is commendable before God** (v. 20).

A cynical adage says that no good deed goes unpunished. We live in a world where the wicked prosper and the righteous suffer. When one tries to behave in an ethical manner, it is inevitable that he or she will suffer unjustly at the hands of godless people. Yet, Peter says, when we do good and suffer and take it patiently, this is commendable before God.

Holy Vocation

Why does God give His smile of approval on those who suffer patiently when they are victims of unjust treatment? Peter gives us the answer: **For to this you were called** (v. 21). It is our vocation. When God calls us to a task, it is our duty to obey it. It is commendable when we suffer unjustly and bear the pain in patience because God has called us to that. Many television preachers today say that God always wills healing and prosperity for His people and, therefore, any pain we suffer comes from Satan and never from the hand of God. This is a pernicious distortion of biblical truth. Just the opposite is the case; our vocation is a call to suffer.

Many years ago I delivered a series of lectures at the MD Anderson Cancer Center in Houston, Texas, on the topic of suffering. One of the lectures I gave, which became part of my book *Surprised by Suffering*, focused on the fact that suffering is a vocation. Suffering becomes bearable when we understand that we are in that state by the providence of God, and therefore, at that time, it is our vocation. The word *vocation* means "calling," from the Latin root *voco*. If we fall ill with a terminal disease, we can curse the fates that have brought us to that stage, or we can see it as the providence of God. There is nothing worse than to suffer pain or grief for no reason, which is why those without Christ are without hope. For them, ultimately, life is an experience of futility, but if their souls become captured by the truth of the gospel, they will know that "all things work together for good to those who love God, to those who are the called according to His purpose" (Rom. 8:28), so there is purpose even in our suffering. That is perhaps the hardest biblical truth to embrace.

When Job's great suffering came upon him, he said, "Naked I came from my mother's womb, and naked shall I return there. The LORD gave, and the LORD has taken away; blessed be the name of the LORD" (Job 1:21). In time his pain grew so intense that his wife told him, "Curse God and die!" (2:9), but Job responded, "Shall we indeed accept good from God, and shall we not accept adversity?" (2:10). As his suffering endured Job said, "Though He slay me, yet will I trust Him" (13:15); and "I know that my Redeemer lives, and He shall stand at last on the earth" (19:25). That is the message Peter is giving. It is commendable to accept suffering with patience because, in the first place, we have been called to that very thing.

Why are we called to suffer? Peter answers that question: **because Christ also suffered for us, leaving us an example, that you should follow His steps** (v. 21). The thinly veiled implication here is that the servant is not above his master. This man who wrote these words under the inspiration of the Holy Spirit is the same man who repudiated Jesus with curses the night that Jesus was betrayed. Peter stood by and watched Jesus being led down the Via Dolorosa to His death. He had distanced himself from Jesus. Here, in his later years, he understood what a hellish thing that was, and he is able to say that we are called to suffer because Jesus suffered for us.

In the middle of the decade of the A.D. 60s, Peter and Paul were put to death in Rome by Nero. Peter was sentenced to die by crucifixion. He submitted to that decree, but he made one plea: he asked to be crucified upside down because he did not think that he was worthy to die in the same manner as his Savior. A long time passed before Peter understood what it meant that Jesus had suffered for him.

Suffering Injustice

Peter adds a citation: **"Who committed no sin, nor was deceit found in His mouth"** (v. 22). We all have experienced being slandered, accused of things for which we were not guilty. How loathsome that is. I remember a time when, as a boy, I was taking an exam in a science class. In the middle of the examination the teacher accused me of cheating. I felt violated and offended because I had not been cheating. I suffered an injustice, and I hated it, but I never stopped to think of how many times I had cheated but had not been caught. Jesus never cheated. There was never any deceit in His mouth. He never sinned. How could anyone justify inflicting suffering on a perfect man? The cross of our Lord was the worst injustice in all of human history, yet it pleased the Father that He suffer that injustice at the hands of men so that the Father's justice could be satisfied for the guilty. This side of heaven we will never comprehend the depths of that substitution.

Peter directs our attention to that example: **Who, when He was reviled, did not revile in return; when He suffered, He did not threaten, but committed Himself to Him who judges righteously** (v. 23). It was impossible for Jesus to return evil for evil. His style was to return good for evil, and He calls us to do the same. Is there anything harder? When He suffered, He did not threaten. Instead, He committed Himself to the Father, because He knew that vengeance was His and that He had promised to vindicate His people who cried unto Him day and night. When you are slandered or falsely accused, there is nothing sweeter than to be vindicated, and there is no one who can vindicate like God. Jesus understood that, but how hard it is for us to do the same.

Every sermon that comes from my pulpit starts with the preacher as the target of the sermon. We are all in this together. I do not set myself before my congregation as an example, nor did Peter. Peter pointed to Jesus as the example. He is the model, the example who committed Himself to the One who judges righteously.

Who Himself bore our sins in His own body on the tree, that we, having died to sins, might live for righteousness—by whose stripes you were healed (v. 24). That last phrase is a quotation from Isaiah 53, and it is the supreme proof-text used by those of the so-called Word of Faith ministry, those who proclaim that God always wills healing. Someone recently said, "Do not tell me about Epaphroditus, Paul's thorn in the flesh, or Timothy's upset stomach. Those examples only prove the sinful character of those who didn't have enough faith to believe that God would heal them." Those who hold to this view misapply this verse from Isaiah. If we were to do an exhaustive study of the word *heal* using a theological dictionary, we would see that the primary reference has nothing to do with being cured of physical diseases or ailments. It has to do with being healed of the consequences of sin. When the Suffering Servant was put before the lash in our stead, the beating left grizzly welts on His back that looked like stripes. Those were stripes of punishment, and by those stripes, we escape punishment for sin. The passage does not offer a blanket promise of healing for sickness.

Very few people in the history of the world, no matter how much devotion they practice or piety they exhibit, have escaped the final illness. Enoch was translated; Elijah walked with God and was not. Most succumbed to their final illness, because the healing that is in the cross, with respect to physical disease, is not something that we are guaranteed to receive in this world. We believe in a comprehensive healing of the body at the final resurrection, but what Peter is speaking about here, echoing the teaching of Isaiah, is healing from the punishment due us for sin.

Overseer of Our Souls

Peter ends the chapter with these words: **For you were like sheep going astray, but have now returned to the Shepherd and Overseer of your souls** (v. 25). Sheep imagery is used often in the Bible to describe our behavior. If you have seen a loose group of sheep, you know that it is chaos in motion. They do not stay together. They run to and fro and trip over themselves. They go astray and lose their way. We are all like that. We wander here and there and do not stay on the road that God has set before us.

An extraordinary occurrence once took place in the middle of an academic convocation at a theological seminary where I was teaching. Such convocations are customary in academia. A celebrated scholar is brought in, and he will read a paper or deliver a technical message that explores some esoteric point of theology. It is part of the academic protocol. On this particular occasion, the speaker stood and began reciting a list of titles: "Messiah, Savior, Lord, Son of David, Son of Man, Son of God, Bright and Morning Star, The Rose of Sharon, Emmanuel." He continued for thirty or forty minutes reciting this litany of titles ascribed to Jesus in the New Testament. It was overwhelming. We can make the grievous mistake of rushing over titles given to Jesus.

There are two titles here at the end of 1 Peter 2: "Shepherd" and "Overseer" or, as some translate, "Bishop." Jesus uses the metaphor of the shepherd to define His identity. He describes Himself as "the good shepherd" (John 10:11). He said, "A hireling, he who is not the shepherd, one who does not own the sheep, sees the wolf coming and leaves the sheep and flees; and the wolf catches the sheep and scatters them" (v. 12). The hireling is not a good shepherd but a bad one. In contrast, Jesus said:

> I am the good shepherd; and I know My sheep, and am known by My own. As the Father knows Me, even so I know the Father; and I lay down My life for the sheep. And other sheep I have which are not of this fold; them also I must bring, and they will hear My voice; and there will be one flock and one shepherd. (vv. 14–16)

"The LORD is my shepherd; I shall not want" (Ps. 23:1). He is the Good Shepherd who is constantly watching out for the well-being of His sheep.

Jesus confronted Peter by the shore and said, "Simon, son of Jonah, do you love me?" and Peter responded, "Yes, Lord; You know that I love you." Then Jesus said, "Feed my sheep" (John 21:16–17). Jesus did not ask Peter to entertain His sheep or to poison them. Jesus commanded Peter to feed His sheep.

A friend, who hardly ever darkened the door of a church, came to St. Andrew's once and sat through a service. Afterward he greeted me and said, "Today, R.C., I was part of your flock"; however, it is not my flock. It is Jesus' flock. He is our Shepherd, and when we go astray, He uses the crooked end of the staff to grab us around the neck and draw us back into line. Being corralled by the Shepherd may be uncomfortable, but His rod and staff ultimately bring comfort, because it is part of His care.

The other title Peter uses here is "Overseer," which is sometimes translated "Supervisor." The Greek word is *episkopos*. The root of that word in its noun form is *skopos*, from which we get the English word *scope*, giving us words such as microscope, stethoscope, and telescope. A scope is an instrument by which we are able to see small things or objects that are far away. Scopes enhance our ability to see. The prefix on the word *episkopos*, *epi*, intensifies the force of the root, so that a supervisor or bishop is a super-looker. In the ancient Greek world, the *episkopos* was one who came unannounced to the troops to see if they were prepared for battle. If they were not, he would chasten them; if they were, he would congratulate and reward them. So it is that Christ, as our Bishop, looks at us intently.

We do not know the condition of our souls from one day to the next, nor do we know what our souls require to move to the next level of sanctification. However, our Bishop knows, because His eye is not simply on the sparrow but on His sheep. He knows every step we take and every pain we feel. We are called to imitate Him, because we have been returned by the Shepherd to the Shepherd.

The hymn "The Ninety and Nine" sings of ninety-nine sheep that lie safely in the shelter of the fold, but there is one lost sheep on a hill far away, far off from the streets of gold. The hymn tells the story of the Shepherd who sought to save that one lost sheep. In a sermon, John Guest said that the hymn expresses the polar opposite of what the liberal church expresses in our day. The liberal church says that generally people are not lost, and those who are should be left alone, and eventually they will come home, wagging their tails behind them. The lost sheep does not know how to come home. He does not know where the sheepfold is until the Good Shepherd seeks him and finds him. There is artwork that depicts Jesus holding a lamb over His shoulder, and that lamb represents us—the sheep that was lost but now is found.

10

WIVES AND HUSBANDS

1 Peter 3:1–7

Wives, likewise, be submissive to your own husbands, that even if some do not obey the word, they, without a word, may be won by the conduct of their wives, when they observe your chaste conduct accompanied by fear. Do not let your adornment be merely outward—arranging the hair, wearing gold, or putting on fine apparel—rather let it be the hidden person of the heart, with the incorruptible beauty of a gentle and quiet spirit, which is very precious in the sight of God. For in this manner, in former times, the holy women who trusted in God also adorned themselves, being submissive to their own husbands, as Sarah obeyed Abraham, calling him lord, whose daughters you are if you do good and are not afraid with any terror. Husbands, likewise, dwell with them with understanding, giving honor to the wife, as to the weaker vessel, and as being heirs together of the grace of life, that your prayers may not be hindered.

We have noticed several times already the many parallels between the teaching of the Apostles Peter and Paul. One parallel is their teaching on submission as a manifestation of our growth in sanctification, and an element of that is submission in marriage. To the Ephesians Paul writes:

Do not be unwise, but understand what the will of the Lord is. And do not be drunk with wine, in which is dissipation; but be filled with the Spirit, speaking to one another in psalms and hymns and spiritual songs, singing and making melody in your heart to the Lord, giving thanks always for all things to God the Father in the name of our Lord Jesus Christ, submitting to one another in the fear of God. Wives, submit to your own husbands, as to the Lord. For the husband is the head of the wife, as also Christ is head of the church; and He is the Savior of the body. Therefore, just as the church is subject to Christ, so let the wives be to their own husbands in everything. Husbands, love your wives, just as Christ also loved the church and gave Himself for her, that He might sanctify and cleanse her with the washing of water by the word, that He might present her to Himself a glorious church, not having spot or wrinkle or any such thing, but that she should be holy and without blemish. So husbands ought to love their own wives as their own bodies. (Eph. 5:17–28)

The Feminist Movement

There are a number of parallels between Paul's words in Ephesians and Peter's words here. Through almost two thousand years of reflection on the biblical text, there has been virtually monolithic agreement as to the content of the teaching—that is, until the advent of the feminist movement. Since feminism has swept through the Western world, the axe has been laid at the root of the meaning of these texts. It is now argued that the traditional interpretation of the texts has been controlled by a seemingly incurable chauvinism that has held captive the minds of scholars. The feminist movement heralds the liberation of these texts from the tyranny of such male dominance. People also argue that the marriage teaching of Paul in Ephesians and of Peter in his epistle simply reflect the cultural custom of their day and so has no bearing on the church now. Rather, they say, the texts that require submission of the wife to the husband are no longer applicable.

There are women scholars who claim the Bible as their authority while simultaneously declaring that these particular biblical teachings reflect sinful, chauvinistic attitudes that were imposed upon the church by the Apostles. More conservative advocates of feminism have sought, instead of discrediting the biblical texts, to reinterpret them in order to make them compatible with the goals of feminism.

There are many dimensions to the feminist movement. A strong protest raised within the movement has to do with the claim of some men that the subordination of the wife to the husband, established at creation, was based upon the inherent inferiority of women. That protest is legitimate, I believe, according to the Word of God. In the wake of feminism we have seen a protest against inequities of wages given to women for the same job men hold. We have also witnessed many professions open to women that were, for the most part, previously closed. Today we find women in politics, medicine, jurisprudence, and a host of other avenues that heretofore were closed to them. All these things, I think, are good and necessary.

However, the downside of feminism in our time is the strong influence the movement has had on abortion, which is America's greatest moral shame. In that respect, the influence of feminism has been destructive. Feminism has also created unbelievable turmoil within the family and in homes the country over. It seems that we are facing an endless power struggle between men and women and between husband and wife. All of that has produced disastrous results, but it is incumbent upon us as Christians not to interpret the text on the basis of contemporary movements or on what is deemed politically correct. Rather, we are to be sober in seeking to understand what the Bible teaches and, once we understand it, to be submissive to it.

When I was a young boy, my mother would have boxed my ears if I had failed to open a door for a woman, or if I had failed to give a woman my seat on a bus or in some crowded venue. At times today, however, I have held open a door for a woman, to which the response was thinly veiled hostility: "I'm perfectly capable of opening that door for myself. I don't need you to do it for me. I'm not helpless." Today we see a venomous attitude toward those earlier customs. The Bible does not say that men are supposed to give their seats to women or to hold open doors for them; those gestures are cultural customs. Nevertheless, such customs, I was taught, are expressions of respect, not of a patronizing attitude. So all these things have come together and influenced our society.

In Ephesians 5, Paul says that we are to submit "to one another in the fear of God" (v. 21). Within this section of Ephesians, wives are called to submit to their husband, children to their parents, slaves to their master, and the church to Christ. All this is given in a literary form called an "elliptical expression." An elliptical expression is a group of words with certain implied words omitted. Perhaps the greatest example of elliptical teaching is found in the Ten Commandments. The fifth commandment says, "Honor your father and your mother" (Ex. 20:12). Tacitly understood, although not explicit in the text, is the equal importance of the unwritten phrase, "Do not dishonor your father and your mother." The call to honor carries with it the implication that we ought not to dishonor. We are also told not to take the name of the Lord our God in vain (Ex. 20:7), and that negative prohibition carries with it the elliptical implication that we should actively seek to treat the name of God as holy. We understand that without the text spelling out all the implications.

Elliptical expression is applied in torturous exegesis of Ephesians 5 by those who say that verse 21 is the controlling phrase that explains everything that comes after it. In other words, whatever is commanded of one is by implication equally commanded of the other. If wives are commanded to submit to their husband, then husbands must also submit to their wife. In other words, they say, mutual submission is in view here. I call this torturous exegesis, because if it is applied throughout the text, not only would children have to obey parents, but also parents would have to obey children; not only would slaves have to obey masters, but masters would have to obey slaves. Most ludicrous is applying it to the church's submission to Christ, because that would mean that Christ must also submit to the church. In this case, we move beyond nonsense to blasphemy. This is the perfect example of how zeal for a cultural movement takes the Word of God and seeks to twist it.

Another text frequently harnessed by feminists is Galatians 3:28: "There is neither Jew nor Greek, there is neither slave nor free, there is neither male nor female; for you are all one in Christ Jesus." They say that cultural distinctions between male and female, Jew and Greek, and slave and free are obliterated in Christ. Therefore, there no longer exists the necessity for wives to be submissive to their husband, slaves to their master, and so on. I hope you can see the folly of that sort of application. Here in Galatians Paul did not mean that these distinctions have completely passed away; in fact, he frequently continues to make such distinctions. The distinction between Jew and Gentile is one that Paul makes a multitude of times in his writings.

When Paul writes that in Christ there is neither Jew nor Greek, slave nor free, male nor female, he has redemption in mind. In terms of redemption there is no advantage to being a man or a woman, a master or a slave, or a Jew or a Gentile. Those barriers were torn down at the foot of the cross. Men are justified by faith alone, and so are women. Jews are justified by faith alone, and so are Gentiles. Masters are justified by faith alone, and so are slaves. That is the teaching of the Apostle Paul, which has been attested for two thousand years of biblical interpretation.

Peter's Word to Wives

Peter addresses women who are married, in some cases to pagan husbands: **Wives, likewise, be submissive to your own husbands** (v. 1). Paul writes the same way: "Wives, submit to your own husbands" (Eph. 5:22).

Wives are not called to submit to someone else's husband but to their own. Peter continues: **that even if some do not obey the word, they, without a word, may be won by the conduct of their wives, when they observe your chaste conduct accompanied by fear** (vv. 1–2). Fear here means reverence. The practical reason that Peter gives for submission to husbands, particularly if the husband is an unbeliever, is that a submissive spirit might bear witness to the truth of the gospel.

Paul gives a slightly different reason for submission: "Wives, submit to your own husbands *as to the Lord*." We noted earlier that all things are governed by the authority that the Father has given to the Son. All authority on heaven and earth has been given to Him, so when we submit to whatever authority is over us, we are bearing witness to the authority of God Himself. I have talked to women about this and said, "You may struggle with the concept of being submissive to your husband when you think of it strictly in terms of the man you married, but would you have a problem submitting to Jesus if He were your husband?" I have never heard Christian women say no, even though they are quick to add that their husband is not Jesus. We can submit to authority, whether husband, employer, or government, if we understand that by doing so we are submitting to the Lord. If we refuse to submit to authority, we are refusing to submit to Christ. That is a serious matter.

Both Apostles, particularly Paul, root this principle of submission not to the first-century culture but to creation. In creation God made Adam to be head over Eve, yet this is where the issue gets murky. Some men say that since marital submission is a creation ordinance and not a cultural custom, it therefore must mean that wives are inferior. That is wrong. We are joint heirs of Christ. God creates us male and female. The position of headship or leadership is a division of labor, and in a division of labor, being subordinate does not imply inferiority.

An article central to the Christian faith is the co-dignity and co-eternality of all members of the Godhead. The Son has the same essence as the Father; nowhere in Scripture is the Son of God called inferior to the Father. Yet, in the economy of redemption the Father sends the Son, the Son does not send the Father. In the economy of redemption Christ is subordinate to the Father, but nowhere does that imply that He is therefore inferior. When in our home we decide how we are going to handle the cleanup after dinner, and my wife says, "You wash and I'll dry," or "I'll wash and you dry"—whichever way we divide the labor has nothing to do with superiority or inferiority but with the structure of the home.

Marriage is a union where the two become one flesh. If no one has the position of leadership, if no one has the final say, then there will be an endless power struggle in which everyone tries to get the upper hand. In the movie *My Big Fat Greek Wedding*, a father is opposed to the man his daughter wants to marry. The daughter turns to her mother for help and asks, "What can you do so that Papa will allow me to get married? After all, he's the head of the house." The mother replies, "Yes, but I'm the neck that turns the head."

Do not let your adornment be merely outward—arranging the hair, wearing gold, or putting on fine apparel—rather let it be the hidden person of the heart, with the incorruptible beauty of a gentle and quiet spirit, which is very precious in the sight of God (vv. 3–4). This biblical text is not commanding ugliness so that a woman's outward appearance cannot possibly disguise evil in her soul. Rather, Peter is telling women not to be caught up in an ostentatious display of beauty, because the most beautiful thing about them is their soul. What will win a man to the things of God is the hidden person of the heart.

Peter speaks of an incorruptible beauty, an adjective we have seen already in this epistle (1:4, 23). Peter continually focuses our attention on that which is incorruptible—here, a beauty that does not fade. Such beauty consists, Peter says, of "a gentle and quiet spirit." The book of Proverbs paints a picture of a contentious woman and shows us that a quarrelsome woman can destroy a home (19:13; 27:15).

Martin Luther once said of his beloved Katherine von Bora, whom he called Katie and sometimes Mrs. Dr. Luther, that if God had wanted him to be married to a meek woman, he would have had to carve one out of stone. His point was that Katie, who was beautiful and had a great spirit, was no doormat. God does not call women to be doormats, to be slavish in the way they relate to their husband, any more than God calls men to exercise tyranny over their wife.

One of the great calamities of our day is the epidemic of wife abuse. There are lots of sins that I can understand, but I cannot understand how a man can hit a woman. Never let it be said of you, that you would let your anger in a domestic dispute move you to such an action as to actually hit your wife. That is absolutely unconscionable. I have had battered women come to me wondering what to do, and I have told them to call the police immediately. Such a husband belongs in jail, where he cannot beat up on women or children.

Incorruptible beauty is displayed in a gentle and quiet spirit, but this does not mean that a wife is prohibited from giving her opinion. Peter's point is that a quiet spirit is not a tempestuous spirit. Jesus was the strongest man who ever lived, yet He was adorned with a gentle and quiet spirit. Peter says that such a spirit is very precious in the sight of God. It is not just the sort of spirit that can lead a man to the truth of Christ, but something that is precious to God. God is the only one who can see that gentle and quiet spirit in a woman's inner person with perfect vision. He sees the beauty in her soul that no man can see, and it is exceedingly precious to Him.

For in this manner, in former times, the holy women who trusted in God also adorned themselves (v. 5). Peter instructs his readers to consider the examples that God has given from history, those holy women in the past who were adorned with these qualities. There was Ruth, Esther, and Mary the mother of Jesus. These holy women trusted in God. They adorned themselves in the manner in which Peter has just spoken, **being submissive to their own husbands, as Sarah obeyed Abraham, calling him lord, whose daughters you are if you do good and are not afraid with any terror** (vv. 5–6).

Peter's Word to Husbands

Peter then gives an exhortation to husbands, which we will again compare to the words of the Apostle Paul, who wrote, "Husbands, love your wives, just as Christ also loved the church and gave Himself for her" (Eph. 5:25). Women chafe under the mandate to be submissive to their husband, but I would exchange that responsibility for the man's responsibility any day of the week. I believe it is a lot easier for a woman to submit to her husband than it is for a man to love his wife the way Christ loves the church. There is no selfishness in the love that Jesus has for His church. Jesus has never abused, tyrannized, exploited, or belittled His bride. When I ask my wife to submit, I am asking her to submit to me as I am prepared to give my life for her.

The Bible does not tell husbands to love their wife if and when the wife submits to him, nor does it tell wives to submit to their husband when that husband loves them as Christ loves the church. Husbands are called to love their wife whether she submits to him or not. He is to be prepared to give his life for his wife even if she never displays a quiet and gentle spirit. His obligation remains his obligation. She cannot keep it for him, as he cannot keep hers for her.

Husbands, likewise, dwell with them with understanding, giving honor to the wife, as to the weaker vessel, and as being heirs

together of the grace of life, that your prayers may not be hindered (v. 7). Weaker vessel does not mean "weak-minded." Peter is clearly referring to physical strength. I have met women who are physically stronger than their husband, but that is extremely rare. In most cases, men are physically stronger than their wife. Men are called not only to love their wife but to respect her, to give her honor.

Honor is what my mother had in mind when she told me to offer my seat to a woman. It is a shame that such customs are under attack. Not too long ago I saw an elderly gentleman walking down the street wearing a hat, which he tipped to a woman who passed him. She laughed him to scorn. These things ought not to be. The man was trying to make an expression of honor and respect. When someone shows you respect, do not be offended. If someone seeks to honor you, do not reject it. Honor is a behavioral matter that is supposed to be characteristic of every Christian's life. We ought to be people who are quick to honor others.

If we followed these simple instructions that the Bible gives for the division of labor in marriage, and if both sides sought to fulfill their obligations, I do not think the home would be the battleground that it is. It would be the kind of place that God ordained the home to be. What happens in the home, within the family, is the bedrock of society, which is why the church, since its founding, has always considered the family a matter of urgent importance.

Peter calls on husbands to give honor to the wife because they are heirs together of the grace of life. Husbands and wives are in it together, and if both are Christians, they share an inheritance. They are joint heirs with Christ of the kingdom of God. Husbands are to give honor so that their prayers may not be hindered. Again we find an ellipsis. The implication of this text is that if husbands fail to love, honor, and respect their wives, that behavior will hinder their prayers. Likewise, wives, if you resist submitting to your husband, that posture will hinder your prayers. In a sense, it means that God does not want to hear our prayers until we come to Him as humbly submissive people.

11

CHRISTIAN VIRTUES

1 Peter 3:8–9

> Finally, all of you be of one mind, having compassion for one another; love as brothers, be tenderhearted, be courteous; not returning evil for evil or reviling for reviling, but on the contrary blessing, knowing that you were called to this, that you may inherit a blessing.

After Peter's somewhat lengthy discourse on the principle of submission to authority, he comes to a conclusion of practical application, which once again is similar to the teaching of Paul. Here Peter gives five instructions for the church's health and well-being, and they apply not only to the first-century church but also to churches of every place and time.

Unity
Finally, all of you be of one mind, having compassion for one another; love as brothers, be tenderhearted, be courteous (v. 8). Sociological studies of church membership in America have revealed patterns of socioeconomic commonality that draw people to various denominations. The sociologists conclude that the draw to join a particular church is driven not so much by theology or doctrine but by one's comfort with the social, eco-

nomic, and political climate within the congregation. Here Peter tells us that it is imperative for the health of a church that its people be of one mind.

This does not mean that the people are to set aside their own perceptions and viewpoints and slavishly embrace everything that everyone else in the congregation believes. That is what you expect to find in a cult, not in a church. We all come from different backgrounds, and we bring to the church different perspectives; discarding those differences is not required for unity. Peter's plea here is that believers have agreement on substantive matters. We are to share one Lord, one faith, and one baptism.

When it comes to questions about the paraments that hang from the pulpit and adorn the Communion table during the Advent season, we can choose to use blue paraments or white. If we polled the congregation as to preference, some would prefer blue and others white, but this is not something over which to divide; it is a matter of personal preference. Peter is not writing about such insignificant matters; rather, he is saying that we should be single-minded in our understanding of the person and work of Christ. We can—and must—be united in our confession of the essentials of the Christian faith, but there is plenty of room for differences in lesser matters.

I think it is safe to say that there are not two people in a church who would agree on everything. Particularly in my work as an apologist over the years, when I have engaged in discussions and debates with unbelievers, I have sought for what the philosophers and theologians have called an *anknüpfungspunkt*, a point of contact.

When I was involved in labor management disputes, I often spoke to members of the American Communist Party who were outwardly hostile toward Christianity. I would ask, "Do you want to be treated with dignity?" By asking that question, I was able to find something upon which everyone in the room could agree. They all wanted to be treated with dignity. Then I would ask, "On what basis can you have dignity? Is it something that human beings possess inherently?" Many of them, if not most, would say yes.

They believed in human dignity while also believing that they had emerged from the slime as a cosmic accident. They believed that they came from nothingness and have been destined, ultimately, to the abyss of meaninglessness, so the two poles of their existence—origin and destiny—are rooted in what Nietzsche called *Das Nichtigheit*, nothingness. So, I would ask, "If you came from nothing and you are going to nothing, why don't you see yourself as nothing right now?" I went on to say that I agree that people have dignity, but the reason I believe it is that the eternal Creator of this world, who Himself has inherent dignity, has assigned dignity to mankind.

My faith in human dignity is not gratuitous. It is not based on a wish or on the borrowed capital of Christianity but on my conviction of the reality of God, who says we have dignity. I asked them to think about this: if there is no God, their hope of dignity was a fool's errand. They said they had dignity, but they could give me no rational basis for that assertion. It was simply an emotional wish.

We can find things about which to agree with people from all walks of life, yet the worldview we embrace as Christians is on a collision course with the thinking of this world. When I read op-eds in the newspaper, hear the commentaries on television, and listen to the speeches of popular politicians, I find myself much more in disagreement than I do in agreement. Have you found that to be the case in your life? We should not be like-minded with the world. The way we think should be rooted and grounded in the truth of God. The values of Christ should be what shapes and frames our opinions.

Bringing our minds into conformity with the mind of Christ by submitting to the Word of God is a lifelong enterprise. The Word of God gives us the perspective of God, and that perspective is radically different from the perspective of the world. Because we want to share the perspective of God, and because our thinking is being formed by that, this should lead us to a very important like-mindedness as we share our common faith in the truth of God. The like-mindedness that is to mark the communion of the saints is so precious that we need to guard it carefully.

Christians ought not to believe something just because their pastor says it. As members of a church, as part of a flock, God requires that you give honor to the pastor and take his words seriously. God has set him as the shepherd over a particular flock. However, he is an under-shepherd, not the Great Shepherd. The pastor does not speak with the authority or infallibility of Christ. Like-mindedness has to come by submission to God's Word, not to the preacher's word, but like-mindedness is something we should cultivate and guard jealously in the church, lest we allow petty matters to destroy the unity of the body of Christ. Most churches split not because of a theological rift but over what color to paint the church basement. So, unity is the first virtue to which Peter calls us.

Compassion

The second virtue, he says, is having compassion for one another. Other translations read "having sympathy for one another." The idea here is not so much one person's feeling sorry for another; the etymology of the words is more specific. To have compassion is to share common feelings. "I feel your pain" has become a trite expression in our day. However, the ability to feel another's pain and joy is what we are called to do: "Rejoice with those who rejoice, and weep with those who weep" (Rom. 12:15).

After a particular Sunday morning worship service, a member of St. Andrew's greeted me. When he shook my hand, he held on and said, "Pastor, my daughter is in the Air Force, and she is being deployed to the Middle East." He began to tremble, and tears rolled down his cheeks. It was a poignant moment. I sensed the fear and concern he had for his daughter. He was expressing what every parent feels when a son or daughter is called into the midst of warfare. He said to me, "Please pray for my daughter," and I said, "Yes, of course." At St. Andrew's, we have lists of people for whom we regularly pray, but this particular encounter was so urgent that I could not go to sleep that week without first pleading for his daughter before the Lord. It weighed on me because he had communicated the intensity of his feelings.

To have sympathy is *pathos*, or passion that is shared. We should share each other's passion. We have various passions about various things, but passion for the virtuous things of God is a contagious matter. If one of us has great feelings of worship, we should share that with one another.

Brotherly Love

Then, Peter says, we are to love as brothers. The love enjoined upon us by the New Testament is one that transcends the earthly sort of love. Even the concept of brotherly love does not quite capture the kind of love that we are to have for fellow Christians. The family is the chief metaphor that the Scriptures give for the church. God is our Father, and we are His adopted children. If Christ loves you, and you are in Christ, and Christ loves me, and I am in Christ, then what could possibly be more natural than to have at the bottom of this pyramid a connection of love between us? We should love one another if for no other reason than that we share the same Father.

God has blessed me with a family that is a place of refuge. I can depend upon the loyalty of my wife, my daughter, my son, and my grandchildren in times of trouble. I hear horror stories of families that are haunted by disloyalty, competition, and brokenness. If you have experienced family loyalty, which should be at the very basis of our human society, then you get the idea that Peter is talking about here, that we should love each other in the church, in the fellowship of Christ, as family. I have not always agreed with my sister, nor has she always agreed with me, but one thing she will always be is my sister, and I will always be to her a brother.

Tenderhearted

We also are to be tenderhearted. Other translations supply a different word here, but the thought is that, in the church, there should be a certain shared tenderness. Tenderness is the opposite of roughness. The word Peter uses does not describe a physical touch but a visceral one, something that comes from the deepest chamber of our hearts. We know what it means to be kind, and we all have known people who manifest a remarkable degree of kindness. When we recognize someone as being kind, we are recognizing a tender heart—not a hardened, mean, thoughtless heart.

I remember from my days of playing golf what it was like to hit an approach shot onto the green. Once the ball hits the green, the player wants it to stop quickly so that it does not roll off the green. In such situations we used to say that we wanted the ball to land on the green like a butterfly with sore feet. If you have a sore, throbbing wound, you do not want to bump it, because it is tender. That is Peter's meaning here—a heart that is not harsh, cruel, or recalcitrant, but soft, gentle, and tender. That is how we should be one with another.

When Jesus was with the hard-hearted, He asked no quarter and gave none; when He dealt with the Pharisees and the Sadducees, He was not Jesus meek and mild. However, with those of a more lowly estate, sinners and publicans, He was tender and gentle. I served on the board of Prison Fellowship when it was first incorporated, and at a board meeting Chuck Colson and I discussed what to use for a ministry logo. It came to me instantly: a bruised reed. A bruised reed was appropriate because the ministry is directed to broken and bruised people, and it was said of Jesus that the bruised reed He would never break (Isa. 42:3). That became the logo for Prison Fellowship, a stalk of wheat that is bent but not broken. It captures a sense of compassion for those in prison. Those were the kind of people that Jesus treated with tenderness.

Courteous

The fifth virtue is courteousness. The word *courtesy* came into common usage in England during the Elizabethan period. It was derived from two words, *court* and *etiquette*. Court etiquette, shortened to "courtesy," was defined in terms of how honor and respect were to be given to the royal family, and those principles of etiquette were practiced in the court. Honor and respect became the ideals for those who served the crown.

Sinclair Ferguson, the great Scot theologian, tells the story of an occasion when the royals Elizabeth and Margaret were still young ladies. Elizabeth had not yet risen to the crown. The sisters were going out to a social function, one of their first as young women, and before they left the palace the Queen Mother said to them, "Remember, girls, royal manners. Conduct yourselves as princesses." Etiquette, sadly, has become almost a lost art in our society, and it would be good for Christian families to give refresher courses in etiquette to their children.

I came to the South from the Northeast, and for a time I taught in Mississippi. During that time, I was invited into people's homes, and I noticed that children addressed their parents as "ma'am" and "sir." I noted at the time that such address is uncommon in the Northeast. It was not uncommon, however, for one of my grade-school gym teachers. One day that instructor asked a student a question, to which the student replied, "Yeah." The teacher was visibly upset and said, "You can say 'yeah' on the playground, but not in this class. When I ask you something, you are to say, 'Yes, sir.'" All these years later, I remember that lesson about simple respect and courtesy.

To be courteous means to respect other people. We are to respect their feelings and their position, which is simply an extension of the principle of honor. The ethic of the church is that we are to honor others above ourselves, which flies in the face of what Nietzsche called the "fundamental primordial will to power that beats in the human breast," whereby humans are constantly seeking to gain the esteem of others rather than offering it. Conversely, Christian ethics teach us to esteem our brothers as higher than we esteem ourselves. That is a high calling.

These five virtues to which we are called as a church describe the ideal church. We are not an ideal church. We do not always share feelings with our friends. We are not always of one mind. We do not always love each other as family, nor are we always tender, courteous, and respectful, but these are the values that God loves.

Heavenly Perspective

Then Peter changes from the positive to the negative, first telling us what we should do, then telling us what we should not do: **not returning evil for evil or reviling for reviling, but on the contrary blessing, knowing that you were called to this, that you may inherit a blessing** (v. 9). There is some ambiguity about this verse. We could read Peter as saying that we are not to return evil with evil or reviling with reviling, but to respond with blessing because we are called to bless people. That is one way the verse could be read, depending on the structure of the clause "knowing that you were called to this." Peter could simply have meant that we are called to being reviled, because the servant is not above his master. Because they reviled Christ, they will revile us, and when we suffer that reviling as He did, He is quick to bless us, as we are to bless others, in order that we may inherit a blessing. The New Testament calls us repeatedly to a heavenly perspective. We are not to forget the inheritance laid up for us in heaven. The incentive here is that when we return good for evil and blessings for cursing, we stockpile an inheritance of blessing.

12

IN PURSUIT OF PEACE

1 Peter 3:10–17

For

"He who would love life
And see good days,
Let him refrain his tongue from evil,
And his lips from speaking deceit.
Let him turn away from evil and do good;
Let him seek peace and pursue it.
For the eyes of the Lord are on the righteous,
And His ears are open to their prayers;
But the face of the Lord is against those who do evil."

And who is he who will harm you if you become followers of what is good? But even if you should suffer for righteousness' sake, you are blessed. "And do not be afraid of their threats, nor be troubled." But sanctify the Lord God in your hearts, and always be ready to give a defense to everyone who asks you a reason for the hope that is in you, with meekness and fear; having a good conscience, that when they defame you as evildoers, those who revile your good conduct in Christ may be ashamed. For it is better, if it is the will of God, to suffer for doing good than for doing evil.

eter has just given us principles on how we are to relate one to another in the church (vv. 8–9). We were told to be of one mind and to have a compassionate heart. We are to love with a tender heart and be courteous, not returning evil for evil or reviling for reviling. Now he reaches the conclusion of this matter with a citation from the Old Testament, which is chiefly from Psalms, that begins, **"He who would love life and see good days . . ."** (v. 10). We are going to consider not only the content of this citation but also its literary structure, so that we may be instructed by it in a way that will be useful to us when we come to other passages in sacred Scripture.

Good Days

The Bible teaches that we are not to cling to the things of the world but to set our hope on eternity; we are to look beyond the borders of the world into that heavenly inheritance that has been preserved for us. At the same time, we are not to despise the life we have in this world. When the Apostle Paul was torn between two straits—to depart and be with the Lord or to remain on earth and minister—he wrote, "I am hard-pressed between the two, having a desire to depart and be with Christ, which is far better. Nevertheless to remain in the flesh *is* more needful for you" (Phil. 1:23–24). The tension with which the Apostle wrestled was not a tug between good and bad; it was between good and better. He was not contrasting that which is far better with that which is bad. We are to love life. Our Lord said of His own mission, "I have come that they may have life, and that they may have it more abundantly" (John 10:10).

We would think it unnecessary to have to tell people that they ought to love life, because by nature we do everything we can to preserve our existence. However, that is only part of the story. Henry David Thoreau said somewhat cynically that the vast majority of men live lives of quiet desperation. A cloud of despair hangs over our heads like the sword of Damocles, and that weight is exceedingly heavy and burdensome for those who go through life without Christ and without hope. We are not without Christ or without hope, so we are to cultivate within our souls a love for life.

Some people seem to have an ongoing love affair with life. Their excitement and optimism about each day are contagious because they communicate a passion for living life to the fullest. That is the way we are supposed to be as Christians. We have a tendency to define our pilgrimage in this world in terms of good days and bad days—"I had a good day at the office" or "I had a bad hair day"—but we should enjoy a multitude of good days, because we are in touch with the Author of good days.

A Restrained Tongue

The Apostle applies his earlier admonition with this recitation from the Old Testament to loving life and seeing good days: **"Let him refrain his tongue from evil, and his lips from speaking deceit. Let him turn away from evil and do good; let him seek peace and pursue it"** (vv. 10–11). This appears in the form of a couplet, two statements. There is no basic difference between refraining a tongue from speaking evil and refraining lips from speaking deceit. We see here a common literary device of Hebrew literature, particular characteristic of poetry. The Bible's wisdom books, such as Psalms, Proverbs, and the Song of Solomon, present a large number of passages in poetic form. Whereas English poetry often rhymes or contains some kind of meter, the principle form of Hebrew poetry is parallelism. There are several kinds of parallelism in Hebrew poetry, but there are three main types: synthetic parallelism, synonymous parallelism, and antithetical parallelism.

Synthetic parallelism is structured so that several verses are set on top of each other and build toward a conclusion. Each line draws from various elements in order to create a synthesis from the information. Synthetic parallelism is a bit difficult to discern in the text, and this form of poetry is in the minority compared to the other two forms.

Synonymous parallelism occurs when the two statements of a couplet say the same thing in two (and sometimes three) different ways. An example of synonymous parallelism is found in the famous Jewish benediction:

> The LORD bless you and keep you;
> The LORD make His face shine upon you,
>   And be gracious to you;
> The LORD lift up His countenance upon you,
>   And give you peace. (Num. 6:24–26)

All three statements communicate the same idea. To be blessed of God is to have Him make His face shine upon us; to be blessed of God is to experience His lifting up the light of His countenance upon us; and when we are blessed by God, we experience God's preserving us. He keeps us, and when He keeps us, He does not do so because we deserve to be kept; it is an expression of His grace. When He keeps us, He is being gracious to us. God's grace was given to the Jew supremely through God's giving him peace. So, all three stanzas are virtually synonymous.

Antithetical parallelism is common. We find it in statements in which ideas are set in vivid contrast. "Do not lead us into temptation, but deliver us from the evil one" (Matt. 6:13) is an example of antithetical parallelism. This example is found in the Lord's Prayer, yet James writes that God tempts no one (James 1:13). Since it is absolutely clear that God never tempts anyone, why would we ask God not to lead us into temptation? The answer is found in the remainder of the couplet: "but deliver us from the evil one," which is the exact opposite of being led into temptation.

I find it regrettable that many English translations, because of the tradition of the way in which the Lord's Prayer has been recited for centuries, cave into popular usage and mistranslate the text. The original text does not say, "deliver us from evil." If so, that would be "evil" in the abstract sense and would require the use of the neuter gender, but the term "evil" in the Lord's Prayer appears in the masculine gender, so its proper translation is actually this: "Lead us not into temptation but deliver us from *tou ponērou* [from the evil one]," which supplies the title in the New Testament for Satan. Jesus encourages us to pray that the Father will not do to us what He did to Jesus, that He will not expose us to the assault of the Devil but instead deliver us from the Evil One.

In the book of Job, Satan came into the presence of God after walking to and fro upon the earth, and he boasted about the failures of the human race. God said to Satan, "Have you considered My servant Job?" (1:8). Satan responded cynically, "Does Job fear God for nothing? Have You not made a hedge around him, around his household, and around all that he has on every side? You have blessed the work of his hands, and his possessions have increased in the land. But now, stretch out Your hand and touch all that he has, and he will surely curse You to Your face!" (1:9–11). That is the substance of what Jesus tells us to pray in this petition of the Lord's Prayer. We are to ask the Father to put a hedge around us, to surround us with His protection and keep us from the fiery darts of the enemy. However, recognizing the antithetical parallelism in this phrase helps us understand how the petition is nuanced.

Such statements are also found throughout Isaiah. People have told me they believe that God created evil because the Bible says so: "I form the light, and create darkness: I make peace, and create evil: I the LORD do all these things" (Isa. 45:7 KJV). The verse is clearly a form of antithetical parallelism, so if you want to understand what is meant in the first part of the couplet, you have to understand what is meant in the second. Although there are eight nuances to the Hebrew word for *evil*, when Isaiah says that God creates evil, he is not talking about moral evil. Through Isaiah, God is essentially saying that He is the one responsible for all that happens. There is no hint in that text of God's creating moral evil, which can be understood by recognizing the presence of parallelism in the text.

If you want to love life, if you want to see good days, then refrain your tongue from evil and your lips from speaking deceit. The Bible is very much concerned about the evil that comes from our mouth. When Isaiah saw the transcendent majesty of God, he saw himself in stark contrast and pronounced an oracle of doom on himself: "Woe is me, for I am undone! Because I am a man of unclean lips, and I dwell in the midst of a people of unclean lips; for my eyes have seen the King, the LORD of hosts" (Isa. 6:5). Isaiah's first sense of guilt upon seeing the holiness of God concerned what was coming out of his mouth, and he recognized that he was not alone in this corruptive mouthing of deceit. The nation was a people with dirty mouths.

With our lips, we are called to bear witness to the truth of God and to speak praise, honor, and glory to Him. Instead, we slander and blaspheme. With our mouths we put the dagger into the back of our friends. James devotes much space in his epistle to this "little member," saying, "See how great a forest a little fire kindles!" (James 3:5). Paul quotes the Old Testament:

> There is none who does good, no, not one.
>> Their throat is an open tomb;
>> With their tongues they have practiced deceit;
>> The poison of asps is under their lips;
>> Whose mouth is full of cursing and bitterness. (Rom. 3:12–14)

One way to recognize poisonous snakes, at least of a certain variety, is by the diamond shape of their head. Such snakes are called "pit vipers" because their jaws contain sacks that store venom, which the snakes release into their prey when they strike. The deadly strike of the asp, the one that killed Cleopatra, was used as the metaphor to describe the mouth of fallen human beings. We have venom in our mouth. If we would love life and see good days, we have to restrain our tongue. The specific evil in view here is the evil of deceit.

Satan himself is called the father of lies (John 8:44). There is no truth in him. He makes his living through deception and falsehood. By use of the lie, he does everything he can to undermine the sanctity of the truth of God. When Pilate asked Jesus whether He was a king, Jesus said, "You say rightly that I am a king. For this cause I was born, and for this cause I have come into the world, that I should bear witness to the truth. Everyone who is of the truth hears My voice" (John 18:37). A Christian is defined by Christ as someone of the truth, and we should guard with our lives the sanctity of that truth. Our yes should be yes, and our no should be no (James 5:12), which simply means that people ought to be able to trust what we say. As we put restraints on our tongues, deceit treads less across our lips.

"Let him turn away from evil and do good; let him seek peace and pursue it"—this is another couplet that expresses, once again, synonymous parallelism. What is said in the first verse is reinforced in the second by saying that which is virtually synonymous. We are told in a general sense in verse 11 that someone who would love life and see good days is not only to refrain his tongue, but he is to turn away from evil. We have here a metaphor of turning. Paul wrote, "They have all turned aside; they have together become unprofitable; there is none who does good, no, not one" (Rom. 3:12). The basic pattern of unconverted human beings is to walk along the path of this world. That way of traveling involves turning away from God. Peter tells us that if we want to have a good life, then we have to turn in the opposite direction. We have to turn away from evil rather than toward it. Notice, however, that refraining from evil is not sufficient; we are called to do good. It is good to be accused of being a "do-gooder," because that is what we are called to be—those who turn away from evil and do good.

Seeking Peace

Peter reinforces this: "Let him seek peace and pursue it." This does not mean simply that we are to be peaceful. We we are to look for peace, which is not a casual undertaking. It is a search marked by passion. Such seeking should come from a heart on fire to reach peace. Seeking after peace involves a pursuit.

I have a picture that was taken of me one Christmas morning during my childhood. In the picture I am seated in front of the Christmas tree in a toy plane. That plane, my most prized present that year, was called a "pursuit plane." A pursuit plane was used by the Air Corps not simply to escape but also to chase the enemy. That image was cast in the language Peter uses here. We are to seek peace by actively pursuing it, not simply opting not to stand in the way of it. We have to chase it.

Our Lord said, "Blessed are the peacemakers, for they shall be called sons of God" (Matt. 5:9). The peace we are to seek is the peace of Christ, the peace of God. There is false peace, and there are false peacemakers. Adolf Hitler once said to his colleagues, "We can lie to the people now because after we are victorious, they will forget it." The great negotiator Neville Chamberlain went to Munich to pursue peace with Hitler. This same man, Chamberlain, once said, "We have achieved peace in our time." At the very moment he made that announcement, Hitler was mobilizing his blitzkrieg.

The Bible warns us about a kind of peace monger, someone who seeks a peace that Luther called "carnal peace," which is a peace of the flesh that lacks integrity. We see this sort of peace in the false prophets of Jeremiah's day, about whom God said, "They have also healed the hurt of My people slightly, saying, 'Peace, peace!' when there is no peace" (Jer. 6:14). There is such a thing as false peace. At times we do not want to rock the boat or disturb the peace, but no one ever disturbed the peace more than the Prince of peace, whose very presence provokes spiritual warfare. We are to seek peace, but it is godly peace we are to pursue, not the peace of the flesh.

"For the eyes of the LORD are on the righteous, and His ears are open to their prayers; but the face of the LORD is against those who do evil" (v. 12). This couplet is also synonymous. It says, in the first place, that the eyes of the Lord are watching His people. His eye is upon us—not a jaundiced eye but a tender one. This is not the stare that destroys but the gaze that lifts up. He keeps an eye on the righteous, and His ears are open to their prayers. When children do not want to hear what someone is telling them, they put their hands over their ears. We have almost the same image here. God puts His fingers in His ears when the wicked speak, but He gives an attentive ear to the prayers of His people. James says, "The effective, fervent prayer of a righteous man avails much" (James 5:16). It avails much because God turns His ear to the prayers of His people.

It is fitting that this particular section of the text ends with a politically incorrect statement. Some years ago in the course of a debate at the Southern Baptist Convention, the head of the convention was asked if God hears the prayers of unbelievers. He said no—a volatile response indeed. It is radical to say that we ought not to encourage godless people to pray because the prayers of the godless are an insult to God. Such prayers do not come from contrite hearts but from those that have a vested self-interest. They make their appeal to a heavenly bellhop, putting in their order. God shuts His ears to that kind of prayer, and He turns His face away from the unrighteous.

When Israel fell into apostasy, God said, "I hate, I despise your feast days, and I do not savor your sacred assemblies. Though you offer Me burnt offerings and your grain offerings, I will not accept them, nor will I regard your fattened peace offerings" (Amos 5:21–22). God is not mocked, and He is not interested in listening to the petitions of those who are insincere when they address Him. However, if you pray to Him with a penitent heart in a spirit of worship, He cannot wait to hear everything that you say, because the prayers of His people are a sheer delight, and their offerings are to Him a sweet aroma and a fragrance of beauty.

We are to be people who love life and see good days, but we have to watch our mouths and turn away from evil. We have to seek peace and pursue it, knowing that God is eager to hear the righteous person and to pour His blessings upon His people. These are the practical things that Peter sets before the church in the first century, a church in the midst of suffering but that also had an unquenchable taste for the glory of God.

13

APOLOGETICS

1 Peter 3:15

But sanctify the Lord God in your hearts, and always be ready to give a defense to everyone who asks you a reason for the hope that is in you, with meekness and fear.

Scholars use the technical phrase *locus classicus* for particular texts of Scripture. The term is simply a fancy way of calling attention to what is deemed to be the classical location of a particular text that is used to support a doctrine. The discipline of apologetics finds its classical, biblical location in 1 Peter 3:15. Apologetics has to do with providing an intellectual defense of the truth claims of Christianity.

But sanctify the Lord God in your hearts (v. 15). This first clause of verse 15 pertains to the responsibility of every Christian with respect to their heart. In view is not the mind but the heart. We read in the Old Testament, "As he thinks in his heart, so is he" (Prov. 23:7). The Jewish concept in that passage is not simply that our thoughts determine how we live; in mind here is the sort of thinking that goes beyond the intellect and penetrates the core of our humanity, which is our heart. There are lots of things that we accept with our mind that never get to the deepest dimension of our heart. Therefore, what we profess to understand with our mind is not what determines how we live; the determiner is what penetrates our hearts—what we call our core values or beliefs.

Over twenty-five years ago I collaborated with my mentor John Gerstner on an academic book in the field of apologetics titled *Classical Apologetics*. The book involved setting forth the historic position that Christians have taken to defend the truth claims of Christianity. The second half of the book offered a critique against a twentieth-century movement that rejected classical apologetics and sought to substitute a new approach. The book provoked quite a bit of discussion in the intellectual world. I hold a minority view of apologetics in the contemporary Reformed community; however, the view I hold was the majority view in church history.

In the beginning of that work, I made a paradoxical statement: when it comes to the Christian faith, we have to affirm the priority of the heart and of the mind. That comes across as something of a contradiction; how can two things hold an equal spot of top priority? I took time to qualify that paradoxical statement, explaining that each holds a top priority in a different sense. In the final analysis, it is the disposition of our heart toward the things of God that weighs more heavily than the correctness of our theology. So, although the priority of the heart is first in importance, the priority of the mind is first in sequence. In other words, the truth of God cannot get to our heart unless it is first processed by our mind. Our heart cannot embrace what the mind finds unintelligible. It is important to make that distinction, because if we divorce the heart from the mind and try to get to the heart by bypassing the mind, we are left with a blind emotionalism that has no valid content to it.

There are many attempts to do just that in contemporary worship, to appeal to feeling without thought. Some say it does not matter what we believe as long as we have a warm feeling in our heart for Jesus. People have said to me, "I have no creed but Christ. It doesn't matter what you believe as long as you embrace Jesus." That bubble is burst as soon as we ask the question, Who is Jesus? The moment we try to answer that question and say something intelligible about the identity of Jesus, we are engaged with thinking, and our mind is brought into the matter.

The priority of heart over mind is spelled out here in this text, where the first thing the Apostle says is that we are to sanctify our hearts to the Lord. *Sanctify* means "to set apart," or "to consecrate in an act of devotion." The Apostle Paul tells us to present our bodies as a living sacrifice (Rom. 12:1); here, the Apostle Peter says that the first thing we must do to grow in our faith is to set our heart in devotion to Jesus. That is top priority.

Ever Ready

Peter continues: **and always be ready to give a defense to everyone who asks you a reason for the hope that is in you, with meekness and fear** (v. 15). We are told always to be ready. In a sense, Peter's motto is much like that of the Boy Scouts—"Be prepared." Our preparation is to make us ready to give a defense and a reason for the hope that is in us. If we are dragged before magistrates, if we are on trial for our faith, we are to be prepared to say why we believe what we believe. If your neighbor says, "I notice that you are a Christian. What is it that you believe?" are you ready to explain not only what you believe but why you believe it?

Some Christians tell those who inquire that we simply take a leap of faith with no bother about the credibility or the rational character of the truth claims of the Bible, but that response goes against the teaching of this text. The only leap of faith we are to take is out of the darkness and into the light. When we become Christians, we do not leave our mind in the parking lot. We are called to think according to the Word of God, to seek the mind of Christ and an understanding of the things set forth in sacred Scripture. The Bible is a big book, and every bit of it, I believe, has been inspired by God the Holy Spirit. Ultimately, the author of this Book is God. He gave it to us to be understood, and we cannot understand it if we close our mind to the careful study of it.

Peter says that we are to stand ready to give what the English translation calls "a defense" to everyone who asks for a reason for our hope. The Greek word translated "defense" is *apologia*, which may be translated as "apology." Every Christian is to be prepared to give an apology to all. This does not mean that we are to apologize to people—"Please, excuse me for being a Christian; I'm sorry that I'm so irrational; I just can't help it"; it means that we are to give a defense.

History of Apologetics

The science of apologetics began in the New Testament when the Apostle Paul went into every town on his missionary journeys. He went first to the synagogue and also to the marketplace, and he reasoned with the people and declared the truths of Christianity. He gave a defense of the faith. The most clear example of that is when Paul was in Athens and went to the meeting place of the philosophers at the Areopagus. There he disputed with the Stoics and the Epicureans, the philosophers of the day, and entered into intellectual argument with them.

In the first century, after the Apostles had passed from the scene, the science of apologetics developed even further, on into the second century. Justin Martyr, for example, was one of the most important early Christian apologists. His most famous writing was simply titled *The Apologia*, or "The Apology," which he addressed to Emperor Antonius Pius. Apologetics at that point was, in the first instance, a defensive activity done in order to defend the church against the false charges being spread abroad in the Empire against them.

In Justin's day, Christians were accused of being atheists because they did not embrace the pagan polytheism of Rome or the emperor cult. Because they would not worship the emperor, they were accused of sedition, of being traitors to the Empire. They were also accused of cannibalism. Rumors circulated that the Christians met together in secret to devour someone's body and blood, a rumor that was nothing more than a serious distortion of the celebration of the Lord's Supper.

Justin Martyr clarified what the Christian church believed, and he told the emperor that Christians are not atheists but committed theists. He explained that Christians believe in a God who is one and not many, as was the case in the mythological religion of the Roman pantheon. Justin Martyr said that while Christians do not worship Caesar, they are scrupulously obedient to the civil magistrate. They pay taxes, and they pray for those who rule over them. However, he said, they do not consider Caesar as a deity, because Jesus is Lord. He went on to explain the nature of the Lord's Supper, which was far from cannibalism.

So the first task of the apologist in the early church was to correct the misapprehensions and distortions that were spread abroad about Christianity. Beyond that, Justin Martyr and other apologists entered into discussion with the great philosophers of Greek thought and developed a positive, rational defense of the truth claims of Christianity.

The greatest Titan of theology in the first thousand years was Augustine. He labored to defend Christianity against pagan philosophers and to show the intellectual superiority of Christianity over Neo-Platonism, Manichaeism, and other philosophical rivals to the faith. In his defense Augustine talked about the role of reason in the Christian faith, and he said, for example, that God's revelation is completely unintelligible unless it is understood by the mind. Reason is part of the constituent makeup of human beings, who are made in the image of God. God thinks, and His creatures also are called to think, clearly and rightly.

Augustine did not believe that naked reason has the power to climb up to eternal truths without the aid of God's revelation. He said that we are dependent upon God's revelation for all our understanding of truth, whether it be biblical truth, theological truth, or scientific truth. Augustine argued that we are as dependent on God's revelation for understanding the truths of science as the eyes are dependent on a source of light to see anything. We have been equipped with appropriate organs, optic nerves and the like, to be able to see things. All that we need to see is built into our human structure, but without the external manifestation of light, we cannot see anything. Therefore, Augustine said, the Christian ought to learn as much as he can about as many things as he can, because all truth is God's truth, and God's revelation is not limited to the pages of Scripture. Scripture itself tells us that God reveals Himself in and through nature.

I used to ask my seminary students, "Do you believe that biblical revelation is infallible?" They would all raise a hand. Then I would ask, "Do you believe that the revelation God gives in nature is infallible?" No hands were raised. Then I would remind them that all revelation is God's revelation. How could His revelation be fallible? It is not fallible when it comes through the medium of Scripture. Just so, it is not fallible when it comes through the medium of nature. We are the fallible ones, not God.

Faith and Reason

Augustine dealt with the fact that the New Testament speaks of faith in distinction from reason. As the author of Hebrews says, "Faith is the substance of things hoped for, the evidence of things not seen" (Heb. 11:1). There is a distinction between faith and reason, but this biblical text talks about faith as being something of substance. The faith of which the Scriptures speak is not empty; it is not ephemeral. It is substantive, and it is the substance of things hoped for, the evidence of things not seen. "By faith we understand that the worlds were framed by the word of God" (Heb. 11:3). There are certain things that we believe without having complete knowledge about them. We do not have the total scientific evidence to know that the universe was created by the word of God. We have the testimony of Scripture to that end, but none of us were eyewitnesses of creation. We do not have firsthand experience of it, so we take it on faith that what the Bible says is true. Augustine wrestled with that and said, "Is that, therefore, unreasonable?"

Following knee surgery, I was given a negative report of the condition of my knee and told by the surgeon that I would likely need a knee replacement. I sought the opinion of other doctors, some of whom advised for the surgery and some against it. Since I am not an expert in medicine, I seek out the opinion of those who are experts, and at some point, I have to trust them. Every day we all have to put faith in sources of truth that we cannot personally verify.

However, is it reasonable to trust God when He tells us things for which we have no verifiable evidence? The answer, which is critical to the Christian understanding of faith, is that there is nothing more reasonable than to trust the integrity of God's revelation. I cannot think of anything more irrational than to elevate our sight as the final arbiter of truth. God has demonstrated in His Word and in history that He is eminently trustworthy. Augustine said that we trust things we cannot see with a provisional acceptance; in other words, we trust unless or until the idea is proven false. Faith, however, is based on trustworthy evidence.

John Calvin in his classic work *Institutes of the Christian Religion* gave a defense of the Bible as God's Word. He devoted a chapter to the reasons for which the church believes that the Scriptures come from God. These reasons he called the *indicia*, the indications that something may be true. The word we use is *evidence*. Calvin went on to say that the heart of man is so opposed to the truth of God that, despite overwhelming evidence, man refuses to submit to it. Unless or until the Holy Spirit works with that evidence and opens our eyes to see this truth, we will not submit. The point Calvin made is of vital importance. He said that when the Spirit changes the disposition of our soul and brings us out of the darkness that has held us captive against the truth of God, we do not then believe against the evidence, but we acquiesce into the evidence. The Spirit causes us to submit to that which is objectively true.

John Warwick Montgomery, a Lutheran apologist, tells the story of a man named Charlie, whose wife tried to rouse him from bed to go to work. Charlie would not get out of bed and said, "I can't go to work today because I am dead."

His wife said, "Charlie, that's the most ridiculous excuse you've ever given to avoid work. You're perfectly well. Now, get out of that bed and go to work."

He continued to protest, saying, "I can't. I'm dead."

No matter how Charlie's wife reasoned, she was unable to convince her husband that he was alive and well. So she called the doctor, and the doctor came and checked all his vital signs and said, "Charlie, you're alive and well. Now you need to get out of bed and go to work."

Charlie said, "I'm sorry, Doctor. Your instruments are wrong. I'm dead, and I know it."

The doctor thought about how to convince Charlie that he was alive, and finally he said, "Charlie, when a person dies, the heart stops beating, and when the heart stops beating, it no longer pushes blood through the blood vessels. Dead people don't bleed."

The doctor took Charlie to the coroner's office, where he poked a needle into the cadavers to prove to Charlie that dead people do not bleed. Afterward the doctor said, "Now, Charlie, do you believe me that dead people don't bleed?"

Charlie said, "Yes, you've proven it to me."

The doctor said, "Come here, Charlie. Give me your finger," and the doctor pricked Charlie's thumb with a pin, and Charlie's thumb began to bleed. "So, what do you think now, Charlie?"

Charlie looked at his bleeding thumb and said, "Well, I'll be! Dead men bleed after all."

That is what John Calvin meant about the difference between proof and persuasion. Proof may be compelling, but because of hardness of heart people will not submit to it.

Competing Views

In our day, there are three competing schools of thought with respect to apologetics. One view, broadly held in evangelical circles, usually among Arminians, is called "evidentialism." The evidentialist position is based on sense perception. Evidence for the existence of God is raised to such a high probability that only a fool would refuse to submit to it. The evidentialist says that the rational and empirical evidence for the existence of God is so overwhelming that the probability for the existence of God is astronomical. There is no legitimate reason to reject it in light of the abundance of evidence. However, as dramatic as that evidence may be, it falls short of absolute logical proof of the existence of God.

Classical apologists, on the other hand, from Thomas Aquinas and many others down through the ages, such as Benjamin Warfield, Charles Hodge, J. H. Thornwell, and Robert Dabney, all believe that the evidence for the existence of God is compelling, and that one must opt for irrationality to deny the existence of God. That was the approach of Anselm and others, and it is my approach. I believe that the case for the existence of God is not just highly probable but is absolutely logically compelling.

The third view, presuppositionalism, has swept the allegiance of Reformed people throughout America. It holds that the only way one can come to the conclusion that God exists is by presupposing that God exists in the first place. All people have presuppositions upon which they build their thought processes, and, therefore, the godly presupposition to begin with is the existence of God. The Bible does not seek to prove the existence of God. It simply declares it in the first verse of sacred Scripture: "In the beginning God created the heavens and the earth" (Gen. 1:1). To even argue from nature and reason for the existence of God is, in their view, to fall into the trap of a kind of humanism that exalts the human mind above the Word of God. That is the prevailing view in most Reformed circles today, and it is a circle around which I have not been willing to dance.

Reason

Peter says that after we sanctify the Lord God in our hearts, we are to be ready to give an *apologia*, a defense, to everyone who asks us a reason for our hope—not a feeling, but a reason. The issue has become so muddled in our day that some modern translators supply "word" instead of "reason." The word Peter uses is *logos*, the Greek term often translated "word," as in the prologue to John's Gospel: "In the beginning was the Word [*logos*], and the Word was with God, and the Word was God" (John 1:1). The Latin text supplies the word *rotionem*, which means "reason," because one of the translations of *logos* is "reason." We get the word *logic* from the Greek word *logos*.

The late Gordon Clark, a Christian philosopher of the twentieth century, even went so far as to translate the preamble to the Gospel of John this way: "In the beginning was logic, and logic was with God, and logic was God." His point was that rationality comes from God Himself, that God is a rational being and He relates to His people in a rational way.

A while ago I was involved in a serious controversy involving a professor who had been teaching that biblical truth cannot be understood by reason but through some kind of mystical intuition. That is the position that was taken by the heretical Gnostics in the second and third centuries. They believed that their mystical apprehension of truth was superior to the Apostles' because the Apostles relied on the mind. Relying on the mind is criticized by some who say that if you rely on the mind to understand the content of the Christian faith, you have submitted to the heresy of rationalism.

I asked this particular professor, "When you talk about rationalism, what do you mean? Are you talking about the Cartesian rationalism of the seventeenth century? Are you talking about the Enlightenment rationalism of the eighteenth century? Are you speaking about the Hegelian rationalism of the nineteenth century that deified reason itself?" He was completely unaware of those radically different types of rationalism. To say that you are a rationalist because Christianity is rational simply does not follow. One can be rational without being a rationalist, just as one can be human without being a humanist, or can exist without being an existentialist, or be feminine without being a feminist.

On the basis of Scripture, we must never negotiate the principle that the truth we receive from God is rational. It is not irrational or illogical. To say that the Word of God is irrational, contradictory, or absurd is to accuse the Holy Spirit of speaking with a forked tongue. As Peter said, "For we did not follow cunningly devised fables when we made known to you the power and coming of our Lord Jesus Christ, but were eyewitnesses of His majesty" (2 Pet. 1:16). What they had witnessed was the sober truth of the Word of God, which is intelligible and reasonable for any reasonable person to embrace. We are called to give an apology—a reason for what we believe—and, as we will see, we are to do it with meekness and fear, not with an arrogant spirit or a cold heart.

When I was in seminary, I read a book written by an Anglican apologist that contained a chapter on what he called "the treason of the intellectual." He pointed out that the crisis of faith in the church today is not because atheists have taken Christ away where we cannot find Him but because so-called Christian professors have committed treason against their Lord. The answer to that is not to surrender the rationality of the faith to the skeptic and the cynic, but to stand toe-to-toe with them and demonstrate their folly.

14

SUFFERING

1 Peter 3:15–20

But sanctify the Lord God in your hearts, and always be ready to give a defense to everyone who asks you a reason for the hope that is in you, with meekness and fear; having a good conscience, that when they defame you as evildoers, those who revile your good conduct in Christ may be ashamed. For it is better, if it is the will of God, to suffer for doing good than for doing evil. For Christ also suffered once for sins, the just for the unjust, that He might bring us to God, being put to death in the flesh but made alive by the Spirit, by whom also He went and preached to the spirits in prison, who formerly were disobedient, when once the Divine longsuffering waited in the days of Noah, while the ark was being prepared, in which a few, that is, eight souls, were saved through water.

In our last study we looked at the classical New Testament text for the science of apologetics that has occupied much of the church's intellectual activity for over two thousand years. We saw that the responsibility of giving an answer and a reason for the hope that is in us at any time is not simply the province of the technical scholars or theologians; we all are called to be ready to give a reason for our faith. We are not only to know what we believe but also why we believe it, so that we may articulate that reason to those who inquire. We are also told that when we give that answer, we are to give it **with meekness and fear** (v. 15).

I cannot read this text without thinking of a discussion I had many years ago with a professor of philosophy. He was skeptical about whether we can give a significant reason for the existence of God. In our discussion I set forth classical arguments for the existence of God that I believe are compelling. He finally said to me, "Well, I can't argue with you, but you are an intellectual bully." I was surprised by his remark. He had good academic credentials, and I didn't think that he should have been so intimidated. It bothered me all the same, and I realized then that our defense of the faith has to be done with gentleness and meekness. Obviously, I was not gentle enough for his taste at that time, and I felt the rebuke of his accusation.

When we engage in debates and arguments, we sometimes allow ourselves to be overcome with the heat of the moment and generate more heat than light. However, at the same time that we are called to give a reason, we are also called to give it with this spirit of meekness and fear, **having a good conscience, that when they defame you as evildoers, those who revile your good conduct in Christ may be ashamed. For it is bet-ter, if it is the will of God, to suffer for doing good than for doing evil** (vv. 16–17). We are not to be reviled for bad conduct but for good. When we are slandered for Christ's sake, it will shame the slanderer.

The Suffering of Christ

When Peter introduces the matter of suffering for the sake of good, he brings immediately to our attention the suffering of our Lord: **For Christ also suffered once for sins, the just for the unjust, that He might bring us to God, being put to death in the flesh but made alive by the Spirit, by whom also He went and preached to the spirits in prison, who formerly were disobedient, when once the Divine longsuffering waited in the days of Noah, while the ark was being prepared, in which a few, that is, eight souls, were saved through water** (vv. 18–20). Peter's language brings to mind again the teaching of the Apostle Paul, who wrote that Christ took upon Himself the punishment due to us and bestows on those who believe the reward that accompanies His righteousness. Since God requires punishment for sin, He receives satisfaction not from us, the unjust, but from Christ, the just One so that God might be both "just and the justifier" (Rom. 3:26).

God is just insofar as He does not wink at human sin. He is just because He requires the penalty for sin to fulfill all righteousness, which righteousness was accomplished by Christ Himself. It is through His righteousness that we are made just in the sight of God. The only ground for our justification, now and forever, is the imputation of the righteousness of Christ to all who believe. The righteousness by which we are justified is what Luther called a *iustitia aliena*, an alien righteousness, a righteousness that, properly speaking, is not our own. It comes *extra nos*, from outside of us. It, properly speaking, belongs only to the One who is just, but it is precisely that foreign righteousness that God accounts to us when we put our trust in Jesus.

Peter's words "made alive by the Spirit" can also be translated "made alive *in* the Spirit," so we might wonder whether it is a reference to Jesus' human spirit or to the Holy Spirit. Another question concerns the clause "by whom also He went and preached." There is no debate over the fact that Jesus, at some point and in some manner, preached to somebody. Peter says that He preached "to the spirits in prison, who formerly were disobedient," and then he makes a reference back to "the days of Noah." So, the passage generates a number of questions: Which spirit is in view here, the human spirit or the Holy Spirit? Who are the spirits in prison? What does the prison indicate, or where is that prison? When did this preaching mission take place? Finally, why did this preaching mission take place? Each of those questions has various answers supplied by biblical scholars. My view of the meaning of this text is in the minority. I would hasten to add that most views about the passage are in the minority, since there is no majority view on the meaning of this text. Yet I am in a minority of the minority in how I understand it.

Much discussion of the text is provoked by a clause within the Apostles' Creed: "He [Jesus] descended into hell." This clause, the *Descensus ad Infernos*, was not in the earliest manuscripts of the creed. Its absence from those early manuscripts is why many churches put an asterisk next to it. Calvin believed that it was suitable to say in our confession of faith that Jesus descended into hell; however, he suggested that the order or the sequence of the phrases be changed this way: "[Jesus] suffered under Pontius Pilate and was crucified, descended into hell, dead, and buried." Calvin argued that there was a real descent into hell but that it did not take place after Jesus' death or between His death and resurrection, but on the cross. Calvin and others would not speak of a later descent or a descent between death and resurrection because at the end of His time on the cross, our Lord said, "It is finished." He used the word *tetelestai*, a word drawn from the commercial language of the day indicating that the final payment had been made. Since there was no more satisfaction to render than that which was rendered on the cross, there was no need for Jesus to experience any further punishment.

The second reason that classical Protestantism does not believe that Jesus went to hell between His death and His resurrection is that the Bible makes clear where He was. His human body was in the tomb, and His human soul was with the Father. In His dying breath Jesus said, "Father, into Your hands I commit My spirit" (Luke 23:46).

Throughout history some have embraced "trichotomy," which says that man is made up of a threefold nature comprising body, soul, and spirit. Virtually every time that this doctrine of anthropology has emerged in church history, it has been used to carry the baggage of some heresy. In any case, if you believe in duality rather than in trichotomy, there is no part of Jesus that could have been in hell between the cross and the resurrection, because the Scriptures make it clear where He was.

The New King James Version says that while Jesus was put to death in the flesh, He was "made alive *by* the Spirit," which, as we already noted, can also be interpreted as "made alive *in* the spirit," thereby distinguishing between Jesus' body and His soul or, in this case, His spirit, so that He suffered death in the body but not in His spirit. I have a problem with that, because the spirit of Jesus did not have to be made alive; it already was alive. If this is a reference to Jesus' human spirit, it would indicate an incorrect understanding of what happened to Jesus at His death, some kind of spirit death along with a bodily death. I do not think that is what Peter means here. I think it is referencing the Holy Spirit, so that the power by which Jesus was raised from the dead was the power of the Holy Spirit Himself. That is consistent with what the Scriptures teach elsewhere, that He was raised by the Spirit of God.

Spirits in Prison

What follows from this becomes more entangled. Peter adds, ". . . by whom [that is, the Holy Spirit] also He went and preached to the spirits in prison, who formerly were disobedient." There is a question as to who these spirits were and what the prison refers to. The majority of commentators understand the prison to be a reference to hell or, at least, to the "limbo" of the fathers. Somewhere about A.D. 300 Clement of Alexandria postulated the thesis that Jesus went to hell to preach the gospel to sinners held captive there so that they might repent and be saved. Augustine objected to that later because the New Testament teaches that we have only one opportunity: "It is appointed for men to die once, but after this the judgment" (Heb. 9:27). Historic Protestantism does not believe in a second chance after death.

At the end of the sixteenth century, one of the leading theologians of the Roman Catholic Church, Cardinal Robert Bellarmine, said he believed that

Jesus went to the limbo of the fathers in order to release the saints who were caught in this preserved state. Supposedly, limbo is not a rigorous portion of hell but a place on the edge of hell, where the flames of pain do not reach. The thinking was that Jesus went there to preach the gospel to Old Testament believers, who had to wait until the time of Christ before they could enter into heaven. That view, of course, is also rejected by classical Protestantism, which believes, as Paul labors in his letter to the Romans, that the moment a person puts his trust in Christ, he is in a state of justifying grace. To make his case, Paul reached back to Abraham, who was counted righteous the moment he believed in the promise of God (Rom. 4:3). We believe that the saints of the Old Testament went to heaven, not to a holding place. The principle is that the work of Jesus is applied by God both backward and forward. They trusted in the future promise; we trust in the fulfilled promise.

My friend John MacArthur and I rarely disagree on matters of biblical interpretation, but we do disagree on this text. MacArthur believes that this text refers to a mission Jesus made to the evil angels, incarcerated since their evil activities in the days of Noah. We read in the early chapters of Genesis how the sons of God intermarried with the daughters of men and produced a race of corrupt people (Gen. 6:2). Dr. MacArthur interprets the Genesis text as indicating an actual intermarriage between heavenly beings and earthly beings. I disagree with his thinking there. I think that "sons of God" in Genesis refers to the descendants of the line of Seth who maintained their integrity and the descendants of the line of Cain who were filled with corruption. The genealogies in Genesis give us these different lines and place a strong emphasis on their differences until the sons of God married the daughters of men. The obedient line intermarried with the radically corrupt line, and the whole world was cast into remarkable corruption.

Concerning the spirits in prison, people argue as to whether they are angelic spirits, the departed souls of righteous believers, or the departed souls of evil, ungodly people. Those are the three basic options, but I am going to suggest a fourth. Before I do that, I want to mention that much of the speculation about this text is based on the fact that the reference to Jesus' going on this preaching mission occurs after the reference to His death. Because it is mentioned later, the automatic assumption is that it must refer to something that took place after His death; but the text does not say that. This becomes of critical importance, as we will see.

A case is also made for it on the basis that this reference occurs after the reference to the suffering in the flesh, but that is a case in which an argument proves too much, because the mission of preaching to the spirits in prison is mentioned after the resurrection. We see the suffering in the flesh, then Christ made alive by the Spirit, and then we have mention of His going on a preaching mission to the spirits in prison. If we are going to follow the logic that these things happened in that order, we would have to say that this preaching did not take place between Christ's death and resurrection but afterward. Many people agree that this took place after the resurrection and maybe between the resurrection and the ascension. Others argue that it happened at the ascension. We are still left with the mystery of when this preaching actually took place. I suggest that the text does not tell us. It simply mentions that Jesus preached to the spirits in prison by the same Spirit that raised Him from the dead.

The fourth option as to whom Jesus preached is not without difficulties. When I think of Jesus preaching by the power of the Spirit, the first thing that comes to mind is His inaugural sermon in the synagogue, when He read from the prophet Isaiah: "The Spirit of the LORD is upon Me" (Luke 4:18). After Jesus read the text, He said, "Today this Scripture is fulfilled in your hearing" (v. 21). At Jesus' baptism He was anointed by the Holy Spirit and empowered for His earthly ministry, and the majority of His attention while He was on earth was given to His own people, Israel. When John the Baptist was thrown into prison, he sent a message asking, "Are you the Coming One, or do we look for another?" Jesus answered, "Go and tell John the things which you hear and see: The blind see and the lame walk; the lepers are cleansed and the deaf hear; the dead are raised up and the poor have the gospel preached to them" (Matt. 11:3–5). When Jesus sent that message to John the Baptist, He was in essence telling John to go back and read Isaiah 61. If we look at Isaiah 61, we see that the heart of the Messiah's task was to preach release for the captives, the lost of Israel. So it is possible that what Peter has in view here, as he is writing to Jewish people, are living people. The spirits in prison are not dead people but living people, not people in hell but people who are held captive by their sin.

The Bible does use the term "spirit" to refer to living people. We do it ourselves when we refer to living people as "souls." We say such things as, "Not a soul was at the event last evening." In fact, when God breathed into Adam His breath, man became a living *nephesh* or *pneuma*—spirit. Because the Bible refers to people as spirits, living people who are in bondage to sin can certainly be referred to as "spirits in prison."

There is a difficulty, however, with the reference to those who were formerly disobedient in the days of Noah. This might mean that the condition of being captive by sin can be traced all the way back to the days of Noah, when men became wicked and the thoughts of their heart were only evil continuously so that God judged the world in the flood. Then, through the proclamation of Noah, eight were saved, but through the preaching of Christ to this people, who have been held captive for a millennia, they have been redeemed. The context in which Peter writes these things is to encourage us that our suffering is used by God as a testimony for righteousness and is accompanied by the Holy Spirit to bring about the Spirit's purposes of redemption, in the same manner by which our Lord, who was raised by the Spirit, went and preached and saw so much fruit.

I am not prepared to say that this is exactly what Peter meant, but the ambiguity of the language here in this text does not require us to come to the conclusion that it must refer to some kind of post-resurrection preaching mission in hell to angels or to dead people. It may have its primary reference to the earthly ministry of Jesus. This is a text about which I am open to correction and reproof, and I will be quick to ask the Apostle when I see him in glory what he meant by these very enigmatic words.

15

THROUGH THE
RESURRECTION

1 Peter 3:20–22

The Divine longsuffering waited in the days of Noah, while the ark was being prepared, in which a few, that is, eight souls, were saved through water. There is also an antitype which now saves us—baptism (not the removal of the filth of the flesh, but the answer of a good conscience toward God), through the resurrection of Jesus Christ, who has gone into heaven and is at the right hand of God, angels and authorities and powers having been made subject to Him.

The latter portion of 1 Peter 3 has had profound significance in the history of the church. We were first enjoined to be prepared to give an answer or an apology and a reason for the hope that is within us. We saw that this is the classical text upon which the science of apologetics has been based. Then we looked at an extremely difficult text with respect to Christ's preaching to the lost spirits in prison. We saw how it has been related historically to various understandings of Christ's descent into hell and other ministries attributed to Him, either after His resurrection or even before His birth. The text before us now is attended with many difficulties but it has had enormous influence in the development of many ideas throughout the history of the church.

The Divine longsuffering waited in the days of Noah, while the ark was being prepared, in which a few, that is, eight souls, were saved through water. There is also an antitype which now saves us—baptism (vv. 20–21). The Apostle makes a strong link between what God did in His redemptive purposes in the Old Testament through the salvation of Noah and his family on the ark and what came later in the sacrament of baptism. The experience on the ark is seen as a type or symbol of what would come later.

The Days of Noah

God was patient in the days of Noah. During that time, Noah was, as the Apostle Peter wrote, a "preacher of righteousness" (2 Pet. 2:5). After the ark was finished, the rains came, and the flood inundated the whole world, and Peter says that eight people were saved through the instrumentation of the water. If we read between the lines, we can see that, in all likelihood, there were many people who knew Noah and heard his preaching but failed to heed his warning of God's coming judgment. We also can readily assume that some of those who perished in the flood had actually helped Noah in the construction of the vessel. In that historical reference there is a lesson for us: we tend to cling to our folly and put off to some later day the necessary repentance to which God calls us, hoping that time will give us another opportunity. These very people, some of whom helped Noah, even as others who mocked him, perished in the flood; but Noah, we are told, was saved along with eight souls through water.

The eight people spared at the time of the flood were Noah and his wife and their three sons and their wives. Some commentators historically have seen symbolism even in the number of people who were redeemed from the flood, eight being the number of supreme perfection for Jewish people. For the most part, the number seven is considered to be the number of completion or perfection, but in antiquity some people saw that the number seven was made even more perfect and complete by the eighth number. They believed that there were seven planets in the sky, which represented the perfect number of seven, but when the sun was added to the planets, that totaled eight. Later there were some who argued that, after the resurrection, the Sabbath should be commemorated on an eighth day of the week rather than commemorating it on the first day of the week as the Lord's Day. Such numerological speculations have not had a great impact on the history of the church; for the most part, they have been somewhat frivolous.

The idea that these eight souls were saved through water has become a controversial concept in historical theology. The salvation that is described as taking place through water indicates that the water was the instrument of salvation for Noah and his family. If you look at that story of Noah, you see that the water for those who perished was the cause of their destruction. It was the instrument of divine wrath against a world that had gone over completely into godlessness. At the same time, those very waters that destroyed the world carried the vessel in which the family of Noah was housed and carried them to safety. Notice that, with reference to baptism, Peter does not say that the eight were immersed in the water. The ones who were immersed perished. The ones who were carried above the water were saved.

Causality

The Greek philosopher Aristotle applied his scientific inquiry to the subject of causality. What is it that causes one thing to influence another? The study of causal relationships is critical to the entire scientific enterprise. When you are sick and go to the doctor, you want the doctor to find the cause of your illness. Until he knows the cause of your discomfort, he will not know how to prescribe a cure. Aristotle noticed that there are several dimensions in causal activities. His most famous illustration involved the creation of a statue from a block of stone. The material cause for the statue was the stone, he said. If one lacks the stone to work with, he will not be able to create a beautiful statue. There must be something physical out of which to create the statue, and so Aristotle assigned "material causality" to the block of stone. Then he distinguished what he called the "efficient cause," that is, the cause that actually brings about the change from the raw block of stone to a beautiful statue. The efficient cause is the activity of the sculptor, who does his artistic work to shape and form that block of stone into a beautiful statue. There is also the "formal cause," which Aristotle defined as the idea in the mind of the sculptor. The sculptor did not simply attack the stone aimlessly, chipping here and there, but he had some idea, maybe even a sketch on a piece of paper, of how he wanted the finished product to look. The "final cause" he distinguished as that purpose for which the statue was made. Maybe it was created for a beautiful patrician's house or mausoleum or even for a church somewhere. In the midst of all the causes that Aristotle distinguished, he spoke of the "instrumental cause." In the simple case of the making of a statue, the instrumental cause was the instrument the sculptor used to change the surface of the stone and produce the beautiful statuary—a chisel and hammer.

Here, with the instrumental cause, we touch on something that strikes at the very heart of Christian theology. Central to the sixteenth-century Protestant Reformation was the theological question, What is the instrumental cause of our justification? The Roman Catholic Church had declared the instrumental cause of our salvation to be the sacrament of baptism. Through baptism, the church says, saving grace is administered. A person is cleansed from original sin and brought into a state of justification.

Protestants revolted against the system of theology called "sacerdotalism," which holds that salvation comes principally through the sacraments administered by the church. The Protestant Reformation insisted that the instrumental cause of justification was not baptism, but faith. When the New Testament says that we are justified by faith, that word "by," sometimes translated "through," is the instrumental dative that indicates the means by which a person is linked to Christ.

The Reformers did not see faith as the meritorious cause, although some people think that Protestants teach that. Faith is merely the instrument by which we are linked to Christ and receive all the benefits of His work. This text in 1 Peter 3 is one by which the Roman Catholic Church came to the conclusion that people are saved through the instrumental power of baptism. The text says that Noah and his family were saved through water, and clearly the water was the medium through which Noah and his family were saved. In verse 21 Peter says that there is an antitype that now saves us, which is baptism. Just as water was the instrument God used to save Noah and his family, so now baptism is the instrument that God uses to save us. You can see how important this text has been to the debate of whether we are saved by sacraments or by faith.

Within the Church?

Then the plot thickens dramatically. In the third century, one of the most important church fathers was Cyprian. He wrote a book on the unity of the church, and he is known for two statements that have lasted through the ages, one of which is this: "He who does not have the church as his mother does not have God as his father." Far more important is the formula that Cyprian expressed, which down through ages has been known simply as the Cyprianic Formula: *extra ecclesiam nulla salus*. Translated, it means literally "outside the church there is no salvation." Cyprian was speaking not of the invisible church, of which Augustine would write later, but rather of the visible church. Cyprian's thesis was this: only if you are a member of the visible church can you be saved. Being a member of the visible church, which, in that case, was the Roman Catholic Church, was a necessary condition for salvation. Cyprian said that it is just as necessary to be inside the visible Roman Catholic Church as it was for people in Noah's day to be inside the ark in order to be saved. This idea of the necessity of being inside the visible church has persisted for hundreds of years.

The sanctuary of St. Andrew's where I serve is built in the shape of a cross. If you would look at it from above or from the air, you would see the cross-shaped structure of the building. The center section of the church is called the "nave" from which we get the word *navy*, and it is this central portion that symbolizes the ark, the place of salvation. Just as Noah and his family were saved by a naval vessel, so we are saved by this naval vessel, this building called the church.

Cyprian's strict formula of having to be a member of the visible church in order to be saved has undergone some significant modifications throughout church history. One of the most important was given in an *allocutio* by Pope Pius IX, who presided over the first Vatican Council in 1870. That was the council in which the doctrine of the infallibility of the pope was defined. Sixteen years before that, the pope had articulated the doctrine that people had to be inside the church in order to be saved, except for those who were prevented from entering by "invincible ignorance." According to Rome, after the sixteenth-century Reformation, generations of Protestants were raised in the doctrines of Protestantism and were ignorant of the doctrines taught by the Roman Catholic Church. They were so clouded by error that their ignorance was considered invincible, not able to be overcome. The distinction made by Pius IX was between invincible ignorance and what he called "vincible ignorance." Vincible ignorance can be conquered or overcome, and it should be overcome. Yet, he acknowledged, there is an ignorance that is so deeply ingrained that even honest, intelligent people cannot overcome it, so he made a provision for a kind of spiritual inclusion into the holy mother church.

This modification issued by Pius IX was not without a bit of precedence, which occurred at the Council of Trent. In the sixteenth century the Council of Trent articulated its doctrine of baptism and reaffirmed the teaching of Cyprian to the effect that baptism is necessary for salvation or "the desire for it." That tiny qualification at the Council of Trent was the foundation for further elaborations that allowed people outside the confines of the visible

Roman Church to be saved. One was called the *votum baptisma*, "the desire of baptism" or the desire to be baptized.

Consider the case of the thief on the cross. He embraced Jesus and believed in Him, but he died before he had the opportunity to be baptized. In that special case, he went to heaven because he had an explicit desire to do what was required but was providentially hindered from doing it. Or consider the case of a Protestant who takes instruction at a Roman Catholic Church and agrees to be baptized in the Roman fellowship, but on the way to the church he is hit by a bus and killed. He is considered to have been baptized because he had the desire for baptism, which they call the *votum baptisma explicitum*, an explicit desire.

Later, in the twentieth century, this was modified even further. Rome said that someone is considered to be in the church if he or she has an explicit desire to join the church but is somehow prevented. That would be the *votum ecclesia explicitum*. Rome took it even further and said that if a Protestant has a genuine desire to do what is pleasing to God but does not understand that what pleases God is to join the Roman Catholic Church, that Protestant may be considered to have a desire for the church, although the desire is implicit, not explicit—the *votum ecclesia implicitum*. Such people are considered to be within the fold, and they are afforded the benefits of the salvation that is ministered through the church.

In recent years we have heard astonishing further modifications. Some Roman Catholic leaders, including popes, have indicated that even Muslims can be saved, which seems a long way from Cyprian's formula of "outside the church there is no salvation." The Roman Catholic Church is not saying that Islam brings salvation but that this *votum ecclesia implicitum* may be applied even to earnest followers of other religions. They are not saved by Islam, but they are saved despite their Islamic beliefs through being included in the ark of the Roman Catholic Church. This seems to be a shift away from triumphalism to a more humble, gracious, inclusive attitude, but it is not. This extension of salvation beyond an embracing of Christianity can be accomplished because Rome, it says, has the power of the keys. It has the keys of the kingdom and can unlock the kingdom to anyone it sees fit.

This lengthy discussion of the necessity of being in the visible church in order to be saved has its roots back in the third century with Cyprian's formula that outside the church there is no salvation, and that was based in large measure on this text of 1 Peter.

Baptism

Beyond the issue of Protestantism versus Rome, we see major controversies within Protestantism about baptism, because the Roman Catholic Church taught then and continues to teach that the sacrament of baptism works *ex opere operato*, that is, to the very "working of the work"; it works regeneration in the souls of those who receive the sacrament, which is known as "baptismal regeneration." That doctrine has been held to other degrees by Protestant bodies, but in the main, historic Protestantism, particularly Reformed Protestantism, has categorically rejected the idea that baptism automatically regenerates or places a person in a state of salvation, arguing that people who are baptized may indeed not be saved, and it is a mistake to assume that baptism indicates salvation. This was the mistake Israel made with their sign of circumcision. They thought that just because they were circumcised and had the sign of God's promise of salvation that they had the reality toward which that sign pointed.

We believe in our communion that baptism is the sign of God's promise for all who believe, and that the promise is not realized unless we embrace Christ by faith. When we do, all the things that baptism symbolizes become ours. Baptism symbolizes our participation in Christ's burial and in His resurrection. It symbolizes the cleansing of our sin. It symbolizes our regeneration but does not automatically convey it. It symbolizes our sanctification, our being anointed by the Holy Spirit. It signifies our adoption into the family of God, all of which occur the second we have faith.

One reason why the Baptist community has emerged historically as one of the strongest Protestant groups is that historic Baptists rejected the idea of baptismal regeneration. Baptists believe that the efficacy of baptism is so dependent upon faith that it ought never to be administered to anyone who has not made a profession of faith. Inasmuch as infants are not capable of doing so, baptism should be reserved only for those who profess faith in Christ.

A Good Conscience

All these things are involved in the implication of this text in 1 Peter 3. We are told that **baptism (not the removal of the filth of the flesh, but the answer of a good conscience toward God), through the resurrection of Jesus Christ, who has gone into heaven and is at the right hand of God, angels and authorities and powers having been made subject to Him . . .** (vv. 21–22). In a word, without Christ, His death, His resurrection, the imputation of His righteousness to us, and the imputation of our guilt to Him on the cross—without those things, baptism would be utterly worthless. If I thought for one second that baptism put people in a state of justification, I would stand on a corner with a fire hose and baptize as many people as I could. I do not think that is the point being made here. The water that saved Noah and his family saved them because they put their trust in the promises of God, and for those who did not, that same water was the occasion of their utter destruction.

I do not want to demean the importance of baptism, because it is a sacrament, and it does communicate the promise of God to all who believe. We do not despise His Word, which makes His promises verbally, nor do we despise the sacrament that confirms it nonverbally. These are authentic signs and seals of God's promises. The power of the sacrament lies in the integrity of God, not in the priest or the pastor who administers it or in the virtue of those who receive it. It lies in the power of God, whose Word is confirmed in this seal of our redemption.

16

LIFE IN THE SPIRIT

1 Peter 4:1–6

Therefore, since Christ suffered for us in the flesh, arm yourselves also with
the same mind, for he who has suffered in the flesh has ceased from sin, that
he no longer should live the rest of his time in the flesh for the lusts of men,
but for the will of God. For we have spent enough of our past lifetime in doing
the will of the Gentiles—when we walked in lewdness, lusts, drunkenness,
revelries, drinking parties, and abominable idolatries. In regard to these, they
think it strange that you do not run with them in the same flood of dissipation, speaking evil of you. They will give an account to Him who is ready to
judge the living and the dead. For this reason the gospel was preached also
to those who are dead, that they might be judged according to men in the
flesh, but live according to God in the spirit.

It is important to remember that when Peter wrote this epistle, he did not
divide it into chapters and verses. The chapter divisions and versifications
were added much later to make it easier to locate certain passages in
Scripture. My pet peeve about it is that the chapter divisions we find in the
English text were arrived at somewhat arbitrarily. It particularly distresses me
to find a chapter beginning with the word *therefore*, because it is inextricably
tied to what precedes it. We have a tendency to look at a text as if it were an
independent piece of literature, completely isolated and disconnected from

what went before it. The texts we have been studying have engendered fierce controversy throughout the history of the church, but in this portion of the epistle, there is little controversy to be found. However, there is considerable difficulty in it.

Therefore, since Christ suffered for us in the flesh (v. 1). The suffering Jesus endured was experienced in His human body. This reference to Jesus' appearance in the flesh is that He appeared as one like us. When the Apostle Paul rehearsed his call to be an Apostle, he indicated that he was unlike the disciples before him. Those chosen before him had known Jesus *kata sarka*, "after the flesh"; that is, they had known Him in His earthly incarnation. Paul missed out on that companionship with Jesus.

Peter's words here, however, go back to the verses before, where he spoke of "baptism (not the removal of the filth of the flesh, but the answer of a good conscience toward God), through the resurrection of Jesus Christ, who has gone into heaven and is at the right hand of God, angels and authorities and powers having been made subject to Him" (3:21–22).

The Mind of Christ

In light of Jesus' suffering unto death, **arm yourselves also with the same mind, for he who has suffered in the flesh has ceased from sin** (v. 1). Again we see parallels with Paul's teaching. The Apostle Paul enjoined the Ephesians to put on the whole armor of God, and he listed each piece of armor that was worn by soldiers in the ancient world (Eph. 6:13–17). Here Peter uses the same language of preparing for warfare. The reason that Paul called us to put on the armor of God is that "we do not wrestle against flesh and blood, but against principalities, against powers, against the rulers of the darkness of this age, against spiritual hosts of wickedness in the heavenly places" (Eph. 6:12). Likewise with Peter, who, just a few verses earlier, wrote that angels and authorities and powers have been made subject to Christ (3:22). The powers and principalities against which we wrestle have been put in subjection to Christ; nevertheless, the war goes on for us, and in order to succeed in the battle of the Christian life, we need to be armed. The armor for warfare that Paul gives includes helmet, breastplate, and shield. For Peter, the principal item of armor is the mind of Christ. We are called to arm ourselves by seeking the mind of Christ.

WWJD bracelets were the primary component of a fad that swept through the Christian world some years ago. The bracelets were marked with the letters WWJD, which stood for "What Would Jesus Do?" People wore these bracelets to remind themselves to behave in a manner that would reflect

Jesus. I was ambivalent about whether such trinkets are helpful, because, in the final analysis, the question is not what would Jesus do in a particular situation, but what would Jesus have me do? Obviously, Jesus had a mission to fulfill that is well beyond anything we could ever be involved in. He was the Savior of the world, so He is not asking us to redo what He has already done. At the same time, the New Testament does call us to be imitators of Christ, as Christ was an imitator of God. If we are going to be Christlike, if we are going to be armed as Christians for spiritual warfare, what we need is the mind of Christ.

I know no other way to gain the mind of Christ than to immerse ourselves in His Word. Studying the Scriptures is the way by which we learn the mind of Christ, because the Scriptures reveal Christ. We are living in the most anti-intellectual period in the history of the Christian church. The application of the mind to the search for understanding of the things of God is dismissed in some quarters and actually despised in others. Feeling is substituted for thinking. Christians, we are called to think, to seek understanding of the Word of God; there is no other way to get the mind of Christ.

People have tried countless tactics to avoid thinking. I once had a student who was fond of practicing what she called "lucky dipping." She would close her eyes and place her finger on a line of text in the Bible, and whatever the text said was, she assumed, her answer from God. Her method required no study, preparation, or thought whatsoever. Her great passion was to find a husband, so she applied her method to try to determine whether God was going to provide her with a spouse. The text she got was, "Rejoice greatly, O daughter of Zion! Shout, O daughter of Jerusalem! Behold, your King is coming to you. . . . Lowly and riding on a donkey" (Zech. 9:9), which she took to mean that Prince Charming was on his way. I tried gently to disavow her of this practice and explained that she ought not to get her hopes up for this imminent encounter with Prince Charming. She stuck to her guns, and two weeks later she met the fellow that she married. Nevertheless, that is not how we get the mind of Christ. We have to search the Scriptures, and this is a serious matter. We simply cannot find the mind of Christ in fifteen minutes a day. We must immerse ourselves in the Word of God if we really want to progress in this battle.

No Longer
For he who has suffered in the flesh has ceased from sin, **that he no longer should live the rest of his time in the flesh for the lusts of men, but for the will of God** (v. 2). Some commentators say that

Peter was not referring to our flesh but to Jesus' flesh, and that since Jesus suffered in the flesh, He had ceased from sin. However, to cease from doing something means that there was a time when it was being done, and obviously there was no point at which Jesus was ever engaged in sin. The commentators argue that after Jesus' resurrection took place and His glorified state had been secured, He no longer had to endure the temptations that were set before Him during His earthly life, but I do not think that is what Peter meant. Peter's words refer to us. If we suffer in the flesh, we cease from sin.

In Romans 6 the Apostle Paul talks about our having died to sin. There is a sense in which we have died to sin, but there is another sense in which the old man is still very much alive, and we deceive ourselves if we think that we have moved completely beyond the pale of sinning. But something dramatic has taken place. If you are a Christian and the Holy Spirit has regenerated your soul, then in a very real sense your old man has been put to death. A death sentence stands over your sinful nature, and you have been made alive in your soul by the Holy Spirit.

We are taught throughout Scripture that even though we enjoy this new state of affairs, there remains an ongoing struggle from the time of our conversion to the time of our glorification in heaven. In one sense, D-day has already taken place. Historians say that when the Allies landed in Normandy in June 1944, it marked the beginning of the end of World War II. Yet still to come was the Battle of the Bulge, one of the bloodiest battles of World War II, when the forces of the Third Reich made their last struggle. Our conversion is like D-day. The outcome of our spiritual future is no longer in doubt, yet tomorrow might begin for us the spiritual Battle of the Bulge. Even though these powers and principalities have been subdued by Christ and dealt a mortal blow, they still seek to give us one last battle. To win it, we need the mind of Christ.

There does seem to be an oscillation here in the text with Peter's use of the word "flesh." Sometimes the word is used to describe our physical bodies. Other times it is used to describe our fallen, corrupt nature. What Peter means here is that if, in our flesh, we have ceased from sin, we should not live in sin. We should live in light of the change that the Spirit of God has wrought in us, putting the flesh to death and nurturing the new man, the man made by the Holy Spirit. Since we have been released from sin and the hold that it had upon our soul, we no longer should live the rest of our time in the flesh, that is, in corruption, "for the lusts of men." This chapter of Peter's epistle reads much like Ephesians 2, where Paul writes:

And you He made alive, who were dead in trespasses and sins, in which you
once walked according to the course of this world, according to the prince
of the power of the air, the spirit who now works in the sons of disobedience,
among whom also we all once conducted ourselves in the lusts of our flesh,
fulfilling the desires of the flesh and of the mind, and were by nature children
of wrath, just as the others. (vv. 1–3)

When we come to Christ, we come by repentance. There is no other way.
One does not cling to Christ as Savior until he first acknowledges that he
is a sinner who needs a Savior. Even when we are converted and the Spirit
removes the scales from our eyes and changes the hardness of our hearts,
we still know little about the corruption in which we once walked. Before
conversion, we did not have a spiritual bone in our body. We had not the
slightest inclination toward the things of God. We walked according to the
course of this world until the Lord rescued us and delivered us from the
kingdom of darkness and brought us into the kingdom of light.

Aiming Forward

**For we have spent enough of our past lifetime in doing the will
of the Gentiles—when we walked in lewdness, lusts, drunkenness, revelries, drinking parties, and abominable idolatries** (v. 3).
Augustine spent the early years of his life following the pattern that Peter
describes here. Then one day he was in a garden where children were playing a game that contained the refrain *tolle lege; tolle lege*, which means "pick
up and read." With those words ringing in his ears, he picked up the Bible
and his eyes fell upon this passage: "Let us walk properly, as in the day, not in
revelry and drunkenness, not in lewdness and lust, not in strife and envy. But
put on the Lord Jesus Christ, and make no provision for the flesh, to fulfill
its lusts" (Rom. 13:13–14). At that moment, Augustine's heart was stricken
because he recognized himself in the text he was reading. He said in essence,
"I have made every provision I could to fulfill the lusts of my flesh. I need
to change my clothes. God grant that He would dress me in the clothes of
Christ that I may no longer make provision for the lusts of the flesh." Peter
says the same thing. We know the bankruptcy of our former way of life. We
ought to spend our time for the will of God. We have spent enough time
doing the will of pagans, when we walked like they walk—lewdness, lusts,
drunkenness, revelries, drinking parties, and abominable idolatries.

**In regard to these, they think it strange that you do not run with
them in the same flood of dissipation, speaking evil of you** (v. 4).
Peter might have added at this point, "Blessed are you when they speak evil

of you and say all manner of evil against you falsely for Jesus' sake. When that happens, rejoice, for great is your reward in heaven," because he had heard Jesus say such words in the Sermon on the Mount (Matt. 5:11–12).

Sometimes while we are reading Scripture, a passage seems to jump off the page at us and serve as a mirror. When that happens, we wonder, *How does Scripture know so much about me?* When I became converted, I had a strong desire to lead my buddies to Christ. I came home from college and went to see them. They wanted to go out and do the same things we had always done, but I told them I could no longer participate. When they asked me why, I told them that I had become a Christian and that I wanted to tell them about it. They thought I was crazy, and they did not like that I would not participate with them in our usual activities. As the leader of the gang, I was naïve enough to think that they would follow my leadership and commit their lives to Jesus, but they wanted nothing to do with it. If we stop behaving as we used to behave and as the world behaves, and if we march to a different drummer, people are not going to like it. They will speak evil of us, even if we love them. They think it is strange, as Peter says here.

Peter uses the language of ancient orgies and wild parties. The purpose of drinking at these parties was not simple enjoyment of the fruit of the vine. The goal was drunkenness in order to get rid of all moral inhibitions so that there could be a flood of dissipation. This is what characterized the bacchanalias of the ancient world, drunken festivals dedicated to the god Bacchus. The idea was that people could get in touch with their idols by getting rid of their inhibitions. Any remnants of conscience operating as restraints were abolished at these parties. About them Peter writes, **They will give an account to Him who is ready to judge the living and the dead** (v. 5).

Peter continues, **For this reason the gospel was preached also to those who are dead, that they might be judged according to men in the flesh, but live according to God in the spirit** (v. 6). He is not talking about Jesus' preaching to dead spirits; rather, he is indicating the reason that Christ came. Jesus preached the gospel, and many of those who had heard Him and believed had died, so their battle was over and their victory won.

When we get unexpected news of the death of someone we know, we wonder immediately how he or she died. Was she killed in an automobile accident? Did he have a heart attack? When the Bible speaks of people's dying, it is somewhat reductionistic. From a biblical standpoint, there are only two conditions in which someone dies: in the faith or out of the faith.

We die in faith, or we die in sin. Peter understood the urgency of the gospel, so he called people to think about that time of accountability when they would stand before Christ, not in their sins but in faith.

Every day we are judged by people, sometimes fairly and sometimes unfairly, sometimes graciously and sometimes without grace. Yet any judgment made about us in this world—good or bad—ultimately does not count, because it is a judgment made in the flesh. The only judgment that counts is the judgment of God, so we are to live not according to the judgment of people but according to God in the Spirit.

17

THE END OF ALL THINGS

1 Peter 4:7

But the end of all things is at hand; therefore be serious and watchful in your prayers.

We have been looking at one text after another that have had a significant place in the history of Christian theology. All these texts have been the focal point of great controversy. We find another one here. We are going to study verse 7 in the light of some significant historical developments in the theology of the last two hundred years.

There are three distinct possibilities as to what Peter means when he announces that the end of all things is at hand. The first possibility, which seems to be the obvious one, is that the end of the world is near, bringing with it the end of all things on earth. The second possible interpretation is that Peter is referring to the end of all things Jewish, looking toward the catastrophic event that took place in A.D. 70, when the temple was destroyed and Jerusalem was trodden underfoot by the Gentiles. From the Jewish perspective, the end of Jerusalem, and thus the end of temple worship, would be the end of everything. The third possibility is that Peter has in mind the nearness of the demise of those reading the epistle. Any one of those views is a possible interpretation.

Advent of Liberalism

Nineteenth-century church history witnessed the advent of Liberalism. There have always been those with a liberal view toward various issues in the life of the church, but in the nineteenth century, a particular movement came to be known as Liberalism. It was dominant in Europe, particularly in Germany, and it eventually found its way to England and across the sea to the United States. It has had a dramatic impact on colleges and seminaries and particularly on the creeds of the mainline churches. The earlier teachers of Liberalism believed that the Bible had to be naturalized in order to be relevant to modern people after the Enlightenment and the scientific advancements that came out of it. To say it another way, the gospel message had to be de-supernaturalized if it was to have any relevance to modern people.

A neo-liberal of the twentieth century, Rudolf Bultmann, made the observation that modern man cannot avail himself of antibiotic medicine or use the marvels of electricity yet still believe in a three-storied universe (earth here, hell below, and heaven above), in a world inhabited by demons or angels, or in a gospel with teachings such as the miracles surrounding the life and death of Jesus. For the gospel to be relevant today, said Bultmann, it must be demythologized. He said that we must cut through the husk of mythology to find a core of truth that will be useful today.

The Liberals systematically denied all the miracles and supernatural elements of the New Testament. They redefined the kingdom of God and the mission of Jesus and, consequently, the mission of the church. For these thinkers, the kingdom of God was not something that happens in heaven but something that takes place here through progressive education and ethical behavior. Jesus was exalted by this group as the great moral teacher who gave us the pattern for right living. They saw the gospel as social with respect to the necessity of being humanitarian and ministering to the pain and suffering of the world. Of course, this produced a crisis in the church.

Into this milieu of nineteenth-century Liberalism came a brilliant New Testament scholar, Albert Schweitzer. He was a physician, and he also had an international reputation as a world-class organist. He became one of the most famous twentieth-century missionaries in Africa. Schweitzer analyzed the teaching of nineteenth-century Liberalism and found it wanting. At a very key point in his classic work, *The Quest for the Historical Jesus*, Schweitzer chided the nineteenth-century Liberals for failing to understand the message of Jesus, a message, Schweitzer said, that is from start to finish eschatological.

The word *eschatological* comes from the word *eschatology*, which comes from a word in Greek that refers to the last things. The science of eschatology is the study of the future, which includes the study of the return of Jesus, the restoration of the cosmos, the coming of new heavens and a new earth, matters of heaven and hell, and the last judgment. However, when Schweitzer used the term *eschatological*, he meant more than just future events. Schweitzer posited that to understand Jesus, we must realize that Jesus thought that the kingdom of God would be brought to pass in history by the supernatural, transcendent intervention of Almighty God. It would not evolve through a natural process or as the result of increased education; it would come about through something that God Himself would do. Schweitzer devastated the nineteenth-century Liberals with that finding. He said that their attempt to liberalize Christianity was dishonest, because it was reductionistic and failed to take the teaching of Jesus seriously.

Schweitzer said that when Jesus sent out the seventy disciples and empowered them to preach and to announce the coming of the kingdom, Jesus expected the kingdom to come then, but it did not happen. Therefore, Schweitzer said, Jesus had a growing realization that drastic steps would have to be taken in order to move the Father to bring this kingdom to pass. Schweitzer said that Jesus allowed Himself to be arrested, tried, and taken to the cross from which He awaited the climactic moment of the end of history, when the Father would intervene and save Him and deliver the kingdom. When that did not happen, Jesus' disappointment in His eschatological dream was manifested in the despair that pierced His soul when He cried, "My God, My God, why have You forsaken Me?" (Matt. 27:46; Mark 15:34). The substance of the teaching of Albert Schweitzer was that Jesus was a remarkable man, a great teacher, and a visionary who died in disillusionment because the kingdom did not come.

I grew up in a church that followed the teachings of nineteenth-century Liberalism. The questions of the Westminster Shorter Catechism were altered to suit our minister, who made up his own questions, one of which was, "Who is the greatest living Christian?" The answer we were taught to reply was "Albert Schweitzer"—Albert Schweitzer, whose book is a monument to unbelief in the deity of Christ. Schweitzer did, however, expose the folly of his predecessors who had tried to understand Jesus purely in ethical terms, not in terms of the central importance of the kingdom of God.

Schweitzer and others wrestled with a problem they called "*parousia* delay," the delay of the return of Jesus. Every page of the New Testament seems to breathe an expectation of the nearness of the return of Jesus, and, they said, it is generally thought that the believers of the first century expected Jesus to return in their lifetime. In the Olivet Discourse, Jesus talked about the destruction of Jerusalem and His own appearing. When His disciples asked when those things would happen, He responded, "Assuredly, I say to you, this generation will by no means pass away till all these things take place" (Matt. 24:34).

Twentieth-century scholars said that Jesus expected His return to occur within a forty-year period, and, because of that, His disciples also expected it within that time frame. They were disappointed when it did not happen, so, in the latter writings of the New Testament the scholars look for an adjustment in the theology of the future, where provisions are made for postponement of the consummation of the kingdom.

Bertrand Russell wrote in his book *Why I Am Not a Christian* that Jesus taught that He would return within the space of forty years but failed to keep His word. Therefore, Russell did not think Jesus was worthy of his belief. When I was in seminary, I was taught that the Bible is not to be trusted and that Jesus Himself was wrong in His future predictions. I wrote a book as a response to those claims called *Jesus' View of the Last Day*, which focuses attention chiefly on the Olivet Discourse, because I believe that everything Jesus predicted would take place within forty years did take place within forty years.

Already and Not Yet

The next major milestone took place when a British New Testament scholar by the name of C. H. Dodd wrote an analysis of the parables of Jesus as well as of the Gospel of John and introduced to the church a theory called "realized eschatology." Dodd's thesis was that Jesus' future kingdom actually did come to pass in the first century. Concerning Jesus' words, "Assuredly, I say to you, there are some standing here who shall not taste death till they see the Son of Man coming in His kingdom" (Matt. 16:28; cf. Mark 9:1; Luke 9:27), Dodd said that this references the ascension of Christ and things related to it, such as Pentecost and the outpouring of the power of the Holy Spirit. In the ascension, Dodd said, Jesus was elevated to His position as the King of kings. He ascended to His coronation, and all that He taught during His earthly ministry about His kingdom was fulfilled in those few years from the announcement to its realization. Dodd became famous for taking the opposite position from Schweitzer and the skeptics, saying not only was the kingdom of God not postponed but that it had actually come to pass in its fullness at that time.

However, other scholars said that if we carefully examine the concept of the kingdom of God in the New Testament, we must take seriously the manifold passages that teach that the kingdom will not take place in the distant future, as the dispensationalists believe, but that the kingdom was inaugurated during the ministry of Jesus, the ascension, the outpouring of the Holy Spirit, and the destruction of Jerusalem. Yet, these scholars say, elements of a future eschatology have not yet taken place, such as the resurrection of the dead from their graves that will occur at the time of the return of Jesus in glory, and therefore the church is to adopt a posture of diligent and vigilant expectation.

This idea was championed by the Swiss scholar Oscar Cullmann, who gave us the D-day analogy we looked at in an earlier study. He said all that pertained to the consummation of the kingdom of God was accomplished during the ministry of Jesus. It was like D-day, he said, in that, for all intents and purposes, the war was over, but there were still things that had to take place before hostilities would cease. However, D-day occurred in June 1944, but the Germans did not surrender until the spring of 1945. There was no two-thousand-year lapse between D-day and the end of the war, which rather strains Cullmann's analogy.

Cullmann's analogy was further argued by a Dutch New Testament scholar, Hermann Ridderbos, who wrote a book entitled *The Coming of the Kingdom*. In the book Ridderbos dissects the different theories of the Liberals and concludes that in order to understand the biblical concept of the kingdom, we must grasp the "already and not yet," by which he meant that a large dimension of the kingdom has already come to pass—we are right now living in the eschatological era of the kingdom of God—but we still await the final consummation of all things.

Peter writes, **But the end of all things is at hand; therefore be serious and watchful in your prayers** (v. 7). The Greek word translated "all things" is *panta*. The Greek word he uses for "the end" is *telos*, which is often translated as "goal," "purpose," or "aim." So, we could translate these words as "the goal of all things is at hand." The Latin uses a form of the word *omnia* for "all things." Someone with all knowledge is "omniscient," and someone with all power is "omnipotent." The concept of all things is rooted here in the text, and when Peter refers to the end or the goal of all things, he uses a form of the word translated "near." It is nearby.

If Peter had in mind the end of the world, the final consummation of the kingdom, there is a problem with that. The biblical view of the consummation of the kingdom of God and the completion of the work of Jesus is not the end of the world. The future of this planet, according to the New Testament, is not annihilation but restoration and renovation. We look for new heavens and a new earth. We could say that since there will be new heavens and a new earth, then the end of all these present things is going to take place, but it is not in God's plan to destroy the planet. As Paul tells us, "We know that the whole creation groans and labors with birth pangs together until now. Not only they, but we also who have the firstfruits of the Spirit, even we ourselves groan within ourselves, eagerly waiting for the adoption, the redemption of our body" (Rom. 8:22–23). God's work of redemption is cosmic in scope. He is not just going to save us out of the world; He will redeem the world and everything in it.

Peter could have been thinking of the consummation of the kingdom at the return of Jesus. In his second epistle he inquires as to why the Lord delays in returning, and he answers, "The Lord is not slack concerning His promise, as some count slackness, but is longsuffering toward us, not willing that any should perish but that all should come to repentance" (2 Pet. 3:9). The reason the culmination of the kingdom has not happened yet is that all of the elect have not been gathered in. Indeed, if the kingdom of God had been finished at the end of the first century, you and I would have missed it.

Peter might have been referencing the radical nearness of a crisis event that few in Christendom have taken seriously, probably the most significant extrabiblical event to take place in world history—the destruction of Jerusalem and the temple. Up until A.D. 70 the Christian church was considered a subdivision or sect of Judaism. It was not recognized on its own terms until after the temple was destroyed and the Holy City was given into the hands of the Gentiles. In Luke's version of the prophecy of that event, the destruction and occupation would not be forever but only until the fullness of the Gentiles came in. That is, there is an interim in world history between the age of the Jews and the age of the Gentiles; and after the age of the Gentiles is fulfilled, as Paul teaches in Romans 11, God will deal again with ethnic Israel. Whenever we hear Jesus speaking about the end of the age, we tend to fill in the blanks and think that the end of the age means the end of time, when in all probability he was speaking of the end of the age of the Jews, which would take place in a very short time.

Ready and Waiting

The third option is simply the impending demise of all people. In light of the reality that our days are numbered, we are called in the New Testament to redeem the time, to make every day count, and that every day would be one in which we prepare ourselves by being sober, serious, and watchful in our prayers.

So, whether Peter had in mind the coming destruction of Jerusalem, the coming end of our lives, or the ultimate consummation of the kingdom of Christ, it is still appropriate to heed his advice to be serious and watchful in our prayers, because in this age, and through all the centuries of the church, the church is called to be ever watchful, always waiting for the final return of Jesus. We are warned that, for us, Jesus should not come as a thief in the night and find us in a state of business as usual, neglecting our prayers and our devotion to His kingdom. We are to be ever vigilant, ever watchful, ever ready for the Lord, for we know not when the Lord comes. "Even so, come, Lord Jesus!" (Rev. 22:20).

18

COVER OF LOVE

1 Peter 4:8–11

And above all things have fervent love for one another, for "love will cover a multitude of sins." Be hospitable to one another without grumbling. As each one has received a gift, minister it to one another, as good stewards of the manifold grace of God. If anyone speaks, let him speak as the oracles of God. If anyone ministers, let him do it as with the ability which God supplies, that in all things God may be glorified through Jesus Christ, to whom belong the glory and the dominion forever and ever. Amen.

In our last study we looked at verse 7, where Peter introduced a sense of urgency, declaring, "The end of all things is at hand." We wrestled with the possible different meanings and with application of the verse. Because of the nearness of the consummation of all things, Peter calls us to be serious and watchful in our prayers. Whether the meaning of "the end of all things" is the end of our life, the end of the Jewish age, or the end of all redemptive history, we are to be vigilant in prayer. In this study we find a continuation of that same vigilance.

Fervent Love

And above all things have fervent love for one another, for "love will cover a multitude of sins" (v. 8). The Torah contains 613 specific laws. People would like to know the priority of those laws, from the most important to the least. We have a tendency to want to organize our duties and responsibilities in such a manner. In the New Testament from time to time we see priorities set forth. Jesus said, "Seek first the kingdom of God and His righteousness, and all these things shall be added to you" (Matt. 6:33). Our first priority is the seeking of the kingdom of God and His righteousness. We are to do that "first," *prōtos*—not first in a chronological sense but first in the order of importance. James in his epistle gives a similar admonition: "But above all, my brethren, do not swear, either by heaven or by earth or with any other oath. But let your 'Yes' be 'Yes,' and your 'No,' 'No,' lest you fall into judgment" (James 5:12). James filled his letter with all kinds of ethical injunctions, but near the end of it he said that above all, a Christian should be known as someone whose word can be counted upon.

Peter uses this same method of accentuating something of supreme importance when he says, "Above all things have fervent love for one another." Gone are the days when Hollywood would exploit religious themes without trashing Christianity, as they do today. In several of those older films, the Apostle Peter was depicted. I remember one in which Christians would gather at night and say, "The fisherman is here," when the character of Peter walked before the people. As I watched the movie, I could sense the excitement and joy, and a holy hush fell over the people because they were about to hear from someone who had been with Jesus throughout His entire earthly ministry—Peter, who had been known for his impetuosity.

Peter had denied Jesus three times and then wept bitterly, but afterward Jesus talked to him on the seashore and asked him three times, "Simon, son of Jonah, do you love Me?" "Yes, Lord, You know that I love You." Then "Feed my sheep" (John 21:15–17). When I read this epistle from the pen of Peter, I can hear Jesus saying to him, "Peter, when you write to the people, remember that they are My sheep, and I want you to feed them." Peter fed the sheep with the teachings of Jesus, and he remembered what a high priority the Lord had put upon the love of the brethren. "By this all will know that you are My disciples, if you have love for one another" (John 13:35). Christian love is not just about an individual's love for God or for Christ. He who loves God cannot love God and hate his brother. We manifest our love for God by a fervent love for each other. There is a big difference between tolerance and zealous love.

Covering Love

Peter does not simply repeat Jesus' admonition, but he gives the reason for it, quoting from Proverbs (10:12). Peter writes that we are to have fervent love for one another, for "love will cover a multitude of sins" (v. 8). The metaphor of covering is of central importance to our understanding of salvation. The image of covering is found in the Old Testament. On the Day of Atonement, blood from a sacrificed animal was taken by the High Priest into the Holy of Holies and sprinkled on the mercy seat, which was the covering of the ark of the covenant, the most holy vessel in the *sanctus sanctorum*. The blood of the sacrifice was poured over the throne of God to cover the sins of the people.

The practice began even earlier than on the Day of Atonement, way back at the fall. After Adam and Eve sinned, they felt ashamed. They became aware of their nakedness, and in their shame they tried to hide; they desired covering. When God came into the garden and found His trembling creatures cowering in shame, weighed down by the burden of their guilt, He made clothing from animal skins and covered their shame. This was the first act of redeeming grace, and throughout the rest of Scripture, the idea of redemption is understood in terms of God's covering His naked, guilty people.

Supremely, we see this metaphor in the doctrine of justification. Our own righteousness is nothing but filthy rags and lacks the capacity to cover our sin, but we have been clothed with the righteousness of Jesus. God takes the righteousness of His Son and uses it as a cloak to cover His sinful creatures. The only way we can stand before God is if we wear the covering of the righteousness of Jesus.

Here in Peter's epistle, there is talk of another covering—not the covering that God provides to His naked creatures, or the covering of our sin in the Holy of Holies, or even the cloak of Jesus' righteousness, but of a special love that covers a multitude of sins. It is our love for each other.

Several years ago I was asked by some students why my ministry was almost exclusively one of education and teaching rather than pastoring and preaching. I told them the reason is that I am too thin-skinned. Pastors receive significant criticism, which can cause them much hurt. With teaching, however, I critique the students; they do not critique me. The fear of public speaking is the primary phobia among American people because their entire person is on display and open to critique, much of which at times can be petty and negative. Preachers open themselves to scrutiny and criticism; it is unavoidable. I have been able to deal with that over the years; it is the pettiness that is difficult to handle.

Nothing will destroy a church faster than pettiness, people picking at each other over trivial things. In the New Testament we are told that when Christians commit gross and heinous sins, they must be disciplined as part of the spiritual nurture of the church. However, our Lord was very careful to specify the sins that require discipline, understanding that no one in the church of Christ is finished with sanctification. We all bring different baggage into the Christian life; we are each at a different point in our progression. We can destroy one another by nitpicking. If one of your brothers or sisters has an annoying habit, it may irritate you, but it has been covered by Jesus. We all have to endure people who criticize us over insignificant, petty things. Let the world be petty, but let it not be said of Christians. Let us love one another with such a fervency that we have the love that covers a multitude of sins.

Covering love is how families survive. Family members know each other's foibles, weaknesses, and failures, and the bond of a family will not last long if there is constant, petty complaining in the home. The church is a family too.

Back in the sixties I met some people who were involved in the charismatic movement. They expressed excitement about the fellowship within the movement. They had made a pledge to be scrupulously honest and open with one another and never to have an unexpressed thought about the behavior of all the others, right down to the clothes they wore. One woman in the group told me that the goal of such candidness was to stimulate their growth in the Lord. That particular group lasted less than six months because they focused on pointing out one another's failures. That destroys the church. If something is a small matter, it is to be covered.

That is what it means to love. When we think of what God has covered for us, can we not cover for our brothers and sisters in the Lord? "Love will cover a multitude of sins." Some people interpret this verse to mean that if we love enough, it will serve almost as an atonement for our sins; but that is not what it means. The meaning is that love does not seek to expose our neighbor for every petty weakness but to cover him or her from the attacks of the world.

Hospitality

Be hospitable to one another without grumbling (v. 9). The Israelites for most of their history were semi-nomads. They had no permanent place of residence but lived as wanderers, in tents. As a result, they placed a high premium on hospitality. It was highly valued in the ancient world; in fact, it is still valued highly in the Near East. One of the great virtues of love is to show hospitality.

The New Testament begins with a failure to show hospitality to Joseph and Mary on the night of the birth of Jesus, even though the law of God commands that hospitality be given to sojourners. Peter knew that his readers were well aware of this mandate, which was such a part of the Old Testament ethic. Here, Peter adds something to the law: hospitality is to be offered without grumbling. We sometimes tend to feel that guests are like fish: after three days, they begin to smell. There are people who do exploit the hospitality and kindness of those who practice it, but that does not matter. Even if we are exploited, we are not to grumble. We are to open our homes or whatever else we have for those in need.

Good Stewards

As each one has received a gift, minister it to one another, as good stewards of the manifold grace of God (v. 10). Notice that Peter doesn't say *if* each one has received a gift, but as each one *has* received. Peter is saying exactly what the Apostle Paul taught the Corinthians, that every believer is gifted by God. Every believer is a charismatic in the sense that the Spirit has endowed him or her with some gift to be used for the edification of the church. Some have the gift of preaching. Some have the gift of teaching. Some have the gift of evangelism. Some have the gift of healthcare. Some have the gift of administration. Some have the gift of giving. The list that Paul gave to the Corinthians was not exhaustive, but representative. One problem I have with the neo-Pentecostal theology of our day is that it posits that there are two types of Christians: those who have gifts and those who do not. That flies in the face of the teaching of the New Testament, which says that every believer is endowed by the Holy Spirit for ministry.

When Martin Luther taught the priesthood of all believers, he did not thereby mean the end of any distinction between clergy and laity. He meant that the ministry of Christ's church is not to be carried on simply by ordained clergy. The whole congregation is to be involved in ministry, because everyone in the congregation has been endowed by the Holy Spirit with His power.

Do you know what your spiritual gift is? I talk frequently to Christians who tell me they do not know. You may have a spiritual gift or gifts of which you are completely unaware. One function of the church is to help people find their gifts and give them an opportunity to use them. There have been times in my life when I have been discouraged in teaching, and I have told my wife, Vesta, that I am ready to quit. At such times Vesta has quoted to me, "Having then gifts differing according to the grace that is given to us, let us use them: . . . he who teaches, in teaching" (Rom. 12:6–7). If the Lord has gifted you to teach, you had better teach. If He has gifted you to preach, you had better preach. If He has gifted you to give, you had better give.

In verse 10 Peter introduces the notion of stewardship, which, in New Testament Greek, is subsumed under the word *oikonomia*. The English word *economics* comes from *oikonomia*, which means literally "house law." The steward in biblical times was not the owner of the house but the one hired to manage household affairs. When we speak in the church today of stewardship, we almost always restrict it to matters of finance. Financial stewardship was clearly taught by Jesus, and certainly how we manage our finances is an important aspect of stewardship, but that is not the stewardship that Peter is talking about here. Peter says we are to be good stewards of the plentiful, abundant grace of God for the edification of the body of Christ.

Countless times I have heard people complaining after a church service, "I didn't get anything out of it." I want to ask them what they put into it. They come to have their needs met, but the preacher does not preach to meet the felt needs of the people. The church is there to meet people's real need, which is to understand who God is. We all have a responsibility to be stewards of God's gifts, which is what Peter has in mind here. God has given you and me grace, which is a gift, but with the gift comes a responsibility.

Maybe you do not have a vocation to be an evangelist or a missionary. Maybe you have not been called to preach or to sing in the choir. Every one of us, however, is called to make sure that the ministry of evangelism is done, that the ministries of preaching and teaching are accomplished, that the ministry of worship occurs, and that the missionary enterprise is accomplished. We might not be the ones who go, but how can God use our gifts to make all the church ministries effective? We all have a stake in this, and Peter says that this is the deepest manifestation of the love that God has poured out upon us.

If anyone speaks, let him speak as the oracles of God (v. 11). Another way to say this is, "If anyone speaks, let him speak the Word of God." A church that wants to grow to twenty thousand members can toss aside the Bible and entertain people instead, offering the latest psychobabble and tickling people with itchy ears. In Romans, Paul wrote about how the Jewish people had fallen away. Their circumcision had become uncircumcision, so, Paul asked, "What advantage then has the Jew, or what is the profit of circumcision?" (Rom. 3:1). He answered his question, "Much in every way! Chiefly because to them were committed the oracles of God" (v. 2).

The greatest gift that the church has is the Word of God. When travel keeps me away from St. Andrew's on a Sunday, I seek a church where the Word is preached. I am starved for the Word of God. I want to go to a church where the Scriptures are expounded. Our minds are informed and our souls are set aflame by the power of the Word of God.

If anyone ministers, let him do it as with the ability which God supplies (v. 11). "Whatever your hand finds to do, do it with your might" (Eccles. 9:10). Every talent and ability you have is a gift from God, and you have a responsibility to exercise it.

19

GOD'S GLORIOUS
SELF-EXISTENCE

1 Peter 4:11

If anyone speaks, let him speak as the oracles of God. If anyone ministers,
let him do it as with the ability which God supplies, that in all things God
may be glorified through Jesus Christ, to whom belong the glory and the
dominion forever and ever. Amen.

In what does the glory of God consist? What is this concept of glory that
we encounter so many times in sacred Scripture, and what precisely is
it about the nature and character of God that makes him so glorious?
In the Old Testament, the Hebrew term translated "glory" is *kavod*. The
word in its ancient etymology called attention to the weightiness of God,
not in a physical sense but in having such substance and significance that His
very being is filled with eternal dignity and importance. When considering
profound matters, we might say, "That's a weighty concept." Conversely,
things that we consider trivial we refer to as "light." The Israelites thought
of God's glory in terms of weightiness.

On a dark day in the history of Israel, the people's most sacred vessel,
the ark of the covenant, fell into the hands of the Philistines. The ark was
taken and set up in the temple of Dagon. On that day, Hophni and Phineas

were killed and their father, Eli, perished. When the news was brought to the people that Eli and his sons had perished and the ark of the covenant had been carried away, they gave Eli's grandson the name Ichabod, meaning "the glory has departed from Israel" (1 Sam. 4:21). No worse calamity could befall the Jews in antiquity than for God to withdraw His glory and depart from their midst.

God's Glory

In the New Testament we find the Greek word *doxa*, which corresponds to the Hebrew *kavod*. *Doxa* comes into use when we sing the doxology. A doxology ascribes praise and honor to God, either in speech or song. In fact, when we look at the origin of worship in biblical categories, its very essence is to bring the sacrifice of praise to God. We sing:

> Praise God, from Whom all blessings flow;
> Praise Him, all creatures here below;
> Praise Him above, ye heavenly host;
> Praise Father, Son, and Holy Ghost.

On the occasion of the celebration of the Lord's Supper, we sing another song with regard to the glory of God. This doxology, the *Gloria Patri*, comes from the Latin word that we translate as *gloria*:

> Glory be to the Father, and to the Son:
> and to the Holy Ghost;
> As it was in the beginning, is now, and ever shall be:
> world without end. Amen.

The *Gloria Patri* was not originally used in the sanctuary in the context of corporate worship but on the battlefield during a time of crisis when the Arians, who denied the deity of Jesus, wanted to spread their heresy. The Arians composed somewhat bawdy songs and sang them across the river, insulting the Christians who believed in the Trinity and the full deity of Jesus. In response to these salacious songs, the Christians lined up on the other side of the river and sang, "Glory be to the Father, *and* to the Son, *and* to the Holy Ghost. As it was in the beginning, is now and ever shall be, world without end." This fight song then came into the church and became an integral part of our liturgy.

I want to go beyond mere word definitions and look at what makes God so glorious. I recall the story of two little boys who were having a theological discussion. One boy said to the other, "I wonder where the trees came from."

The boy replied, "God made the trees."

So the first boy said, "I wonder where the sun came from."

The second boy said, "God made the sun."

The first boy said, "I wonder where you came from."

His friend replied, "God made me."

Finally, the first boy asked, "Well, who made God?"

His friend replied, "God made Himself."

The boy's reply was not fundamentally sound. The young boy, in his attempt to be profound, made a nonsensical statement. Even God cannot make Himself; in order to do so, He would have to be before He was. He would have to be and not be at the same time in the same relation, and even God in all His glory is not capable of that.

Cause and Effect

In the middle of the twentieth century a famous debate took place between two scholars. One was Frederick Copleston, a Roman Catholic philosopher, and the other was the British skeptic Bertrand Russell. When Bertrand Russell wrote his book *Why I Am Not a Christian*, he reviewed a crisis point in his thinking about God that had taken place when he was a teenager. Up to the time of this event, he had followed the traditional idea that there must be a cause behind all things that exist in the universe and that the ultimate cause for all things is God. Then, as a teenager, Bertrand Russell read an essay by John Stuart Mill that argued against the existence of God with a simple rejoinder that if everything requires a cause, then God Himself must have a cause; and if God Himself has a cause, then God Himself would be dependent upon it and would therefore not be ultimate.

If everything has a cause, the very law of causality, which has been used for centuries to argue for the existence of God, is actually, said John Stuart Mill, an argument against the existence of God. This persuaded young, impressionable Russell, and he held to the force of that argument until the day he died. Copleston pointed out, however, in their public debate, that the law of causality does not teach nor has it ever taught that everything has a cause. Rather, the law of causality says that every effect must have a cause.

If I say that everything has an antecedent cause, I am saying that everything is ultimately the effect of something else; effects by definition require causes. The point of the existence of God is that He is not an effect, so, therefore, He does not require a cause. In trying to manifest that obvious distinction to Russell, Copleston reminded him that everything we know about in this finite universe does not have a sufficient reason for its existence within itself, which is just a fancy way of saying that everything we know of in creation is contingent or dependent upon something outside of itself. Think of your own life. When you die and are buried, there will likely be a tombstone with brief information etched into it. It will likely mention your name, the date of your birth, and the date of your death.

There was a time when we did not exist and a time when this book did not exist. For this book to exist, it had to have been made or manufactured by something other than itself. The book did not exist in nothingness and suddenly decide to make itself a book and pop into being. If it had, we would not call that philosophy, science, or theology; we would call it magic, which is exactly where science has deteriorated. Scientists ask us to have faith in their conclusions, which renders us only credulous creatures who believe in magic, where the universe came into being out of nothing.

In that debate, Russell tried to argue from the standpoint of the "infinite regress," in which whatever we see was produced by something antecedent to it, and that, in turn, was produced by something before it and that before it. We have an infinite series of finite causes. The problem, as Copleston so ably pointed out, is that the idea of an infinite regress of finite causes is absolute nonsense. It is a thinly disguised argument from self-creation. In fact, it is self-creation eternally compounded because it takes the error of self-creation and posits it infinitely.

Virtually every argument that has been lodged against the existence of God, in the final analysis becomes some type of an argument of self-creation. In the final analysis, the universe creates itself. When the Hubble spacecraft was sent into outer space, an American astrophysicist said, "Sixteen to eighteen billion years ago, the universe exploded into being." He knew that the universe is not and cannot be eternal, because it does not have sufficient reason for its own being. Every particle of it is the result of something antecedent to it, and therefore it manifests contingent being. Scientists understand that, so they have to posit that there was a time when things started. The usual argument is that sixteen to eighteen billion years ago, all the energy and matter in the universe was compressed into an infinitesimal point of singularity, which remained in a perfect state of organization until, at a particular moment in time, it exploded.

Of course, the law of inertia says that things at rest tend to remain at rest unless acted upon by an outside cause, or things in motion tend to stay in motion unless acted upon by an outside cause. The law of inertia is what makes the game of golf so frustrating. The ball goes into motion against the forces of gravity, but other forces stop its progress much sooner than the golfer would like. At the same time, if the law did not exist, if there was nothing to act against that ball in motion, the golfer would have only one shot—the original tee-shot, which would go on forever. Eighteen holes would take an eternity to accomplish.

Many years ago I corresponded with Carl Sagan about this matter, and I asked him about the outside force that supposedly produced the big bang. He said that we can take it back to the final nanosecond before everything changed, and he was satisfied to stop his inquiry at that point. I suggested that stopping at that point is where he stopped being a scientist because he did not care to seek a sufficient reason for the theory.

Scientifically and philosophically, there are only two categories: being and nonbeing. Nonbeing is everything outside the category of being, and nonbeing is just a synonym for nothing. Nothing is that which has no being to it at all. What happened, according to a particular astrophysicist, is that there was nothing out there, no being, which suddenly exploded into being.

Some time ago a Nobel Prize winner said that we can no longer believe in that earlier form of self-creation called "spontaneous generation," in which things supposedly just pop into being. We now know, he said, through better scientific analysis that spontaneous generation does not happen. In fact, it cannot happen because we cannot get something from nothing quickly; it takes time, he said, so we must consider "gradual spontaneous generation." Such intelligent people seem to be educated beyond their intelligence when they make such arguments. It is laughable to think of nothing producing something in any circumstance, yet such thinkers say that Christians are weak-minded for believing that a self-existent, eternal, omnipotent being created the universe out of no preexisting matter.

God's Self-Existence

This brings us back to our original question: what about God makes Him so glorious? The universe in which we live, in the final analysis, is the result of either some form of self-creation or a creation by something or someone self-existent. There are two ideas before us: self-existence and self-creation. The very idea of self-creation is formally false; it is a self-referential absurdity. On the other hand, someone self-existent is not dependent upon anything else. To put it another way, He has the power of being eternally in Himself. That idea violates no law of science or logic.

The great philosopher and theologian Thomas Aquinas understood this clearly when he argued for the existence of God as what he called "necessary being." The universe and everything in it could exist without us. We are not necessary to the existence of all things. The fact that we are not necessary creatures means that we have a contingent, derived, dependent existence. Thomas Aquinas said that God has the power of being in and of Himself. He is eternal and has necessary existence in the sense that He cannot not be. God did not die on the cross, because God cannot die. God is immutable because the power of being eternally exists within Him by necessity.

Aquinas was saying that God, as necessary being, is not only necessary ontologically, that is, in His being, but that His being is also logically necessary because without the existence of a self-existent being, nothing could possibly exist. If something does exist, logic gives formal, demonstrative proof of the existence of a self-existent being. This is one of the most powerful arguments that is proven by the impossibility of the contrary. It is logically impossible for a self-existent, eternal being not to be. We know that God exists not merely by a leap of faith or by evidence around us but by the sheer force of the logical necessity of it. That kind of argument is absolutely irrefutable.

I presented that argument at Yale University about twenty-five years ago, and one of the professors, the son of a world-famous British empirical philosopher, also a skeptic and an atheist, approached me afterward and told me, "I've never heard that in my life. I can't argue with that, and it is quite compelling." Of course it is compelling, but it is not profound. It has been known for centuries.

If the only benefit we derive from this study is a deeper confidence in the reality of the object of our faith, we have failed to get the point. The reason why God is glorious is that He is the only being who has the power of being in Himself and the One from whom all other things derive. The marvelous transcendence of God, who alone is dependent on nothing, has not derived His being from something before Him or outside of Him. He is not subject to any possibility of decay, degeneration, or death. In Him all things live and move and have their being (Acts 17:28). That is glorious and transcendent. That describes a Being who is so far above anything finite, anything created, that to worship a tree or any aspect of the created order is manifest nonsense and idolatry by way of contrast.

Early in my study of philosophy, I came to the theories of a pre-Socratic philosopher named Parmenides. My professor told the class that Parmenides is known for a statement from his writings: "Whatever is *is*." Parmenides was getting at pure being, which has no mixture or alloy of nonbeing. Pure being has not an ounce of contingency or a speck of dependence.

God is before all things and above all things. In His being He is perfect. Nothing is lacking. He is filled with a countless multitude of excellencies. That is why the angels in heaven never tire of singing doxology to Him. That is why the people of God should never be bored in bringing Him the sacrifice of prayer and praise. His is a singular greatness that transcends all lesser things, even those things that impress us so deeply about this world. They are all like grass, which fades away. The One who has the power of being in Himself has, with that same power, the ability to speak worlds into existence. He said, "Let there be light," and there was light (Gen. 1:3). That was not magic. It was the light that comes out of the very being of an eternal, immutable, omnipotent God.

Here is why we minister: **that in all things God may be glorified through Jesus Christ, to whom belong the glory and the dominion forever and ever. Amen** (v. 11). To God the Father, God the Son, and God the Holy Spirit glory is an inherent property. We glorify God because He is a being who possesses eternal glory, and that is why Peter begins to sing. Glory belongs to God. Dominion belongs to God. Not for a moment, but for eternity.

We get caught up in the excitement of competitive sports and success. We have our sports heroes and our idols. Yet sometimes, a year after a professional athlete wins the World Series or the Super Bowl, they wonder, "Is this all there is?" These athletes have extraordinary talent and skill and have disciplined themselves to win a prize, but the glory of the ticker tape parade in New York City fades with the next sunset, and the fans clamor, "What are you going to do for us next year?" The glory and the dominion and the power that are possessed inherently by the Trinitarian God last forever, "for Yours is the kingdom and the power and the glory forever. Amen" (Matt. 6:13).

20

SUFFERING AND THE GOODNESS OF GOD

1 Peter 4:12–19

Beloved, do not think it strange concerning the fiery trial which is to try you, as though some strange thing happened to you; but rejoice to the extent that you partake of Christ's sufferings, that when His glory is revealed, you may also be glad with exceeding joy. If you are reproached for the name of Christ, blessed are you, for the Spirit of glory and of God rests upon you. On their part He is blasphemed, but on your part He is glorified. But let none of you suffer as a murderer, a thief, an evildoer, or as a busybody in other people's matters. Yet if anyone suffers as a Christian, let him not be ashamed, but let him glorify God in this matter. For the time has come for judgment to begin at the house of God; and if it begins with us first, what will be the end of those who do not obey the gospel of God? Now

"If the righteous one is scarcely saved,

Where will the ungodly and the sinner appear?"

Therefore let those who suffer according to the will of God commit their souls to Him in doing good, as to a faithful Creator.

Throughout our study of 1 Peter 4, we have seen passage after passage that has generated untold controversy over doctrinal and philosophical issues. In our last study we focused on a portion of verse 11 that deals with the glory of God. We looked briefly at the glory and majesty of God's eternal, self-existent being, which so transcends everything creaturely that it causes us to fall on our knees before Him. In the midst of this symphony of celebration of the glory of God, a dissonant note is sounded, a bit of discord that enters Peter's text when he turns his attention from the glory of God to the suffering of God's people in the world. **Beloved, do not think it strange concerning the fiery trial which is to try you, as though some strange thing happened to you** (v. 12). Twice here Peter speaks of something strange, a sort of anomaly in the Christian life—the presence of pain and suffering under the watchful eye of God.

Evidence for God

Earlier I mentioned Bertrand Russell, who became an atheist as a teenager after being exposed to an essay by the philosopher John Stuart Mill. In that essay Mill argued against the existence of God, saying that if everything has a cause, then God must have a cause, and if God must have a cause, then He is just like any other part of creation. I pointed out that such thinking represents a fundamental misrepresentation of the law of causality, which does not teach that everything must have a cause, but simply that every *effect* must have a cause.

Another man, the son of an evangelical Methodist minister and scholar, also became an atheist as a teen. The reason for his atheism was the influence of the same philosopher, John Stuart Mill. This young man was captured by a statement Mill made that God cannot be both omnipotent and good. If God is omnipotent and yet allows the atrocities that befall human beings, then He has the power to stop the suffering. Since He does not, it is proof that He is neither good nor all-loving. On the other hand, if He is good and all-loving and does not want to see the savage brutality that afflicts the human race, then it must mean that He simply is incapable of stopping it and, therefore, is not omnipotent. That fifteen-year-old boy felt the weight of Mill's argument and came to the conclusion that there must be no God, certainly not the God of the Bible.

Later on, this same boy told a story, which became a famous parable. It is a story of two explorers who were working their way through a jungle in Africa, uninhabited, far removed from any civilization. As they were hacking their way through the undergrowth with machetes, they came upon a clearing, and in the clearing they found a magnificent garden. The garden contained flowers and vegetables perfectly arranged in rows, not a single weed invading its beauty. It appeared to be perfectly tended. One explorer said to the other one, "Isn't this incredible? I wonder where the gardener is. Let's wait for him and ask him how he came to plant this magnificent garden in the middle of this seemingly uninhabitable place." So they waited, but no gardener came.

One of the explorers said, "We must have been mistaken. There must not be a gardener. The garden must have happened by accident; it is just an inexplicable freak of nature. So let us go on with our work of exploring."

The other said, "No, maybe this gardener is different from other gardeners. Maybe this one is invisible, and he is busy tending the garden, and we are just not able to see him."

As they were having this discussion, one said, "Let's set a trap for him. We will set up a wire around the perimeter of the garden and attach bells to it. If he in his invisible presence comes to tend the garden, he will bump the wires and the bells will ring, and we will know that he has been here, even though we cannot see him."

So they carefully prepared their trap, and they waited, but the bells did not ring. One explorer said, "See? There is no invisible gardener."

The other replied, "Wait. Maybe this gardener is not only invisible but also immaterial. Perhaps he does not have a body that will bump up against the wire and make the bells ring."

The author of the parable, philosopher Antony Flew, was saying that the concept of God has died the death of a thousand qualifications. In the final analysis, he asked, what is the difference between an invisible, immaterial God and no God at all? Of course, the answer to that screams that the difference is the garden. How does one account for the perfect design of the garden apart from a designer?

Some time ago, I interviewed Ben Stein for the *Renewing Your Mind* radio program. At the time, Stein was heavily involved in the production of a Hollywood movie titled *Expelled*. In that movie, Stein addressed what is happening to professors and teachers on college campuses in America, and also in high schools, who have the audacity to suggest that the universe may be here as a result of intelligent design rather than as the result of a cosmic accident. Throughout the history of Western science, the work of philosophy and the philosophical foundations of science have promoted free inquiry on any question of this type with the virtue of having the courage to allow one to go wherever the evidence leads. Yet now in America there is an inquisition against free inquiry. The Orange County school board ruled any teaching of intelligent design out of bounds in the public schools. An editorial that appeared at the time in the *Orlando Sentinel* strongly agreed with this decision.

Yet that is an unintelligent decision, because what is at stake is not just religion or theology but scientific inquiry.

In the midst of this debate about intelligent design, something remarkable happened. Antony Flew announced to the world that he had changed his mind and come to the conclusion that the evidence for God is compelling. Intelligent design is not simply an optional theory, he said, but a philosophical necessity. It has been interesting to see how the world of atheists has responded to Flew's conversion. His character has been all but assassinated by philosophers and scientists who say that the only reason he changed his mind is that he developed dementia in old age. Flew then wrote a book, *There Is a God: How the World's Most Notorious Atheist Changed His Mind*,[1] explaining why he changed, and if you read it, you will see that it does not contain the writings of a demented person.

What made Flew become an atheist in the first place was not the parable of the garden in the wilderness but the problem of suffering. When he was fifteen years old, he read Mill's statement, that God cannot be both all-loving and good and at the same time be omnipotent, and Flew could not answer that criticism of Christianity. Nineteenth-century critics of Christianity called the problem of pain the Achilles' heel of the Christian faith. Flew came at it from a different angle. He said that when the existence of something is asserted, whatever evidence works against it must be taken into account. For example, in order to say that the world is round, all the evidence that appears to render the world flat must be considered. The idea of a round earth took a long time to supplant the idea of a flat earth, because it was strange—so strange that it seemed much easier to continue believing that it is flat.

Scientists know that scientific theories change as quickly as weather patterns. Many things I learned in high school have long since been put aside. In the scientific world, there are paradigms or theories that attempt to describe all of reality; but so far, no scientific theory for understanding everything in the world has been free of contrary evidence. Think, for example, of the well-established claim that uniformitarian geology is a scientific truth. This holds that the changes in the surface of the earth have developed over vast periods of times in a uniform and gradual way, not as the result of a sudden, catastrophic moment that changed everything.

Albert Einstein's friend Immanuel Velikovsky wrote two books about the anomalies of that, mentioning, for example, the problem of the mastodons that were frozen in the icecap with their bodies completely intact. When

---

[1] Antony Flew and Roy Abraham Varghese, *There Is a God: How the World's Most Notorious Atheist Changed His Mind* (New York: HarperOne, 2003).

scientists thawed and dissected them, they found undigested tropical food in their bellies. Tropical food did not get to the arctic gradually, so the perplexed scientists looked for a theory to account for it.

I am not picking on the uniformitarians. I am saying that every theory, whatever it is, has counterevidence, and if the counterevidence becomes too severe, too multiple, or too profound, the theory has to change, which is what Antony Flew said. Flew read of the holocaust in World War II, about the camps in which so many millions were extinguished, and he became aware of the slaughter that had occurred through Joseph Stalin. Today we read that Saddam Hussein killed more Arabs than any man in human history, sometimes just for the fun of it.

There is unspeakable evil in this world and unbelievable pain and suffering. When we see that, we have to ask the question that the people in the Old Testament raised more than once in the Wisdom Literature: why do the wicked prosper and the righteous suffer? It just makes no sense. There are few people who, in the midst of suffering, can say, "Naked I came from my mother's womb, and naked shall I return there. The LORD gave, and the LORD has taken away; blessed be the name of the LORD" (Job 1:21). One must have a profound understanding of the character of God and a profound trust in His goodness.

Why Consider It Strange?
Both Jesus and the Apostle Peter answered the question as to why the wicked prosper and the righteous suffer. Here Peter asks us why we are taken by surprise. Why do we consider it strange? The Jews were unable to believe that Jesus was the Messiah, because He suffered. What kind of a God would send His own Son to Golgotha? They came to Jesus and asked about the Galileans whose blood Pilate had mingled with their sacrifices, and about the eighteen on whom the tower in Siloam fell and killed them (Luke 13:1–4). Jesus did not respond that those situations were anomalies for which there is no answer, or that people would have to adjust their understanding of the character of God. He did not say that the promises of Scripture are poetic hyperbole. What Jesus did say was this: "Unless you repent you will all likewise perish" (v. 3).

Jesus said to His disciples, and through His disciples to us, something that we almost never think about: why should God have prevented the temple from falling on the heads of those people? They had been in utter rebellion against their Creator. The question, it seems to me, is not why there is so much suffering in the world but why there is so little. Why, in light of our blasphemous hostility to our Creator, are we not all suffering in hell this very moment? One reason that there is suffering in this world—in fact, *the reason why there is suffering*—is not that God is not good, but because He is. A good God will not allow evil to go unpunished. Jesus said that they were asking the wrong question.

Peter says that we are not think it "strange." The word he uses here is the one from which we get the term *xenophobia*, which is a phobia or a fear of strangers, people who do not fit into our mold. He wants his readers to understand that our trials are not without purpose. The God who has redeemed us counts our soul more valuable than gold, and as gold is refined in the fire, so are we refined. Though we suffer for a moment, the goal of God in our suffering is our redemption, not our destruction. What about those who perish in hell? God can create people, knowing in advance that they will sin and die for it, because He is holy. The problem of suffering is based on two things that we fail to know: the character of God and the seriousness of sin. Those are weighty matters.

John Stuart Mill said that if God is good, He has to be all loving, but why does a good God have to love evil people? In fact, though there are some respects in which God does love evil people, there are other respects in which He does not. The Bible says that God's love is poured out to the whole world—His benevolence, His beneficence, goes toward everyone—yet, at the same time, from another perspective, the Bible tells us that God abhors the wicked. We have no inherent claim on the love of God. We would not be here today apart from it, but the fact that He loves us is not because He owes us or because our character demands it. It is only because of a mercy and grace that transcend our understanding.

Do not think it strange, Peter says, **but rejoice to the extent that you partake of Christ's sufferings, that when His glory is revealed, you may also be glad with exceeding joy** (v. 13). Rejoice, Peter says, that our sufferings come as a result of our participation and identification with the suffering and humiliation of Jesus. We suffer because He suffered, and He asked us to join Him in that. His suffering is redemptive; ours is not, but in our suffering we bear witness to the glory of His. This is similar to what Paul wrote to the Colossians: "I now rejoice in my sufferings for you, and fill up in my flesh what is lacking in the afflictions of Christ" (Col. 1:24). Paul did not mean that there was merit lacking in Jesus' passion, but rather that Christ has invited all who are in Him to taste of His suffering. To the extent that we have a share in the suffering of Christ, this should be an occasion, Peter says, not for consternation but for exceeding joy.

Our Faithful Creator

If you are reproached for the name of Christ, blessed are you, for the Spirit of glory and of God rests upon you (v. 14). In our last study we looked at the glory of God; here we are looking at suffering. Peter sees no conflict between the glory of God and the suffering that exists in this world. **On their part He is blasphemed, but on your part He is glorified** (v. 14). Then Peter warns that we are not to suffer as a result of participating in evil, and he concludes by saying, **Therefore let those who suffer according to the will of God commit their souls to Him in doing good, as to a faithful Creator** (v. 19).

Several years ago I was invited by the president of the American Cancer Society to deliver a series of lectures on suffering to people who were terminally ill with cancer. I titled that series of lectures "Surprised by Suffering," which later became a book. In those lectures I applied Peter's concept to receiving a medical report of incurable disease. I talked to them about vocation, saying, "I don't know what your vocation was before you came to this place—banker, physician, schoolteacher, or truck driver—but I know what it is now. Your vocation now is to suffer for the glory of God, because you are not here by accident. You are here according to the will of God." Some of them bristled at that, but I told them that if God had nothing to do with their illness, then they have no hope.

If we think that our suffering is a result of blind chance and a collision of atoms outside the will of God, we are of all people the most to be pitied. However, if we know that our pain comes to us by our heavenly Father, then we ought to be able to say with Job, "I know that my Redeemer lives, and He shall stand at last on the earth" (Job 19:25). That is the very heart and soul of Christianity. Our Christian faith means nothing until we come to the valley of the shadow of death.

If God calls us to suffer, we have to commit our souls to Him, not as to a capricious, vengeful, tyrannical deity, but as to a faithful Creator. The hardest time to believe that God is faithful is when His hand is heavy on your back. Yet we are told that though we suffer—and the pain may be excruciating—it is only for a moment and not worthy to be compared with what God has prepared for us for eternity.

No scientific paradigm reaches the point of omniscience, of knowing what will take place tomorrow. We cannot judge the final goodness and power of God until we see the new heavens and the new earth, where pain is exiled, suffering is vanquished, and death is forever banished. We can trust God, because He is worthy of our trust. He is faithful, and trusting Him is the only answer that I know of to the reality of suffering in this world.

21

FAITHFUL SHEPHERDS

1 Peter 5:1–4

The elders who are among you I exhort, I who am a fellow elder and a witness of the sufferings of Christ, and also a partaker of the glory that will be revealed: Shepherd the flock of God which is among you, serving as overseers, not by compulsion but willingly, not for dishonest gain but eagerly; nor as being lords over those entrusted to you, but being examples to the flock; and when the Chief Shepherd appears, you will receive the crown of glory that does not fade away.

Earlier in the epistle Peter wrote, "The time has come for judgment to begin at the house of God; and if it begins with us first, what will be the end of those who do not obey the gospel of God?" (4:17). Judgment begins with us. Christians demonstrate a tendency at times to try to serve as judges of the world, but God is the judge. We are called to be vessels of His mercy, even to those outside the community of faith. If we do judge, we must begin with ourselves, for we bear a greater responsibility than those who are in the world. As we are taught, "Everyone to whom much is given, from him much will be required" (Luke 12:48). We who enjoy being special recipients of the grace of God should have no room for a judgmental spirit. "There but for the grace of God go I," says the old adage. In speaking of one of his rivals, Winston Churchill once said, "There but for the grace of God goes God." We live by grace and by grace alone.

With that in mind, Peter directs his attention to those in a position of leadership within the church. Specifically, he mentions the elders. There are many different kinds of church government or polity. Churches in which the authority resides in the congregation are called congregationalist. They tend to function as pure democracies. Churches that are governed by elected elders are called presbyterian. The most common form of government down through church history has been the episcopal type, in which individual pastors serve in local churches but are ultimately governed by a bishop who presides over a certain number of pastors within a given geographical area. From what we can discern about early-church government, it practiced some form of episcopal government. This later developed into the monoepiscopacy in which one bishop is set above the rest. The Roman Catholic Church emerged with this monoepiscopal form of government.

Christians differ about what constitutes the best form of church government. How the Lord intended the church to be governed is not as clear as some other matters of biblical doctrine. Of course, those who favor an episcopal form of government argue that the Bible supports that, and those who argue for a presbyterian form of government insist that this is the biblical way. Still others argue from Scripture for some form of congregational government. The difference between the word *elder* or *presbyter* and the word *bishop* or *episkopos* has been much debated. The matter is made all the more difficult by the many passages in Scripture where it seems that the terms are used interchangeably.

Because of the difficulties of biblical interpretation here, we ought to be patient and forbearing with our Christian brothers and sisters who favor and adopt a different form of church government from our own. We believe in the *communio sanctorum*, the communion of saints, so however we may be divided organizationally and governmentally, every Christian in every church has communion with every other Christian in every other church based upon the biblical principle of the mystical union that every believer has with Christ. Insofar as we are all are united to Christ, we are united one to another. Although there are legitimate reasons for specific denominations, our spiritual union transcends all those boundaries. Therefore, it is possible to have fellowship under one Supreme Ruler, even Christ Himself, who is the head of His church.

Apostles and Elders

Elders specifically are addressed here: **The elders who are among you I exhort, I who am a fellow elder and a witness of the sufferings of Christ, and also a partaker of the glory that will be revealed** (v. 1). We could understand the term *elders* as people functioning in local church government as distinguished from pastors, or we could see the primary meaning as referring specifically to pastors. It is interesting that Peter calls himself an elder. Peter's office in the early church was that of an Apostle. In the hierarchy of the structures of authority in the New Testament, at the top is God the Father, who then delegates all authority on heaven and earth to His Son, the head of the church. His Son, in turn, authorized some to speak with His authority, the Apostles.

Sometimes we use the terms *disciple* and *Apostle* interchangeably, but they are not synonymous. A disciple is a student, one who studied at the feet of Jesus, and an Apostle is one sent as a delegate to speak with the authority of Christ Himself. When He appointed His Apostles He said, "He who receives you receives Me, and he who receives Me receives Him who sent Me" (Matt. 10:40). The Apostles spoke with nothing less than the authority of Christ. In our day there are people who attempt to set the teaching of Paul over against the teaching of Christ, but to do that is to violate Christ's commissioning of His Apostles. People who do not receive Paul do not receive Christ.

There were certain criteria, set forth in the New Testament, for the role of Apostle. To be an Apostle, one first had to have been a disciple under the teaching ministry of Jesus and an eyewitness of the resurrection. Another criterion—the most important—was a direct and immediate appointment to the office by Christ Himself. It is because of those criteria that the apostolic authority of Paul was so often challenged in the New Testament. He had not been a disciple during the earthly ministry of Jesus, nor had he been an eyewitness of the resurrection. Jesus did not appear to Paul until after His ascension into heaven. To the Corinthians Paul wrote, "[Christ] was seen by Cephas, then by the twelve. After that He was seen by over five hundred brethren at once. . . . After that He was seen by James, then by all the apostles. Then last of all He was seen by me also, as by one born out of due time" (1 Cor. 15:5–8). Three times in the book of Acts Luke records the rehearsal of the circumstances surrounding Paul's conversion on the road to Damascus and his being called by Christ to be an Apostle. One reason for that was likely the challenge to Paul's apostolic authority.

Paul's call to be an Apostle was so extraordinary that it had to be confirmed by those whose apostleship met all the obvious criteria. That is important, because there are people today who claim to be Apostles and to speak with as much authority as did Peter, Paul, or John. No one today could possibly meet the criteria of apostolic authority set forth in the New Testament, because nobody alive today was a disciple during the earthly ministry of Jesus. No one alive today was an eyewitness of Christ's resurrection in the first century. Some argue that God can call someone to be an Apostle today by giving them the charismatic gift of apostleship and with it the authority of the Apostle, but, unlike Paul, such a person would not be able to have his apostleship confirmed by the original disciples of Jesus.

The dimension of charismatic authority given to the Apostles did not continue past the first century, so we make a distinction between the extraordinary office of the Apostle and the ordinary offices of church officials. The Apostles established churches and within them the ordinary offices of elders, deacons, and bishops. There was a clear distinction, even in the New Testament era, between those who governed by the special measure of authority given to the Apostles and those who ruled at a lower level, under the authority of the Apostles. We speak first of the apostolic age and then of the sub-apostolic age, which generation was not on par with the authority of the Apostles.

In Paul's first letter to the Corinthian church, he wrote to referee internal disputes about who held greater authority among them, and one of the great disputes had to do with the use of the gifts of the Holy Spirit. Some in the Corinthian community who had experienced marvelous gifts of God had made themselves authorities in the church rather than remaining submissive to the duly structured authorities that the Apostles had established. Paul rebuked them for this in both 1 and 2 Corinthians. Near the end of the first century, Clement, then the bishop of Rome, was asked to intercede in ongoing disputes in the Corinthian church, and in a letter to the Corinthians, he called the people of Corinth to submit to the authority of the Apostles. We see, therefore, that terms such as *elder, bishop,* or *deacon* reference the ordinary offices of church government rather than the extraordinary office of the Old Testament prophet or the New Testament Apostle.

Peter gives an exhortation to the elders among the recipients of his letter as a fellow elder and a witness of the sufferings of Christ, and also as a partaker of the glory that will be revealed. A theme proclaimed frequently, not only by Peter but also by Paul, is that our baptism communicates that we are indelibly marked as those called to participate in the death of Christ and in His resurrection. If we are not willing to participate in the abasement that Christ suffered, if we are not willing to be united to our Lord in His humiliation, then we will by no means participate in His exaltation. This point is again brought up here when Peter points out that he was an eyewitness of the suffering of Christ but also a partaker of the glory that will be revealed. This glory is not something postponed until the future; Peter is saying that he was already participating in that glory.

Peter was an eyewitness of the humiliation of Christ. Indeed, he was a participant in it by virtue of his betrayal of Jesus. He also was an eyewitness to the glory of Christ (2 Pet. 1:16–19). John writes at the end of the prologue in his Gospel: "We beheld His glory, the glory as of the only begotten of the Father, full of grace and truth" (John 1:14). Peter's letter is no casual correspondence from a first-century Christian but is from an eyewitness of the suffering of Jesus. Peter was there on the Mount of Transfiguration, and he saw Jesus in His resurrection. He earned the right to teach us.

Shepherds of Christ's Flock

The admonition Peter gives to the elders is this: **Shepherd the flock of God which is among you, serving as overseers** (v. 2). Here we see the bishop as an overseer, a superintendent. The term *bishop* (*episkopos*), has a common Greek root that is intensified by the prefix *epi*. From the root, *scopis*, we get the English word *scope*. A telescope or microscope is an instrument we use to look at things. *Episkopos* means "to look at something with the most careful scrutiny." The verb form, *episkein*, is translated in the New Testament as "to visit." The incarnation of Jesus is celebrated as the visitation of God to His people, the "day of visitation." The word used there came from the Greek military. The visiting general, the *skopos*, came to review the troops to see if they were battle worthy.

From the word *episkopos* we get the concept of "supervisor." The word *vision* is involved here; supervisors are overseers. The purpose of the bishop is not to look at the flock and find the faults of the sheep but, rather, to shepherd the sheep. The image in Scripture of the shepherd, which is drawn from the work of Israelite shepherds, finds its zenith in Jesus' declaration of Himself as the Good Shepherd who lays down His life for His sheep. His sheep know His voice (John 10:27). When someone comes to service our air handler in our yard, our large dog is frantic to get at this seeming intruder. However, when I am out in the backyard, our dog just stands still and watches me. She does not bark, because she knows me; she knows my voice. The sheep knew the voice of the Great Shepherd, and when the Shepherd spoke, the sheep listened and followed the Shepherd.

Peter says that those of us in positions of ministry are to be shepherds of God's flock. The sheep do not belong to these shepherds; they belong to

God. Surely ringing in Peter's ears when he wrote this were Jesus's words of reinstatement following Peter's denial: "He said to him the third time, 'Simon, son of Jonah, do you love Me?' Peter was grieved because He said to him the third time, 'Do you love Me?' And he said to Him, 'Lord, You know all things; You know that I love You.' Jesus said to him, 'Feed My sheep'" (John 21:17). A shepherd protected the sheep from wild animals and from thieves, and his rod and staff provided comfort and safety, but the principal task of the shepherd was to feed the sheep. Peter had learned that and understood it well. Jesus did not tell the shepherd to entertain the sheep, and He certainly did not tell the shepherd to poison the sheep.

In churches today, particularly in America, enormous expectations are imposed upon the office of minister. Because of that, sixteen thousand pastors leave the ministry every year. Today a pastor is expected to be psychologist, theologian, biblical scholar, administrator, preacher, teacher, and community leader. The minister spends so much time on secondary matters that he has little time to do his principal work, which is to feed the sheep through preaching and teaching. The greatest service your minister can do for you is to feed you, not with his opinion but with the Word of God.

Peter reminds those who shepherd the flock of God to serve **not by compulsion but willingly, not for dishonest gain but eagerly** (v. 2). Ministers are not to shepherd from a sense of duty but from delight. The salary for most ministerial positions is low. In Old Testament times there was no income tax save for the tithe. God imposed a 10 percent tax on all the people out of which they were to pay the preachers and the teachers. God places a higher value on the care of our soul than we do, so He provided for the feeding of our soul through our gifts and tithes. Despite that, thousands of pastors in our country are exploited. I have heard businessmen say, "I don't think the pastor should make what I make," to which I respond, "Why not?" We need to readjust our thinking. Pastors leave the ministry often not because the salary is low but because of the implied message that their work is of little value. That is often the message sent, and it is a travesty on the kingdom of God.

Nor as being lords over those entrusted to you, but being examples to the flock; and when the Chief Shepherd appears, you will receive the crown of glory that does not fade away (vv. 3–4). God in Christ is going to bestow a crown upon His servants who feed His sheep, that is, if they execute the office according to the Word of God. Above all things, a pastor must feed Christ's flock the Word of God.

22

HUMILITY

1 Peter 5:5–14

Likewise you younger people, submit yourselves to your elders. Yes, all of you be submissive to one another, and be clothed with humility, for

"God resists the proud,

But gives grace to the humble."

Therefore humble yourselves under the mighty hand of God, that He may exalt you in due time, casting all your care upon Him, for He cares for you. Be sober, be vigilant; because your adversary the devil walks about like a roaring lion, seeking whom he may devour. Resist him, steadfast in the faith, knowing that the same sufferings are experienced by your brotherhood in the world. But may the God of all grace, who called us to His eternal glory by Christ Jesus, after you have suffered a while, perfect, establish, strengthen, and settle you. To Him be the glory and the dominion forever and ever. Amen. By Silvanus, our faithful brother as I consider him, I have written to you briefly, exhorting and testifying that this is the true grace of God in which you stand. She who is in Babylon, elect together with you, greets you; and so does Mark my son. Greet one another with a kiss of love. Peace to you all who are in Christ Jesus. Amen.

I find it fascinating that, throughout the New Testament, the use of garments portrays our redemption. Most importantly, of course, is that cloak with which we are clothed by the righteousness of Jesus. We are told in Scripture that all our righteousness is as filthy rags (Isa. 64:6), and if we stood before God on the basis of our own righteousness, we would be as those who were naked and ashamed.

The very first act of God's grace and redemption was to Adam and Eve. When guilty of the first sin, they fled from the presence of God and hid themselves because they were naked and ashamed. Instead of consigning Adam and Eve to perpetual shame and embarrassment, God in His mercy condescended to make clothes for them and hid their nakedness and covered their shame. In a sense, that first act of redemption foreshadowed the supreme act by which we would be clothed—not with the skins of animals but with the righteousness of Christ Himself.

Submission to Authority

Here Peter admonishes his readers not only to wear the garment of the righteousness of Christ but also to be clothed in humility: **Likewise you younger people, submit yourselves to your elders. Yes, all of you be submissive to one another, and be clothed with humility, for "God resists the proud, but gives grace to the humble"** (v. 5). Our entire being is to be covered with the virtue of humility because "God resists the proud, but gives grace to the humble." There is an antithetical parallelism in that quotation. The humble are given grace, which stands in stark contrast to the proud, who meet with the fierce resistance of God. Who can stand against that resistance? Yet when we approach God in a spirit of humility, He does not resist us but adds grace upon grace.

Peter goes on to say, **Therefore humble yourselves under the mighty hand of God, that He may exalt you in due time** (v. 6). Another metaphor, so rich throughout Scripture, is the hand or arm of the Lord, which signifies His strength. Mary said, "My soul magnifies the Lord, And my spirit has rejoiced in God my Savior. . . . He has shown strength with His arm; He has scattered the proud in the imagination of their hearts. He has put down the mighty from their thrones, and exalted the lowly" (Luke 1:46–52).

In the Old Testament, when the Israelites were tired of eating manna, Moses interceded for the people. They cried, "Who will give us meat to eat?" (Num. 11:4). Moses wept before the Lord and begged Him to provide meat for the people to eat, and God said, "You shall eat, not one day, nor two days, nor five days, nor ten days, nor twenty days, but for a whole month, until it comes out of your nostrils and becomes loathsome to you, because you have despised the LORD who is among you" (vv. 19–20).

Moses was scared and said, "The people whom I am among are six hundred thousand men on foot; yet You have said, 'I will give them meat, that they may eat for a whole month.' Shall flocks and herds be slaughtered for them, to provide enough for them? Or shall all the fish of the sea be gathered together for them, to provide enough for them?" (vv. 21–22). God said to Moses, "Has the Lord's arm been shortened? Now you shall see whether what I say will happen to you or not" (v. 23).

"Humble yourselves under the mighty hand of God"—in that simple phrase we have a microcosm of the entire Christian life. Obedience means submitting to the arm of the Lord, acknowledging Him as Lord and acknowledging His eternal and everlasting authority to require of us whatsoever is pleasing to Him.

When we do so, He will exalt us in due time. The exaltation will come at the hour that God has appointed. We are told repeatedly in Scripture that God indeed has appointed a time when He will judge the world by His Son, a time when He will vindicate His people, a time when He will share the glory of His Son with those who have embraced His Son.

Submission to God's Call

Casting all your care upon Him, for He cares for you (v. 7). This idea comes from the fishing industry, not from casting into the water with rods and reels but with nets, as fishermen did in antiquity and still do today. The net must be thrown. It is weighted down so that it will sink and fish will swim into it and get caught. Here, this metaphor of casting is used with respect to our anxieties and concerns, the things that weigh us down. Peter says that we are to cast all such cares upon God, and we are to do so because He cares for us.

One of the most important philosophers of the twentieth century was Martin Heidegger. In trying to analyze the human condition, he said that all human beings experience the feeling of *geworfenheit*, of having been thrown chaotically into whatever state one finds oneself. It seems as though fate has just blindly hurled us out there, and Heidegger defines life in the state of having been thrown as being marked by the singular emotion of a *bersorgen*, the kind of care that weighs us down and drives us to despair. He understood that people carry a burden of quiet desperation and that this care and concern is a part of our human predicament and not easily overcome. God says that we are to take all such care and throw it to Him, because He is the God who cares. Sometimes we feel that nobody cares. If you feel that nobody cares, this is the text you must read to be reminded that the God we serve is a God who cares for us.

The fellow who led me to Christ sang a hymn with simple lyrics that went something like this: "No one ever cared for me like Jesus." When I heard it in chapel one day, I wept. The truth of the lyrics came home to my soul. People have loved and cared for me, but nobody has cared for me like Jesus has.

A Roaring Lion

Peter goes on to say, **Be sober, be vigilant; because your adversary the devil walks about like a roaring lion, seeking whom he may devour** (v. 8). The sobriety Peter has in mind here is not simply being free from drunken stupors but to be awake and alert. The reason for that is our adversary the Devil. One great error we make is to underestimate the power of Satan. Those who do not believe that Satan exists fall into his hands because they do not believe in his power. Others become so obsessed with Satan that they see a demon behind every bush, and it seems that their faith is more in the occult than in the truth of God. We need a sober and a vigilant understanding of the nature of Satan, of his person and work.

In the sixteenth century, Luther spoke of the three great obstacles to Christian growth—the world, the flesh, and the Devil. He experienced an unbridled, relentless attack from Satan. Some have thought that Luther's acute sensitivity to the presence of Satan was madness, but if ever there was a man in history, apart from Jesus, who was the target of the Devil, it was Martin Luther. The Devil did not want to see the gospel of the free grace of Christ recovered from the darkness of the Middle Ages.

The metaphor that Peter uses for Satan here is rather strange—he describes Satan as a lion. In Scripture the typical metaphor for Satan is that of serpent or snake, the one who lies, seduces, accuses. The image of a lion in Scripture is usually associated with something more positive, more kingly. We noted earlier that Judah received a benediction from his father, Jacob:

> Judah is a lion's whelp;
>> From the prey, my son, you have gone up.
>> He bows down, he lies down as a lion;
>> And as a lion, who shall rouse him?
>
> The scepter shall not depart from Judah,
>> Nor a lawgiver from between his feet,
>> Until Shiloh comes. (Gen. 49:9–10).

The descendants of the tribe of Judah looked forward to the full manifestation of the lion that would come from the seed of David, the Lion of Judah, the title given to Jesus. Here in Peter's epistle, Satan receives that marvelous metaphor of the lion that was usually reserved for Christ.

Peter describes Satan as our adversary. He is our supreme opponent, the one who stands against us and seeks our ruin. So often, we think that the principal role of Satan is to entice or tempt us to sin. Indeed, he does that, but even more devastating is his role of accuser. In the book of Zechariah, we find a vision of the high priest whose clothes were soiled. Satan came to accuse him, and the Lord said, "The LORD rebuke you, Satan! The LORD who has chosen Jerusalem rebuke you! Is this not a brand plucked from the fire?" (Zech. 3:2). Satan focused on the sins of the high priest in order to discredit him, but that high priest was clothed with the righteousness of Christ. Satan comes to us at times and says, "Are you sure you're a Christian? How can you be a Christian and do the things that you do, think the things that you think, and say the things that you say?"

A parishioner said to me recently, "The Christian life is really hard," to which I replied that it is hard indeed. Life in this world does not become complicated until we become Christians. Before then, we willingly obey Satan. We follow him and do his bidding, so there is no real conflict, but once we have been rescued and our life has been taken by Jesus, Satan lets go of the prize with great resistance and will seek to cause us to trip. More importantly, he can take away the assurance of our salvation. If he can take away our confidence, then he can render us spiritually impotent.

Satan does not simply slander us, though he does that and will often accuse us of things for which we are not guilty. How can we tell the difference between the ministry of the Holy Spirit, who is sent to convict us of our sins, and the work of Satan, who comes to accuse us of our sins? Both point to the same sin but for radically different reasons. When Satan accuses us of sin, it is to ruin us, to cripple and destroy. When the Holy Spirit convicts us of sin, it is to redeem and cleanse us. Being convicted of sin by the Holy Spirit can be an exceedingly painful process, and true repentance can be painful, but there is always something sweet about it. When the Spirit convicts us, and we recognize it, He takes us to the Savior for forgiveness, not destruction. Satan's goal is not our redemption but our ruin. He is our adversary, and he "walks about like a roaring lion, seeking whom he may devour" (1 Pet. 5:8).

There was a time in Peter's life when he grossly underestimated the power of the Devil. At the Last Supper when Jesus told the men that one among them would betray Him, each asked him, "Is it I?" (Matt. 26:22; Mark 14:19). To Judas, Jesus said, "You have said it" (Matt. 26:25). Then He announced Peter's betrayal and said to him, "Simon, Simon! Indeed, Satan has asked for you, that he may sift you as wheat. But I have prayed for you, that your faith should not fail; and when you have returned to Me, strengthen your brethren" (Luke 22:31–32). That night in the courtyard, Satan sifted Peter like wheat. Now, in his later years, Peter is writing to this young flock with warning. Peter knew, and we must know, that we are no match for Satan. That is why we need the whole armor of God.

Elsewhere in Scripture we are told, "Resist the devil and he will flee from you" (James 4:7), and "He who is in you is greater than he who is in the world" (1 John 4:4). We are no match for Satan, but once we are equipped with the whole armor of God, Satan is no match for us. This stalking, roaring, threatening lion will flee with his tail between his legs.

If we are going to be sober and vigilant about the wiles of the Devil, we must be aware of how he is described elsewhere in Scripture. Satan does not appear like a roaring lion or a sneaky snake; he manifests himself as an angel of light. He masks his evil with counterfeit good, which is why he is deceptive. No sin can ever bring us happiness, but sin can bring us pleasure. The Devil comes as an angel of light and promises us pleasure in sin so that we begin to think that what God forbids is not only allowable but good.

Resist him, steadfast in the faith, knowing that the same sufferings are experienced by your brotherhood in the world (v. 9). People interpret these words in different ways. Some say we are to resist him by a steadfast or solid faith, which is a possible rendering of the text. However, I think Peter meant that the way we resist him is by having ourselves deeply rooted in the content of the Christian faith or doctrine. Doctrine has to do with God's revealed truth, and those who master the doctrine of the Word of God have a solid foundation by which they are empowered to resist the devouring enemy.

Peter also says here that our problems are not unique. We are not alone in our experiences of suffering and affliction. Suffering is the natural course of things. We must remember that Peter began this section with, "Beloved, do not think it strange concerning the fiery trial which is to try you, as though some strange thing happened to you" (4:12).

God of All Grace
But may the God of all grace, who called us to His eternal glory by Christ Jesus, after you have suffered a while, perfect, establish,

strengthen, and settle you (v. 10). Every good thing we experience comes to us from the benevolent hand of God. We live by grace alone. We move from faith to faith, life to life, and grace to grace, and God is the author of all of these graces. He is not just the God of grace or just a gracious God, but He is the God of *all* grace. God's eternal glory, which is in Him alone from all eternity, He will not share with any man. Nevertheless, by His grace He has called us to participate in it. The only one who can perfect us is God. The only one who is able to establish us is God. The only one who can give us abiding strength is God. The only one who can settle us is God.

Augustine said, "Almighty God, you have made us for yourself, and our hearts are restless till they find their rest in you." Augustine was saying that the human spirit remains perpetually unsettled. As long as we are estranged from God, who made us for Himself, we cannot possibly be settled in our spirits. To be settled is an act of divine grace, so Peter's plea is that God would settle us. Then Peter gives a benediction: **To Him be the glory and the dominion forever and ever. Amen** (v. 11)—*soli Deo gloria*. Peter had been there for the Sermon on the Mount. He had heard Jesus explain how to pray: "Yours is the kingdom and the power and the glory forever. Amen" (Matt. 6:13).

After the benediction comes Peter's farewell: **By Silvanus, our faithful brother as I consider him, I have written to you briefly, exhorting and testifying that this is the true grace of God in which you stand** (v. 12). Who is Silvanus? Most commentators agree that the name Silvanus is another way of spelling the name Silas, the man who traveled with Paul on his missionary journeys and rose to great importance in the early church. Presumably Peter entrusted this epistle to Silas to deliver to the recipients.

She who is in Babylon, elect together with you, greets you; and so does Mark my son (v. 13). Some have speculated that "she who is in Babylon" was Peter's wife. Earlier, Jesus had healed Peter's mother-in-law, so we know that at some point Peter was married. However, the "she" here almost certainly refers to the church, which is given a feminine title throughout the Bible. Babylon is the code name, as it were, among biblical writers of the first century, for the city of Rome. If Peter is writing this epistle from the city of Rome, he is telling its recipients that not only does he greet them but that the whole church in Rome greets them as well.

In referencing Mark, I doubt very much that Peter is using the term "son" in a biological manner but rather as Paul referred to Timothy. As Timothy was Paul's son in the Lord, so Peter describes Mark as his spiritual son. Peter is almost certainly indicating John Mark, the one who went with Paul on a missionary journey but was sent back home. He did not make it as a missionary; the Apostle Paul had to fire him so that Mark could find his vocation. Afterward Mark went home and wrote the Gospel of Mark, which we believe to be, in a very real sense, Peter's gospel, because Peter stood behind Mark as he penned it. Now Peter makes mention again of Mark and sends Mark's greetings along.

Greet one another with a kiss of love (v. 14). Elsewhere that is called a "holy kiss." It was the way ancient Near Eastern people greeted each other at that time and still do today. We are not obligated to continue that custom in our nation, but we may greet one another with a holy kiss, if we desire.

Peter concludes the epistle the same way that Jesus concluded His teaching to His disciples: giving them the legacy of Christ. Jesus had no earthly estate. His only garment was His robe, which was taken by His captors who gambled for it. All He had left to give His disciples was peace: "Peace I leave with you, My peace I give to you; not as the world gives do I give to you. Let not your heart be troubled, neither let it be afraid" (John 14:27). Although Jews commonly wished peace on one another, it took on a particular sensitivity in the Christian community, so Peter concludes this epistle with this common ending. **Peace to you all who are in Christ Jesus. Amen** (v. 14). Peace to all who are in the Prince of Peace; peace to all who have the inheritance of His peace. Amen.

2 PETER

23

THE AUTHORITY OF 2 PETER

2 Peter 1:1

Simon Peter, a bondservant and apostle of Jesus Christ, to those who have obtained like precious faith with us by the righteousness of our God and Savior Jesus Christ.

When I begin a study of a book of the Bible, I pause to consider some background questions. I consider who wrote it, when it was written, and to whom it was written, because knowing the context helps us greatly in our attempt to understand its message. It has been said that 2 Peter is the forgotten stepchild of the New Testament. There perhaps have been fewer commentaries written about this book than any other of the New Testament, with the possible exception of Jude. When we encounter this particular epistle, we immediately bump up against all the standard criticisms. The Petrine authorship of the book has been challenged and so has its legitimacy as part of the New Testament canon.

Development of the Canon

The first thing we have to understand is that the Bible is not a single book but a collection of sixty-six individual books. All of those books gathered together into one volume we call the "canon of sacred Scripture." The word *canon* comes from the Greek term *kanon*, which means "measuring rod" or "standard." When the church made its confession of which books to include in the category of sacred Scripture, or which books, properly speaking, belong to the canon, they said that these sixty-six books are the ones that manifest the standard of the Word of God. They are the norm of all Christian literature. Indeed, it is said of the canon that it is the norm of norms and without norm. The development of the canon was a process. In fact, the church was engaged for over three hundred years in debate, discussion, and analysis of various books from the first century in order to establish once and for all which books belonged.

The first collection of books was drawn up by a heretic named Marcion, who had antipathy toward the God of the Old Testament. Marcion did not believe that God was the ultimate God of the universe but was a lesser being, what he called a "demiurge," troubled by ill temper and subject to fits of wrath unworthy of ultimate deity. Any references in the New Testament that were favorably inclined to the God of the Old Testament or that suggested Jesus was the Son of the God of the Old Testament were ruthlessly expurgated from Marcion's canon. By the time he was finished with his scissors and tape, there was little of what we now recognize in the New Testament. Throughout church history, it has been the teaching of heretics that has forced the church to refine and make precise her confession of faith. Because Marcion's false canon was being spread abroad, it was necessary for the church to step into the fray and declare which books had apostolic authority.

One of the most important lists that would determine the canon came in A.D. 175 in what was called the Muratorian Canon. Second Peter did not appear in the Muratorian Canon of the late second century; it was not included until later on in church history.

I once read that a critic of biblical Christianity said there were between two and three thousand books contending for inclusion in the New Testament canon and only a handful of them made it in the final analysis. This particular critic questioned the odds of the right books' making it into the canon when there were so many to choose from. Our Roman Catholic friends say that the right books were selected because the church, which decreed the canon, chose them; however, this rather triumphant claim of Rome is not without its attending difficulties.

First, the church changed her mind on more than one occasion about which books belong. Therefore, which selection was the inspired or infallible one, and which was the wrong one? Since their choices did not always agree, it is difficult to appeal to some kind of transcendent infallibility in the process.

Second, and more important, the church at that time was not creating the canon but simply acknowledging what the canon was, recognizing—receiving—certain books as authoritative books of the New Testament. In other words, the church was acquiescing to a list of books that they recognized had authority over them.

We need have no concern as whether the right ones got in or were left out because, in that historical selection process, of all the books given serious consideration, only three were not included in our present New Testament canon. The vast majority of the contenders for inclusion in the New Testament were clearly and widely known to be spurious, many of them false teachings, usually attributed to the Gnostics. In their effort to supplant the authority of the Bible, Gnostics wrote their fraudulent books and tried to sneak them into the churches by attributing to them apostolic authorship. Those books were never seriously considered. The only three that did not make it into the canon were *The Shepherd of Hermes*, the *Didache*, and the *1 Clement* (Clement was the bishop of Rome in the latter part of the first century), yet even those three books were never strong contenders.

In Clement's letter, it is clear that he saw himself as being under the authority of the Apostles. He clearly understood himself to be second generation, and he appealed to the Apostles that went before him for the truth of their teaching. If you look at that document and the others that were excluded, you will see why they were not included in the canon.

The debate that goes on today is not so much about whether the ones that were excluded should have been included but about whether a few of the books that were included in the final analysis should have been excluded. There were a handful of books in the New Testament about which serious questions were raised. The book of Hebrews was one, because it seems to suggest that people could lose their salvation (see Hebrews 6, 10). That created no small controversy in the early church. The book of Revelation had some questions about it because of the serious difficulty in interpreting its symbols and images. Second Peter was another, as were 1, 2, and 3 John. Nevertheless, the questions were not serious.

Canon Criteria

What process did the church follow in order to reach its decision? The church first looked at the question of whether the writings had been received by the first Christian church, the original Christian community, as being of apostolic authority. From the beginning there was no question that the Gospels were received in the early church as being the Word of God and of apostolic authority. Even though the Gospels of Mark and Luke were not written by Apostles, it was recognized from the beginning that the apostolic authority of Peter stood behind the Gospel of Mark and that the apostolic authority of Paul stood behind the Gospel of Luke and the book of Acts.

That brings us to the second criterion, which is apostolic authorship. If a book could be shown to have been written by an Apostle, that was credential enough for its inclusion in the canon. If a book could be shown to have been endorsed by an Apostle, as was the case with Mark and Luke, that also provided its access to the canon. Concerning the books about which there were lingering questions, their inclusion in the canon was determined by measuring their content and doctrine with the content in the books already determined for inclusion.

An irony of the discussion was that the book of Hebrews made it into the canon when the church became convinced that it had been written by the Apostle Paul, yet today there are few who believe that Paul actually wrote Hebrews (I being an exception). Since 2 Peter bears the name of an Apostle, Simon Peter, we would think that would have been sufficient to bring it into the canon without argument, but not until later decisions of the church were made at the Councils of Carthage and Hippo was 2 Peter fully acknowledged to be authentic in apostolic claim. In other words, the church became convinced that its author, Simon Peter, really was the one who claimed authorship in the first verse. Yet there are still those who argue that 2 Peter was not written by the Apostle Peter and, therefore, does not belong in the canon of Scripture.

Likewise, the authorship of all thirteen of the epistles attributed to the Apostle Paul has been challenged by higher critics during the last century. The guns of criticism have been trained against virtually every book in the New Testament, arguing that some of the Gospels themselves were not composed until the second century. All of that is basically driven by an attempt to undermine the authority of the biblical documents.

Finally, it has been argued that the doctrine of the inerrancy of Scripture was not the position of the early church, or even of the magisterial Reformers of the sixteenth century, but was an abstract doctrine that came in through the rationalism of seventeenth-century Protestant scholasticism. It is true that Martin Luther never said that the Bible is inerrant, but he did say that the Bible never errs. John Calvin did not customarily use the term *inerrancy*, but he did say that we should receive the Bible as if it were heard uttered audibly from heaven, as it is the veritable Word of God.

There was a time in Luther's great controversy over the doctrine of justification by faith alone when his adversaries quoted James 2 against that notion. For a season, Luther became so frustrated that he said in exasperation, "James is an epistle of straw," and he challenged its inclusion in the canon. Some say that since Luther at one point challenged the canonicity of James, he obviously did not believe in the inerrancy of the Bible. However, Luther believed that every book in the Bible is the inerrant Word of God; his question was whether a particular book should be included in the canon. His question about James did not concern the inspiration of sacred Scripture; it was a question of the canonicity of James. In the final analysis he did embrace James and was happy with its inclusion in the canon.

The nature of the Bible and the extent of the Bible involve two different questions. I am totally convinced that, in the final analysis, every book the church acknowledged as authentic was given by apostolic authority and all the books God intended to include in the New Testament are there today.

Authorship of 2 Peter

Simon Peter, a bondservant and apostle of Jesus Christ, to those who have obtained like precious faith with us by the righteousness of our God and Savior Jesus Christ (v. 1). In the Greek, the name Peter gives for himself is not Simon Peter but Simeon Peter. The name Simeon was one of the most common first names of Aramaic-speaking people in the ancient world, and it is the Aramaic form of the name Simon. Nevertheless, some doubt that the Apostle Peter wrote the epistle since the author calls himself Simeon Peter instead of Simon Peter.

More significantly, those who challenge the authorship of this epistle do so on the basis of some striking literary differences between 1 and 2 Peter. Those differences involve three matters. First is the style of the Greek used in each of the epistles. Second is the problem of *hapax legomena*, a term that refers to words found only once in a particular writing or body of writing. For example, we can say that there are *hapax legomena* in Ephesians because there are more than thirty words in that letter that are found nowhere else in Paul's writings. So, people say, obviously someone else had to have written it. In 2 Peter there are fifty-seven words found only in this epistle and nowhere else in the New Testament. Third is that the subject matter of 2 Peter differs from 1 Peter in its philosophical and cultural nature.

We see time after time in the literature of the New Testament that the authors of the books used secretaries or amanuenses to set down their writings. Silvanus, the one whom the Apostle Peter mentioned in his first epistle as his letter carrier, was also likely Peter's secretary in the writing of that epistle. Here, in the epistle written shortly before Peter's death, he is using a different secretary, and the difference in secretary would more than reasonably account for the difference in some of the style and structure.

The issue of the *hapax legomena* falls apart when we consider that it is not at all unusual for writers to vary their vocabulary. When I enrolled in my doctoral studies in Holland, my first assignment was to read twenty-five books in Dutch, a language I did not know. The first two volumes addressed basically the same subject, christology, and were written to the same audience only one year apart. Because I did not know the language, I opened the first book to the first word of the first sentence, and it was, of course, a Dutch word. So I got out my Dutch-English dictionary and looked up the word. I wrote the Dutch word on one side of a little card and the English word on the other. I repeated the process for the second word and the third. That first day I was able to translate only a bit more than one page. It was daunting. Every day I spent time adding to the pile of cards and memorizing them. Once I had finished that first volume, I had memorized about ten thousand words. Then I tackled the second volume, and I found five thousand words that I had not found in the first volume—the same author, the same subject, and the same audience. So much for this nonsense of *hapax legomena*.

The Apostle Paul wrote on different subjects at different times to different audiences, yet people doubt his authorship because there are thirty-three words in one of his letters that do not appear elsewhere. They have to think that Paul and Peter were absolutely impoverished with respect to vocabulary.

The third issue has to do with the cultural and philosophical nature of Peter's epistles. If the central theme of 1 Peter is encouragement during times of persecution, this second epistle deals with the threat of the Gnostic heresy. Gnosticism was one of the most serious threats to the life of the church in the later part of the first century and into the second and third centuries. If Peter was aware of the Gnostic threat, then he certainly would have been able to address it in his writings. Peter was not an ignorant man. He understood that the greatest threat to the well-being of God's people is false teaching.

Gnostic Influence

People in our day do not want to take doctrine seriously. They say that doctrine divides, so instead we must focus on relationships, but ironically, in so saying, they mimic the very people that Peter is addressing in this second epistle. The biggest heretical threat in the first two hundred years of Christianity came from Gnosticism. The word *gnosis* is found frequently in the English language. Those who say they do not know whether God exists call themselves *agnostic*, "without knowledge." The Latin equivalent to that, by the way, is *ignoramus*.

The Gnostics argued that truth, particularly ultimate truth, could not be learned through the mind, through the use of rationality, through the five senses, or through scientific investigation. The only way the truth of God can be understood, they argued, is through a mystical intuition that goes beyond the categories of reason and eyewitness testimony. The Gnostics attempted an amalgamation of Greek philosophy and Oriental dualism with a sprinkle of Christianity mixed in. They claimed to have a special pipeline to God such that God revealed Himself only to those in the know, the *gnosticoi*, whose knowledge was supposedly superior to that of the Apostles, since the Apostles sought to understand the message of revelation in an intelligible way rather than through mystical intuition.

The New Testament scholar Peter Jones has written a book entitled *The Gnostic Empire Strikes Back* in which he does a comprehensive study of the way in which gnosticism is alive and well in our day. The chief vehicle for the spread of the gnostic gospel is New Age thought, which has so captured the imagination of the Western world that the gnostic elements pervasive during the time of the early church have been embraced by postmoderns.

Several years ago I was invited to give a convocation address, which is usually a scholarly presentation, at a seminary. I addressed the faculty and student body about the urgent need to require courses in logic in every seminary. We make sure that our students learn Hebrew and Greek and that they study the context and background of the Bible, yet the Scriptures are still misinterpreted because illegitimate inferences are made from the text. There is a failure to understand the laws of immediate inference, that is, a failure to understand the rudimentary principles of logic. The audience was unhappy with my presentation because that seminary community had been drawn into the idea that we understand the things of God not with our mind but through mystical apprehension.

One of the great issues that Peter addresses in this epistle is the nature of the knowledge of God, and he gets into it rather quickly. Even though 2 Peter did not make it into the Muratorian Canon of A.D. 175, early church fathers made allusions that were taken clearly from this book, and the Petrine authorship of it was strongly affirmed by people like Athanasius, Ambrose, and Augustine. The internal testimony of the book and the external testimony of church history are strong, and I teach the epistle from the firm conviction that it comes to us from the apostolic authority of Simon Peter.

24

MAKE YOUR CALLING SURE, PART 1

2 Peter 1:1

Simon Peter, a bondservant and apostle of Jesus Christ, to those who have obtained like precious faith with us by the righteousness of our God and Savior Jesus Christ.

As the Apostle Paul frequently identified himself in his letters, so Peter identifies himself here with a twin appellation; namely, that he is **a bondservant and apostle of Jesus Christ** (v. 1). In the Christian community, the lowest possible layer or stratification of society was that of a slave, and the most elevated office, save for the office of Jesus Himself, was that of Apostle. To the Apostles was given the authority of Jesus to such a degree that He announced, "He who receives you receives Me, and he who receives Me receives Him who sent Me" (Matt. 10:40).

In our day and age, there are multitudes who say, "I believe in Jesus and follow His teachings, but I cannot follow the Apostles. That chauvinistic, Jewish theologian Paul, I can hardly tolerate." However, we do not know anything about Jesus except from the apostolic testimony that comes to us through the Scriptures, so to distinguish between Jesus and the Apostles is foreign to Scripture itself. In the early church Irenaeus had to contend with cynics who said that they appreciated Jesus but would not submit to the authority of the Apostles. Irenaeus said that one cannot have Jesus yet reject the ones whom Jesus appointed to speak in His name, just as one cannot have God yet reject His supreme Apostle, Jesus Himself. During Jesus' earthly ministry, the Pharisees made a similar type of distinction. They claimed to believe in God, yet they rejected Jesus. Jesus said, "He who rejects Me rejects Him who sent Me" (Luke 10:16). That is simple logic. So the highest authority operating in the early church, apart from Jesus, was that of the Apostles.

Here Peter claims the highest authority that anyone could claim in the early church—that of being an Apostle. At the same time, like the Apostle Paul, he identifies himself as a slave. He is simultaneously the highest and the lowest of Christian society. The word Peter uses here, *doulos*, is the same word that Paul uses in Romans; it refers to a purchased slave. There is a close connection in the Scriptures between the word *doulos* and the word *kyrios*. A *kyrios* was the lord or master; one could not be a *kyrios* unless he owned slaves. Carrying the metaphor even further, the Apostle Paul wrote, "You were bought at a price" (1 Cor. 6:20; 7:23).

Peter and Paul saw themselves as slaves of Christ, and that idea extends to everyone purchased by Jesus. We are all bondservants of Christ. The supreme irony is that Jesus comes to set us free from slavery, and He tells us, "Therefore if the Son makes you free, you shall be free indeed" (John 8:36). Those who are delivered from the slavery of sin take on a new kind of slavery; they become slaves to Christ. If you think you are free outside of bondage to Christ, your freedom is so much slavery. We have to lose our lives to find them; we have to give them away to get them back. All of that and more is found simply in Peter's self-designation.

Like Precious Faith

To those who have obtained like precious faith with us by the righteousness of our God and Savior Jesus Christ (v. 1). This second part of verse 1 is worthy of the writing of at least ten books. Peter addresses the epistle to his fellow believers who have received faith. Just like the Apostle Paul, so the Apostle Peter defines faith not as something that originates and is exercised by an unregenerate human heart but as something the believer receives passively. If you have faith in Jesus Christ, you did not conjure it up. When you first heard the gospel and responded favorably to it, perhaps you thought that you decided to believe in Jesus, but saving faith is not the result of a human decision. It is a divine gift. Paul wrote:

You He made alive, who were dead in trespasses and sins, in which you once walked according to the course of this world, according to the prince of the power of the air, the spirit who now works in the sons of disobedience, among whom also we all once conducted ourselves in the lusts of our flesh, fulfilling the desires of the flesh and of the mind, and were by nature children of wrath, just as the others. But God, who is rich in mercy, because of His great love with which He loved us, even when we were dead in trespasses, made us alive together with Christ. (Eph. 2:1–5)

That God has made us alive is the biblical language for regeneration. God made us born again, not after we left the pigsty of the prodigal son and came home but while we were dead in sin and trespasses, while we were still following the course of this world, the prince of the power of the air, and obeying the lusts of our flesh. While we were in that spiritually dead condition, God, in His unspeakable grace and mercy, brought us to spiritual life. When the physical corpse of Jesus was placed in the tomb, the power of God raised Him from death and brought Him to life once more. That is the same power that raises us from spiritual death, if indeed we have faith in Christ. Paul continues:

(By grace you have been saved), and raised us up together, and made us sit together in the heavenly places in Christ Jesus, that in the ages to come He might show the exceeding riches of His grace in His kindness toward us in Christ Jesus. For by grace you have been saved through faith, and that not of yourselves; it is the gift of God. (Eph. 2:5–9)

This is the wonderful benefit of the sovereign election of God, that He gives the gift that we do not deserve. Nobody believes by his own power but only as the result of God's action. That is exactly what Peter is saying.

In our vocabulary something called "precious" has an exceedingly high value. Gems we call precious stones because they are so much more valuable than gravel. Just so, Peter describes the faith by which we are saved as a precious faith. Is there any possession you have more precious than the faith that links you to Christ and delivers to you His entire inheritance? The wisest people divest themselves of all they have in order to possess this precious reality, this pearl of great price.

The Deity of Jesus

There is a bit of awkwardness in the way this second sentence is structured. We have obtained this precious faith "by the righteousness of our God and Savior Jesus Christ." When Paul speaks of our justification by faith alone and about the righteousness of God in that context, the righteousness by which we are justified is not that by which God Himself is righteous, but that which He gives as a gift to all who believe. It is the transfer or imputation of the righteousness of Christ to the account of all who put their trust in Him. There is no doctrine more precious than that of the imputation of the righteousness of Christ to the account of the believer, because the only righteousness by which we will ever be saved before God is the righteousness of Christ.

It may be in this sentence that Peter is making reference to that precious faith that links us now to the righteousness that is the ground of our salvation. The sentence could also be interpreted to mean that it is through God's own marvelous righteousness that He has been pleased to give us the same precious gift of faith that He has given to others. I do not know which of those two possible interpretations is the correct one, but either one ends in the same place. The precious faith we have obtained is "by the righteousness of our God and Savior Jesus Christ." Here the structure is abundantly clear. Peter is talking about the gift that comes to us by the righteousness of our God and Savior Jesus Christ. Peter is referring to Jesus not only as the Messiah, our Savior, but as God Himself. There are few texts in all the New Testament that are as clear as this one in its attributing deity to Jesus.

In the Gospel of John, Jesus appeared to Thomas the Twin, who had resolved not to believe on the basis of the testimony of his fellow disciples. He said, "Unless I see in His hands the print of the nails, and put my finger into the print of the nails, and put my hand into His side, I will not believe" (John 20:25). When Jesus appeared to him, He stretched forth His hand and said, "Reach your finger here, and look at My hands; and reach your hand here, and put it into My side. Do not be unbelieving, but believing" (v. 27). The Gospel does not tell us whether Thomas actually did extend his hand and do that. I do not think he did; seeing Jesus standing before him was sufficient. Then Thomas fell to his knees and made the great confession, "My Lord and my God!" (v. 28).

That confession of the full deity of Jesus is set forth in the prologue of John's Gospel: "In the beginning was the Word, and the Word was with God, and the Word was God" (John 1:1). For the first two hundred years of Christian reflection on the person of Jesus, that *logos* concept in the prologue dominated the thinking of the greatest minds of the early church fathers. They noted the clarity with which the Apostle John declared that the Word was God—not *a* god, not *like* God, but "was God." The grammar of that text makes a clear identity between the Word and God. It is not by accident that the early church professed the deity of Christ.

However, some in church history struggled with the doctrine of the deity of Christ. They were unable to understand how one could be faithful to the monotheism of Old Testament Judaism, which declares, "Hear, O Israel: The LORD our God, the LORD is one" (Deut. 6:4). How can people hold to the oneness of God and at the same time ascribe deity to the Son and to the Father and to the Holy Spirit?

The Arian Heresy

The question of the nature of the Trinity came under attack and at no point more critically than in the fourth century, with the teaching of the heretic Arius. Arius taught that Jesus is worthy to be worshiped despite the fact that He was a creature (despite the fact that worshiping any creature is utterly repugnant to God, no matter how exalted that creature is). Nevertheless, Arius taught that Jesus was the first creature that God made, and through this exalted creature the worlds were made. Jesus is not God, Arius said, because the Bible says that Jesus was begotten of the Father and the firstborn of all creation. Arius pointed out that the Greek word *gennaō* means "to be," "to become," or "to happen," that is, "to have a starting point in time." All created beings at some time in eternity past did not exist, and since Jesus was begotten, that meant there had to be a time when He was not, and if there was a time when He was not, He cannot be eternal, and if He is not eternal, He cannot be God. If He is the firstborn of creation, Arius said, no matter how exalted, He still falls short of deity.

Intense controversy followed in the wake of the teaching of Arius, which culminated ultimately in the decrees of the Council of Nicaea, which produced the Nicene Creed. In the Nicene Creed, one of the most magnificent creeds in the history of Christendom, the church affirmed that Christ is *homoousios*, "one essence," with the Father, of the same being and co-eternal. The Jewish reference to Christ's begottenness does not have the same simplistic understanding that it did among the Greeks. We get a hint of that even in the prologue of John. After John says that the Word was God, he refers to Christ as the *monogenēs*, the "only begotten." No one else begotten of God has been begotten in the sense in which Christ is begotten, because Christ is not begotten at a particular period in time. The second person of the Trinity has no birthday; He is eternally begotten. The Father is always generating the Son.

As the controversy played out, the issues of the debate were presented through slogans and simple songs. Jingles have a way of capturing our imagination, and they allow us to remember things for long periods. "*D-u-z, D-u-z, put Duz in your washing machine. See your clothes come out so clean. D-u-z does everything.*" Powerful little jingles communicate ideas. The Arians composed jingles that were ribald, slanderous, and ugly, and they sang them in a taunting way against the Christians. To combat the Arians, the Trinitarians composed a jingle of their own:

> Glory be to the Father, and to the Son, and to the Holy Ghost.
> As it was in the beginning, is now, and ever shall be, world without end.
> Amen.

The "Gloria Patri" was originally a fight song for Trinitarians, as we noted earlier.

At the Nicaean Council of A.D. 325 and again in A.D. 451 at Chalcedon, the church affirmed the full deity of Christ. They affirmed it not on the basis of philosophical speculation but on the basis of biblical exegesis. The teaching of the deity of Christ is not the invention of theologians; it is the clear teaching of the Word of God. Here in this epistle we have one of those marvelous texts that speak of Jesus Christ as our God and as our Savior. The One who saves us is our God, and our God is our Savior, which means, by way of application, that if God has saved you, you are saved indeed.

25

MAKE YOUR CALLING SURE, PART 2

2 Peter 1:2–4

Grace and peace be multiplied to you in the knowledge of God and of Jesus our Lord, as His divine power has given to us all things that pertain to life and godliness, through the knowledge of Him who called us by glory and virtue, by which have been given to us exceedingly great and precious promises, that through these you may be partakers of the divine nature, having escaped the corruption that is in the world through lust.

As we noted earlier, expressions of grace and peace are common in the salutations of the New Testament epistles. The idea of grace and peace is deeply rooted in Old Testament history. In the Hebrew benediction, God is asked to grant grace and peace to His people: "The LORD bless you and keep you; the LORD make His face shine upon you, and be gracious to you; the LORD lift up His countenance upon you, and give you peace" (Num. 6:24–26). The concept of peace was so important to Jewish people that it became the basic form of personal greeting. To this day, the Jew will greet his friend with *Shalom aleichem*, to which the response is *Aleichem shalom*—"Peace be unto you, and unto you peace."

Grace and Peace Multiplied

Peter does something a bit differently here in his salutation. Instead of simply saying, "Grace and peace to you," he says, **Grace and peace be multiplied to you in the knowledge of God and of Jesus our Lord** (v. 2). He speaks of a multiplication of grace and peace. This text contains a point that was of mighty contention in the sixteenth century. The Roman Catholic Church taught that the grace of justification comes principally through the sacraments, initially through the sacrament of baptism, when grace is infused or imparted to the human soul, or takes up residence in the soul as a *habitus* or habit. Rome speaks frequently of grace in quantitative terms, perhaps only for metaphorical reasons; that is, grace is measured in terms of an amount of substance that is poured into the soul. Rome holds that the grace of justification given initially in baptism can be augmented or diminished (to *augment* something is to add to it; to *diminish* something is to subtract from it). When Rome speaks about an increase of the grace of justification, it means that justification can grow or ebb.

In the Reformation doctrine of justification by faith alone, since justification is not based upon an infusion or a pouring in of divine grace but rather upon a transfer of the righteousness of Christ to the believer, then manifestly there can never be any augmentation or diminution of one's justification, because the righteousness of Christ is perfect and never diminishes. We can never add to the righteousness of Christ. Thus, in the final analysis, the great debate of the sixteenth century came down to two words—*infusion* and *imputation*. Rome held that one cannot be declared just by God until or unless justice or righteousness inheres in that person's soul, whereas the Reformers declared that, according to Scripture, we are justified the moment the righteousness of Christ is transferred to us by faith.

If that is the case—if the grace of justification cannot be augmented or diminished—why then does Peter speak about a multiplication of grace and peace? He does so because the grace of justification is not the only grace that we receive from God. As Paul tells us, "the righteousness of God is revealed from faith to faith" (Rom. 1:17). Although our justification can never be increased, our faith certainly can. The strength of our faith is a fragile thing. It is something that must be fed daily by what we call the "means of grace." Through the study of God's Word, prayer, worship, and fellowship, God fortifies our faith and our sanctification. Certainly sanctification can and must increase as we continue our pilgrimage in faith, but all of God's grace is unmerited by us.

Sufficient Knowledge

Peter links the multiplication of grace and peace to the knowledge of God, which is the central thesis of this epistle. As we noted earlier, one of the obvious threats to the early Christian church was brought by the Gnostic heretics, who claimed to have a superior knowledge. These heretics believed that they had a higher knowledge than that conveyed by the Apostles. Over against the heretical view of knowledge, Peter talks about true knowledge, the knowledge that comes from God, which is, perhaps, one of the most important—if not *the* most important—grace that He disposes upon His people. God gives us knowledge that comes to us from Himself.

The one excuse that will never stand before the bar of God's judgment is that we have not been given enough clear knowledge of God. In fact, it is tragic that we find people with advanced degrees, who, in one sense, have been educated beyond their intelligence. Although they have been exposed to many dimensions of human education, they live their lives as if they were ignorant of the things of God. The fact that God has not kept us in the dark but has been pleased to manifest His being clearly through the things that are made is grace. God did not owe His creatures His self-revelation. He could have made us and walked away and remained in shadow, obscurity, and darkness, giving us no knowledge of Himself. However, He has given us not only knowledge of Himself in creation, which we call "general reve-lation," but He has also given us His Word. Our God is not silent. Though we may not see Him, we hear from Him in His Word. I never cease to be amazed at why so few professing Christians have a passion to know God in His Word.

Not many years ago, a woman wrote a novel about a new convert to Christianity. This new convert wanted to feel the full weight of the teach-ing of sacred Scripture, particularly in the New Testament, so he had his secretary type out the epistles of the New Testament verbatim, one at a time, and then had them sent through the mail to himself, as if he were the one addressed in each epistle. The man received the epistles he had mailed to himself and then read them as if each had been written just for him. If God sent you a letter in the mail, and you went to the mailbox and saw your name on the front of the envelope and the sender being God Himself, you would not throw it away or put it on the shelf to collect dust. If you got a letter written to you personally from God, you would read it repeatedly until you knew every word and every subtle nuance in the text, because you were being informed by a knowledge that comes from God Himself. I am firmly convinced that we have this very thing in sacred Scripture, which is why we never graduate from the school of Christ. We are to be always learning more deeply, more carefully, and hopefully more accurately the things that are contained in this Word.

The Importance of Doctrine

In Jesus' High Priestly Prayer, He prayed for the sanctification of His disciples and of all who would believe through their testimony, which includes you and me. Our Lord prayed, "Sanctify them by Your truth. Your word is truth" (John 17:17). That is what Peter is telling us at the very beginning of this epistle.

Some time ago, I attended a Together for the Gospel Conference in Louisville, Kentucky, that was attended by five thousand pastors. One man gave an address on the importance of doctrine. He confronted the audience with passage after passage from the New Testament that emphasize the importance of doctrine. Basically, that is what the Bible is—the teaching of doctrine. Since that is the case, why do professing Christians say that doctrine does not matter? If you want to have a relationship with Christ, the first question you have to answer is this: "Who is He?" The way in which you understand the person of Jesus is a matter of doctrine. As the speaker pointed out, all Christians are theologians, whether they want to be or not, because every Christian has a theology. The question is not whether we will have a theology but whether the one we have is sound or false. The Bible has not been given to us to make us feel good but to reveal the truth of God to us. It is not an abstract exercise in intellectual pursuit; the Word has been given to us that we might know God and the Savior in the fullness of His glory.

I have spent my life studying theology. I wish I had ten lifetimes to study theology, because it pertains to the knowledge of God. The more we learn of God, the more we know Him, and the greater capacity we have to love Him. There are people who have the creeds in their head but no love in their heart, and I do not understand how that can be. For them, theology has been established as a defense against the piercing of the soul by God, but that is not what the Word was given for. It was given to define for us who Jesus is. For those who say they are concerned only with relationships, how do they determine what a good relationship looks like? How do they determine what a healthy relationship is except by the truth that God gives that teaches us what true relationship should mean?

As his divine power has given to us all things that pertain to life and godliness, through the knowledge of Him who called us by glory and virtue (v. 3). We have already determined that Peter's greeting was given to those who had obtained like precious faith and that the faith we have did not come from our flesh but as a gift from God. Peter hinted at that in the second part of verse 1, and here in verse 3 whatever was left in ambiguity earlier is made abundantly clear.

The most frequent Greek word in the New Testament for "power" is *dunamis*, from which we get the English word *dynamite*. The power that God works in our soul to bring us to faith is dynamite. It is an overwhelming power. It is no human potentiality realized by the flesh but, as Peter tells us, a divine and supernatural work of God in the soul. Regeneration is a result of the immediate, supernatural work of God in our soul, a work that only God can bring to pass. If you are a believer in Christ, if you have an inclination toward the things of God, at some point in your life you encountered the touch of the divine in your soul. That inclination did not arise from your bosom. It came from the Spirit of God—divine power through the knowledge of the One who called us—and He called us by His glory, by His majestic power. By His righteous activity He has made us alive.

Precious Promises

. . . by which have been given to us exceedingly great and precious promises, that through these you may be partakers of the divine nature, having escaped the corruption that is in the world through lust (v. 4). We considered the word "precious" earlier. What makes something precious? We make distinctions in the common areas of life between rocks and gems and between gems and precious gems, and that distinction has to do with the degrees of value and beauty found in various natural substances. When Vesta and I reached the milestone of our twenty-fifth wedding anniversary, I wanted to buy her something special. I talked to a friend who knew a jeweler, and I asked my friend if he could get this jeweler to find me a diamond suitable to give my bride on our twenty-fifth anniversary. The jeweler came to Orlando from New York, and he opened up a package and displayed a diamond, saying, "I've been called upon to rate thousands of diamonds, and I have never rated a diamond as flawless. I am convinced that within the contours of every precious gem, there must be a flaw. However, I have not been able to detect a flaw in this diamond, so I have rated it 'museum quality.'" That was just what I wanted for my wife. She does not have to look hard to find flaws in me, but she has to look hard to find one in her ring, because it is precious.

There are no flaws in the righteousness of Jesus. There are no blemishes in the Lamb who was slain. That is why, during our first five minutes in heaven, I think we will hear the elders singing, "Worthy is the Lamb who was slain to receive honor and glory, dominion and power." He is precious, and His preciousness is a part of Peter's vocabulary.

Jesus said to the Tempter, "Man shall not live by bread alone, but by every word that proceeds from the mouth of God" (Matt. 4:4; Luke 4:4). There are times in the routine of daily life that we scarcely even think about the promises of God, but when our lives are on the line and we can find no way out of trouble, all we have left to hold onto are the promises of God. Yet what greater possession could we have in those times than the promises that Peter speaks about here that are great and precious?

Let us consider the context in which Peter is writing this epistle. It is his swan song. Second Peter is to the Petrine literature what 2 Timothy was to the corpus of the Apostle Paul. At the end of 2 Timothy, Paul tells his beloved disciple that he is ready to be poured out, and he knows that his life is soon to be taken from him. Likewise, Peter announces his imminent departure from the world. At times like that, people begin to think of the promises of God. "Yea, though I walk through the valley of the shadow of death, I will fear no evil; for You are with me" (Ps. 23:4). How can we be afraid of anything if we know that God is with us? That is a precious promise, one worthy to clutch to our bosoms and to die for.

Second Peter 1:4 was greatly misunderstood in the Patristic period of church history. Many of the early theologians believed that Peter was teaching that what happens to us in our salvation ultimately is deification, that salvation makes us like God, and that the temptation given by the Serpent in Eden is fulfilled in our redemption. However, we are creatures now, and we will always be creatures. We will never be gods, because even God cannot make another god. Any god that God could make would, by definition, have a beginning and would therefore be finite, dependent upon the one eternal God for its very existence. God cannot transfer deity to a creature.

I will never forget my first visit to the Capitol of the United States of America. I went into the rotunda, and the guide pointed my gaze to the ceiling on which is a painting of George Washington, the father of our country, being received among the gods. The title of the painting is the *Apotheosis of George Washington. Apotheosis* means "deification," an idea that I cannot imagine anyone would have felt more repugnance about than Washington himself. When Peter says that we are partakers of the divine nature, he is saying that if we are in Christ, then God the Holy Spirit has taken up residence in us. Insofar as we are indwelt by the Holy Spirit, we participate or partake. We do not become divine, but we partake of the presence of God in our very souls.

Several years ago Paul Crouch announced to America on television that, in his view, any person indwelt by the Holy Spirit is as much the son of God as Jesus Himself. A friend of mine wrote a polite letter to Paul Crouch and asked him to retract that statement and pointed out how utterly heretical it was. On the next broadcast, Crouch held up the letter and said, "I just received a letter from a theologian, and he didn't like what I said in my last message, but I will say it again: if you are indwelt by the Holy Spirit, you are as much the incarnation of God as was Jesus Christ." God has one incarnate Son, and though we are indwelt by His Holy Spirit, and by God's grace we are able to partake of His presence, let us not ever deceive ourselves into thinking that we are little gods or, even worse, big gods. It is the grace of God that keeps us from deity.

26

GIVING ALL DILIGENCE

2 Peter 1:5–11

But also for this very reason, giving all diligence, add to your faith virtue, to virtue knowledge, to knowledge self-control, to self-control perseverance, to perseverance godliness, to godliness brotherly kindness, and to brotherly kindness love. For if these things are yours and abound, you will be neither barren nor unfruitful in the knowledge of our Lord Jesus Christ. For he who lacks these things is shortsighted, even to blindness, and has forgotten that he was cleansed from his old sins. Therefore, brethren, be even more diligent to make your call and election sure, for if you do these things you will never stumble; for so an entrance will be supplied to you abundantly into the everlasting kingdom of our Lord and Savior Jesus Christ.

Peter has already spoken about the glorious majesty of the God who has called us by glory and virtue and has given us exceedingly great and precious promises. He then goes on to say, **But also for this very reason, giving all diligence, add to your faith virtue, to virtue knowledge, to knowledge self-control, to self-control perseverance, to perseverance godliness, to godliness brotherly kindness, and to brotherly kindness love. For if these things are yours and abound, you will be neither barren nor unfruitful in the knowledge of our Lord Jesus Christ** (vv. 5–8). Because of what God has done for us, we ought to be "giving all diligence." Before important decisions are made or property is exchanged in the business world, it is incumbent upon those in positions of authority to do what is commonly called "due diligence." To give due diligence is to pay close attention to the matter at hand. Peter uses that word to call us to a posture of diligence as we look into the things of God. Our approach to learning of God is not to be done in a frivolous, capricious, or cavalier manner. With earnest application, careful study, and inquiry, we are to apply ourselves diligently to every word that has proceeded from God's mouth.

Expanding on this diligence, Peter gives us a long list of things that we are to seek diligently. As we look at the list, we cannot help but notice the similarity to lists set forth by the Apostle Paul, most notably the list we call the "fruit of the Spirit" (Gal. 5:22–23). The virtues that follow upon faith are to be manifest in the Christian life. They define for us the very essence of righteousness and true spirituality.

This, of course, should go without saying, but in every generation of Christians, there have been widespread attempts not only to ignore the virtues set forth in sacred Scripture but to supplant them with something far less demanding. There are churches that project a profile of a Christian as someone who does not dance, go to movies, or drink and smoke, as if these were major matters in the kingdom of God. It is much easier to refrain from moviegoing than to acquire a character known for patience, kindness, and meekness. We should be most diligent to acquire the virtues set forth in Scripture.

As we noted earlier, the great enemy threatening the church to which Peter was writing was likely the Gnostic heresy. Gnostics claimed to have a superior type of knowledge above and beyond that possessed by the Apostles, a knowledge gained through a direct mystical perception rather than by diligent thinking. Throughout this epistle Peter brings us back to the acquisition of true knowledge, the true *gnosis*, which is revealed by God and found in His Word. Peter says that those who possess these virtues will not be barren or unfruitful in the knowledge of our Lord Jesus Christ.

Diligent in Knowledge

True knowledge of the things of God is not satisfied with mere abstract proposition but is equipped for virtue. We are to be diligent to seek the knowledge of God—not to get a degree in theology, not to receive the accolades of men, not to be known for our intelligence, but to learn from God and gain the mind of Christ. **For he who lacks these things is shortsighted,**

even to blindness, and has forgotten that he was cleansed from his old sins (v. 9).

I once heard a professor say, "The problem with our culture today is that we have a penurious epistemology that tends to be myopic." A penurious epistemology is a poverty-stricken view of knowledge. It is bankrupt, and it tends to be myopic, which is a more technical term for "nearsighted." It is precisely the problem of myopia that Peter is addressing here. He who lacks these things is shortsighted, even to blindness.

The image of blindness is used repeatedly in the Word of God to describe the natural tendency of those who live in darkness and will not have God in their thoughts. Proclaiming to be wise, such people become fools because their minds are darkened (Rom. 1:21–22). Many people with 20/20 vision are blind to the things of God. We know they are blind because their lives are barren of the fruit of the Spirit and of the virtues that Peter lists here. However, Peter directs this critique not to pagans but to Christians, who can become shortsighted because they forget that they were cleansed from their sins.

David understood the tendency to forget when he wrote, "Bless the LORD, O my soul, and forget not all His benefits" (Ps. 103:2). Think back to the first time you realized that God had forgiven your sin. Recall what that did for you, the freedom it brought to your soul, the peace that came to your conscience, and the joy that came to your heart. Yet how easy it is to forget that God has forgiven us and in Christ has made us clean.

Diligent in Assurance

In his conclusion to these remarks Peter comes to an important teaching that drips theology. **Therefore, brethren, be even more diligent to make your call and election sure, for if you do these things you will never stumble** (v. 10). Peter has called believers to be diligent, industrious, and careful to add virtue to faith, along with perseverance, kindness, and brotherly love, so that they will not be barren or fruitless. Yet he wants believers to be even more diligent about something else. There is an even greater priority, and that is the doctrine of election—not in the abstract but with respect to your own person. The most important question you need answered in your lifetime is this: am I numbered among the elect?

There are multitudes of professing Christians who do not worry about that question because they do not believe in election. In fact, such people appeal to a verse found later in this same epistle to deny the doctrine of election: "The Lord is . . . not willing that any should perish" (3:9). If it is true that God is unwilling that anyone should perish, then who needs to worry about election? We do, because Peter is saying that we need to be all the more diligent to make our calling and election sure.

Peter's first epistle was addressed to the elect. In fact, the doctrine of election permeates both of Peter's epistles. Therefore, we cannot dismiss the doctrine to the machinations of the mind of the Apostle Paul or even to Jesus Himself. It is everywhere on virtually every page of the New Testament. Since that is the case, what does Peter mean when he says we are to be all the more diligent to make our calling and election sure? Many commentators interpret this text to mean that although God has elected to save certain people, their election is not certain until they respond to the call of God; in other words, unless or until people make such a response, their election remains uncertain.

We can do nothing to make an eternal decree of God sure. When God chooses to save someone, his or her election is absolutely certain. God does not choose to save people and then let them decide. There would be no election if that were the case. People would thereby be electing themselves with God standing by as an impotent spectator. If God chooses to elect someone, that election must come to pass. Nothing in heaven or on earth can frustrate the sovereign will of God.

When we argue about this sort of thing, it only exposes how little we know about the nature and character of God. We tend to think of God the way we describe ourselves. As creatures, we change our mind all the time. We make decisions and then reverse them when we get information that we lacked previously or when someone tells us that our decisions were bad; but God is not like that. He does not make foolish decisions that have to be corrected. Obviously, therefore, making our calling and election sure is not making what God has decreed a sure thing. It is a sure thing already. Our diligence can never change something decreed by God.

The question is, for whom is calling and election to be made sure? In this world we can never know for sure that we are not elect, because even though we are not in faith at the present moment, we do not know what tomorrow will bring. We do not know that maybe on our deathbed God will bring us to faith and our election will be realized. We cannot know for sure that we are not elect, but we can know for sure that we are elect. So, Peter is talking about assurance of salvation or the assurance of election.

There are four types of people with respect to the assurance of salvation: (1) unsaved people who know they are not saved; (2) saved people who are unsure if they are saved; (3) saved people who know they are saved; and

(4) unsaved people who are sure they are saved. So, if you are sure that you are saved, how do you know that you are not really unsaved? Jesus gave a warning at the end of the Sermon on the Mount, saying, "Many will say to Me in that day, 'Lord, Lord, have we not prophesied in Your name, cast out demons in Your name, and done many wonders in Your name?' And then I will declare to them, 'I never knew you; depart from Me, you who practice lawlessness!'" (Matt. 7:22–23).

How can we tell the difference between a genuine surety of salvation and a false surety, or, to ask it another way, how can people be unsaved yet believe that they are saved? The first and most obvious reason that people believe they are saved when they are not saved is that they have a defective understanding of salvation. When my son was six years old, I said to him, "If you were to die and stand before God, and God were to say to you, 'Why should I let you into heaven?' what would you say?" My son replied, "I would tell God to let me into heaven because I am dead." He was making a theological assumption of the doctrine of justification by death. He believed at that age that everybody who dies go to heaven. If you believe that every human being who dies is saved, then you will come to the conclusion that you are in a state of salvation. However, if not everyone is saved, then the fact that you are a human being cannot give you any legitimate assurance of salvation.

There are also multitudes who earnestly believe that they are saved by trying to live a good life. They go to church, teach Sunday school, or serve as deacon or elder, and they think that such service saves them. They consider that they have not committed murder or adultery and conclude that they are good and will therefore go to heaven. They have not read the Scripture that says, "By the works of the law no flesh shall be justified" (Gal. 2:16). Their assurance of salvation is false.

False assurance can come to those who lack a correct understanding of how one enters into a state of salvation. False assurance can also come to those who point to a time when they responded to an altar call, or signed a pledge card, or prayed the Sinner's Prayer. Nobody has ever been saved by a profession of faith; you must possess it as well as profess it. We need to consider whether we love Jesus. We certainly do not love Him perfectly or as much as we ought to love Him. The question is whether we have any real affection for Jesus as He is portrayed in the New Testament. We wish we did not disobey Him as much as we do, but we know that we have affection for Him in our heart. This is where our theology is so important. The natural person, the unregenerate, never has an ounce of affection in his heart for God. It is impossible to have any love for Christ unless first the Holy Spirit has changed the disposition of our soul, because by nature not only do we not love Him, but we cannot love Him. Only if we are born of the Spirit is a love for the biblical Christ awakened in us.

Some who are truly saved are afraid that they might lose their salvation. However, if they really have it, they will never lose it; if they lose it, they never had it. The only way we can be born again is if the Holy Spirit changes the disposition of our heart, and the only way that the Holy Spirit changes the disposition of our heart is if He calls us internally by the power of His might. The only way He will do that is if He has elected us to that calling. There are no flaws in God's eternal decrees, so if you have the slightest true affection for Jesus, then your assurance is solid. One of the best ways of gaining assurance of salvation is by understanding what salvation requires, of what it consists, and how it comes to pass. That is why learning theology has such practical implications.

Abundant Supply

If you do these things, Peter says—that is, if you are diligent to make your call and election sure—you will never stumble, **for so an entrance will be supplied to you abundantly into the everlasting kingdom of our Lord and Savior Jesus Christ** (v. 11). Regeneration is *monergistic*, which means that it is not a joint effort between you and God. You cannot cause yourself to be born again. You cannot do anything to help yourself to be born again. Your rebirth is totally dependent upon the sole working of the Holy Spirit, who, in His sovereign and immediate power, raises you from spiritual death. You are utterly, completely passive in that action. However, from that moment until you die, the progress of your Christian life is *synergistic*, which means that it involves a cooperation between you and God. The Apostle Paul tells us, "Work out your own salvation with fear and trembling; for it is God who works in you both to will and to do for His good pleasure" (Phil. 2:12–13). Everything after our rebirth is a cooperative activity.

Peter is saying that if you want to have a fruitful Christian life, if you want to grow in grace, if you want to move forward in your sanctification, then make sure of your election early in your Christian walk. Those who are sure with the sound reasons of assurance are unlike those who are tossed to and fro with every wind of doctrine. Assurance keeps us from being double-minded people who are up one day and down the next. Those with assurance know that their destiny has been settled from the foundation of the world.

Those who argue against election and predestination miss out on the sweetness of these doctrines. To know that your final destination is in God's hands is of great value in the Christian life. The irony is that the more sure you are, the more likely you are to bear fruit in abundance. The purest flower in God's garden is the tulip—*T* for total depravity, *U* for unconditional election, *L* for limited atonement, *I* for irresistible grace, and *P* for perseverance of the saints. The favorite flower of our Arminian friends is the daisy, because the semi-Pelagian never knows for sure. He pulls the petals of the daisy one at a time, saying, "He loves me. He loves me not. He loves me. He loves me not." Such thinking cannot provide hope about our eternal destiny, but when we know the truth of election and the efficacy of God's calling in our soul, the matter is settled, and we begin to bring forth fruit in season, being, as the psalmist said, "like a tree planted by the rivers of water, that brings forth its fruit in its season" (Ps. 1:3).

God grant that it will be so with us.

27

EYEWITNESS OF HIS MAJESTY

2 Peter 1:12–18

For this reason I will not be negligent to remind you always of these things, though you know and are established in the present truth. Yes, I think it is right, as long as I am in this tent, to stir you up by reminding you, knowing that shortly I must put off my tent, just as our Lord Jesus Christ showed me. Moreover I will be careful to ensure that you always have a reminder of these things after my decease. For we did not follow cunningly devised fables when we made known to you the power and coming of our Lord Jesus Christ, but were eyewitnesses of His majesty. For He received from God the Father honor and glory when such a voice came to Him from the Excellent Glory: "This is My beloved Son, in whom I am well pleased." And we heard this voice which came from heaven when we were with Him on the holy mountain.

This passage begins with Peter giving an explanation for the importance of our making our calling and election sure, that we may be fully enabled to work out our sanctification, manifesting the various fruit of the Spirit. The way in which Peter emphasizes these things is once again similar to the emphasis found in the writings of the Apostle Paul. Scripture presents some of its themes repeatedly. We find that to be true in the four

Gospels, in which much of the content is repeated. Why is that? We get a clue to the answer in what Peter says here: **For this reason I will not be negligent to remind you always of these things, though you know and are established in the present truth** (v. 12). Peter's readers know the things he is writing about, and not only do they know them, but they also are firmly established in them. Yet Peter finds it necessary to be repetitive, to remind people of the truths of which they are already aware.

Musing on this passage, I was reminded of my comprehensive exams in college. Those particular exams covered the content of all the courses I had taken in my college major, philosophy. During those four years of schooling, I had gone through the scope of Western philosophy beginning before Plato, advancing through the Middle Ages, and finally to the Modern period. I studied various disciplines in philosophy, such as aesthetics, ethics, and logic. I was apprehensive about those comps, because I was going to be examined on material that I had studied three years earlier; it was no longer fresh in my mind. However, reviewing all the material for that final comprehensive exam was extremely beneficial. It served as an epiphany of sorts because all that I had studied in pieces then fit together. I realized then that we learn through repetition.

That is what Peter is saying here. If he failed to repeat what his readers had already learned, he would be guilty of negligence. He reminds his readers of what they already know because the spirit is willing and the flesh is weak, and no sooner do we learn something about the things of God than we become at ease in Zion. We begin to rest on our laurels and lose any sense of urgency about pressing forward into the kingdom of God. Perhaps the Apostle was thinking of his own pathetic experience. Surely he never forgot the ignominy of his denial of Jesus, the shame that came with it after he had declared, shortly after the transfiguration, that he would never deny Christ. No sooner had he made that emphatic claim than that is exactly what he did—not once, not twice, but three times. Later, Jesus came to Peter after the resurrection and asked him three times if Peter loved Him, and after each affirmation of Peter's love, Jesus told him to care for His sheep. Jesus wanted to burn that into the memory of His Apostle. After our Lord's departure, Peter's primary vocation was to feed the Lord's sheep. We see from that why we have to hear these truths repeatedly.

Death Approaching
Yes, I think it is right, as long as I am in this tent, to stir you up by reminding you (v. 13). The word translated "stir you up" was used when

someone had to be rousted from sleep. In our slumber we are unconscious of holy things. My mentor John Gerstner would say, upon hearing a small theological error from someone who knew better, "Homer nodded." Gerstner was thinking of the errors in Homer's work that resemble "nods," as if he had drifted off to sleep while writing. Peter is saying that so long as he is alive, he will continue to issue wake-up calls. He knows he needs to rouse his readers from slumber and call them to vigilance in working out their faith.

In this passage, as the Apostle Paul did in his second letter to his beloved Timothy, Peter announces his imminent departure from the world. He realizes that his days are growing short; his death is at hand. He had been ministering for many years, yet now the urgency is heightened because he is about to die. Peter refers to his body not as a house but as a tent, **knowing that shortly I must put off my tent, just as our Lord Jesus Christ showed me** (v. 14). He was writing to Jewish people who understood the transiency of their history. They were a semi-nomadic people, always looking for a place where they could have roots—permanence and stability. Yet in the entire history of Israel, the *pax Israeli*, or peace of Israel, has lasted in toto less than one hundred years. It has been a nation always in upheaval, always in transit, never able to send down roots. It is fitting that this Jewish man, writing to other Jews, looked at his body not as a permanent dwelling but as a tent.

When people in the Old Testament moved from place to place, they encamped according to tribe in a circle, and at the center of that circle was the tabernacle, the meeting place. That is why the psalmist wrote that God is in the midst of her (Ps. 46:5). When it was time to move on, when the Shekinah cloud moved, the people loosened the pegs and ropes that kept the tabernacle in an upright position, folded the tent, and moved forward. Living in tents is normally not how we choose to live, but the metaphor indicates that the body that houses our soul is not permanent but transient. Peter is saying that it is time for him to pull up the stakes and move. He did not see himself passing out of existence but moving from one place to another. He was about to pack up his tent and go home.

Verse 14 has been translated and interpreted in different ways historically. One interpretation is that Peter was referencing the example of Jesus, who showed His disciples not only how to live but also how to die. A greater number of exegetes argue that the force of this text is not that Jesus showed Peter how to die but that Jesus had revealed to him that the time of His death was near. We know that Peter died in the decade of the sixties, presumably in Rome under the persecution of Nero. The great fire of Rome that occurred in Nero's reign burned down a major section of the city. There is evidence,

although not conclusive proof, that Nero himself set the fire in an attempt
to clear out some slum land to make room for his new, magnificent palace.
The fire got out of control, however, and burned more than he had anticipated, and looking for a scapegoat, he blamed the fire on the Christians.
Many Christians became human torches in Nero's gardens.

Nero died in A.D. 68, so in all probability Peter died as did Paul somewhere around A.D. 65. Paul, on the other hand, was beheaded, which was
the normal form of execution for Roman citizens.

Majesty, Not Myth

**Moreover I will be careful to ensure that you always have a
reminder of these things after my decease** (v. 15). Again Peter reminds
his readers of the things of God and the truths of the gospel. Some commentators think that the reminder to which Peter refers here is this very epistle.
When the Apostle Paul was removed from active ministry and thrown into
prison, he could do little but write letters. Yet the greatest impact he made
on the world was not through his missionary journeys but through his pen.
Maybe Peter was thinking about that here, and if so, he was saying that the
purpose of this epistle was to leave them a reminder of his teaching after
he was gone.

As I mentioned earlier, some skeptics do not believe that Peter wrote this
epistle, but the early church father Irenaeus did. Irenaeus thought that Peter
here was referencing not this epistle but the Gospel of Mark, in which Mark
basically served as a secretary for Peter. Whichever it was, Peter was able to
make certain that even to this day we have a reminder of these things.

Verse 16 changes the basic thought of the text, although it is not unrelated
to what has gone before it. **For we did not follow cunningly devised
fables when we made known to you the power and coming of our
Lord Jesus Christ, but were eyewitnesses of His majesty** (v. 16).
Here Peter makes an important declaration. He wants to explain what his
message is *not* and where it has *not* come from before he speaks about what it
is and where it has come from. Some translations render, "We do not teach
cunning myths, but we declare to you what we have seen with our eyes and
what we have heard with our ears." Some of the Gospel writers make the
same declaration, that they are passing on in their writings not folklore but
things of which they had firsthand experience. Here Peter strongly negates
any hint that the apostolic message is rooted in mythology.

One of the most influential New Testament scholars in the twentieth century was Rudolf Bultmann. He was noted for his program of demythologizing

the New Testament. Bultmann created a blitzkrieg in the New Testament world, and for decades New Testament scholars were scrambling to complete the work of removing myth from the text of Scripture. Peter is saying that the Word of God has already been demythologized. It is not based on myths but on sober, historical reality.

During my first year of teaching college, I had a friend on the faculty in the English department. He taught an overview course on classical literature, while I taught theology and biblical studies. The English teacher took great pains to debunk the New Testament as perpetrating the same myths that were found in Greek and Roman mythology. I kept hearing this from his students, so one day I said to this English professor, "You've been quick to point out all the similarities you can find between the New Testament and Ovid's *Metamorphosis*, but can you tell me the difference between the Greek view of history and the Hebrew view of history?" He looked at me like a deer caught in headlights, because he did not know. I reminded him of grade school education, when students learn elementary biology and the fundamental principles of taxonomy, in which living things are divided into kingdoms and species. In the study of taxonomy, creatures are grouped according to their similarities, but when that is complete, the task of science is only halfway done; these same creatures also must be grouped according to their differences. This is, in fact, how language emerges.

It is also how the scientific enterprise was begun in the garden of Eden. When God called Adam and Eve to name the animals, they were involved in taxonomy. All science is involved in taxonomy, as is the medical field. When someone has a stomachache, a doctor does not automatically prescribe aspirin or milk of magnesia. A responsible physician will want to get more specific and consider the differences between stomach cancer and indigestion.

I told my fellow professor that if he did not know the difference between the Greek understanding of history, which is cyclical, and the Hebrew understanding, which is linear, he would be unable to point out to his students that the Hebrew faith was based on what they were convinced happened in time and space, not on some mythical Mount Olympus. The Greeks and the Romans did not care whether their gods really existed. They were myths, and they knew they were myths.

Peter was not ready to put off his mortal tent for a myth but for that which he had witnessed. When Paul gave his case for the resurrection, he showed first the biblical evidence, which should have been enough, but then he went on to recite the appearances of Jesus to the Twelve, then to five hundred others, and finally, Paul said, "He was seen by me also, as by one born out of due time" (1 Cor. 15:8). Paul had seen Him and heard His voice. Just so, when Peter writes that he was an eyewitness of Jesus' majesty, it is not difficult to discern what specific event he was referencing.

On the Holy Mountain

For He received from God the Father honor and glory when such a voice came to Him from the Excellent Glory: "This is My beloved Son, in whom I am well pleased." And we heard this voice which came from heaven when we were with Him on the holy mountain (vv. 17–18). John wrote, "The Word became flesh and dwelt among us, and we beheld His glory, the glory as of the only begotten of the Father, full of grace and truth" (John 1:14). John and Peter both reference the event that took place on the Mount of Transfiguration.

On the occasion of the transfiguration, Jesus had been preparing His disciples to return to Jerusalem, where Jesus was to be handed over and killed. He went aside with the inner circle of the disciples—Peter, James, and John—and suddenly He was transfigured in front of them. The Greek word is *metamorphosis*. A profound change instantly came over the countenance of Jesus. His face became radiant, as bright as the sun, and His clothes were whiter than any fuller or clothes washer could make them. Before their very eyes they saw this radiance of divine glory shining from Christ. The incarnation was, in a real sense, a veil of the divine nature of Christ.

When Moses was on the mountain he asked God to let him see His face. God said, "You cannot see My face; for no man shall see Me, and live. . . . Here is a place by Me, and you shall stand on the rock. So it shall be, while My glory passes by, that I will put you in the cleft of the rock, and will cover you with My hand while I pass by. Then I will take away My hand, and you shall see My back; but My face shall not be seen" (Ex. 33:20–23). When Moses had that momentary view of the back of God, Moses' face began to shine with an intensity that no human countenance had ever exhibited before. Moses' face shone with a reflection of the divine glory that had just walked by him. God's glory was bouncing off the skin of Moses, as it were, and it took quite a few days for that radiance to fade away. However, on the Mount of Transfiguration, the shining countenance of Christ was not reflected glory but a glory bursting from His very deity. When that cloud enveloped Peter, James, and John, they were terrified, and they heard a voice from heaven say, "This is My beloved Son, in whom I am well pleased. Hear Him!" (Matt. 17:5; cf. Mark 9:7; Luke 9:35). In this epistle Peter is pointing out that he, James, and John had seen that. They had heard the voice of

God audibly on that holy mountain. The Apostles were not relaying legends, fables, or myths but the sober truth of what they had seen in the person of the Lord Jesus Christ.

An anthem written by a friend of mine contains the lyrics, "Men of Galilee, why are you standing here gazing into heaven?" They were gazing into heaven on the mount of ascension because when Jesus left, He was lifted up in the cloud of glory, the Shekinah cloud that through the ages always manifested the sacred presence of God. Those things, Peter says, are too precious to forget, so he is reminding his readers of them before he dies. He had seen and heard them, so he was not worried about putting off his tent. His bags were packed and he was ready to go.

28

A LIGHT THAT SHINES

2 Peter 1:19–21

And so we have the prophetic word confirmed, which you do well to heed as a light that shines in a dark place, until the day dawns and the morning star rises in your hearts; knowing this first, that no prophecy of Scripture is of any private interpretation, for prophecy never came by the will of man, but holy men of God spoke as they were moved by the Holy Spirit.

Peter has just finished making reference to his presence on the Mount of Transfiguration, where he was an eyewitness to the unveiled glory of Christ. In the midst of that vision of loveliness, not only was Peter given a magnificent view of the glory of Jesus, but he also heard the word of God pronounced audibly from heaven. Now Peter moves to a consideration of the written Word of God with special emphasis on the prophetic content of the Old Testament: **And so we have the prophetic word confirmed, which you do well to heed as a light that shines in a dark place, until the day dawns and the morning star rises in your hearts** (v. 19).

The Apostles did not need to see the prophetic word of the Old Testament confirmed by what they would learn in the New Testament era. Peter, as with all the Jews of his day, was already convinced of the full authority of the Scriptures of the Old Testament. The context of verse 19 is somewhat encumbered and difficult to unpack, but basically Peter is declaring that what they had heard audibly on the Mount of Transfiguration is confirmed by the Prophets. This is a common motif in the New Testament, that the truth of the New Testament is declared as it represents a fulfillment of something in the Old Testament.

I stress that point, because there is a tendency in the church today to treat the Old Testament lightly, as if we could easily rid ourselves of it and focus merely on the writings of the New Testament. We cannot really understand the New Testament apart from the Old Testament. Augustine said, "The New Testament is in the Old Testament concealed, the Old Testament is in the New Testament revealed." There is an inseparable bonding between the two Testaments. The Old Testament is virtually the autobiography of God. Today there is a lack of a sense of the greatness of God, which, I believe, is linked to the church's ignorance of that autobiography, of God's self-revelation that comes to us in the pages of the Old Testament.

A Light in Darkness

Peter gives an admonition to his readers, which include us by extension, that believers must heed the prophetic Word of God and regard it as a light that shines in a dark place, by which Peter means this fallen world. John wrote, "In Him was life, and the life was the light of men. And the light shines in the darkness, and the darkness did not comprehend it" (John 1:4–5). At the appearance of Christ, His arrival as the incarnate Word of God, the powers of darkness were not able to extinguish that light. Beyond the broader context of a world plunged into darkness, the Bible speaks specifically of people who prefer darkness to light, those who refuse to recognize the light that God manifests in this world and through His Word and have been favorably inclined to live in the dark. As a result, God has given us over in our fallen condition, as it were, to a reprobate mind, and our foolish minds have been darkened.

This metaphor of darkness is applied biblically to the condition of our mind. This is not a matter of one's education but of the condition of one's heart, which is hostile by nature to the light of God. We are by nature children of darkness, so Peter here gives this warning that when the light comes and shines in the darkness, we do well to heed it. There is nothing more foolish than refusing light that comes to us from the source of all truth.

We do well to heed this light that shines in a dark place, "until the day dawns and the morning star rises in [our] hearts." Commentators struggle with exactly what Peter had in mind here. Some say it means that we are to give heed to the light by which we have been illumined until the ultimate victory of light over darkness, which will occur at the consummation of the kingdom of God when Christ shall appear in the fullness of His glory. At such time there will be the final vanquishing of every pocket and corner of darkness in this world. That might be what Peter was talking about, but since nobody will be able to miss it when it comes, Peter cannot be talking about opening our eyes to something but rather about a light that illumines the heart. I am not sure of the exact nature of Peter's reference.

We do know the identity of the morning star in Scripture. If we go back to the prophecies of Balaam, we find this in his fourth oracle: "I see Him, but not now; I behold Him, but not near; a Star shall come out of Jacob; a Scepter shall rise out of Israel, and batter the brow of Moab, and destroy all the sons of tumult" (Num. 24:17). This section of the prophecy of Balaam was treasured in the hearts of Jewish people, because they saw in it the promised Messiah, who would be the Star coming out of Jacob and the One given the scepter.

In the final benediction that Jacob gave to his sons, he said, "The scepter shall not depart from Judah" (Gen. 49:10). The scepter is the symbol of royalty, the sign of authority of the king, and that scepter of kingship is promised to the One who will come from the tribe of Judah, from which comes David and then David's greater Son, our Lord Himself.

The Morning Star

At the end of the Bible, in the last chapter of the New Testament, we read Jesus' words that conclude the revelation that He had given to the Apostle John during John's exile on the isle of Patmos: "I, Jesus, have sent My angel to testify to you these things in the churches. I am the Root and the Off-spring of David, the Bright and Morning Star" (Rev. 22:16). This is one of the loveliest titles for Jesus that we find in the New Testament—the Bright and Morning Star.

Peter speaks of the rising of that morning star in our hearts when the day dawns. Is he referencing the end of the age, or has this already happened? We understand that when the Word of God is embraced by those who are children of darkness by nature, it is because the Holy Spirit has penetrated that darkness and illumined their minds to give them eyes to see. When we are given spiritual eyes to see, we wonder how we ever missed it. When we get a clear understanding of the nature of Jesus, it happens because the Holy Spirit brings light to our heart. It does not happen naturally.

There is an apparent contradiction in Paul's writings. Paul wrote that through nature, through the things that are made, God clearly reveals Himself to all people, but all people have suppressed that revelation and are left without excuse. The final element of the indictment comes down as the Apostle writes that they "exchanged the truth of God for the lie, and worshiped and served the creature rather than the Creator, who is blessed forever. Amen" (Rom. 1:25). That indictment, which Paul gives as background for the vital importance of the gospel, makes clear that God is known through His general revelation, His revelation of nature, by every creature. Every person knows of the existence of God. Paul does not mean that every person will affirm the existence of God or welcome that knowledge; on the contrary, the fundamental sin of man is the refusal to acknowledge what he knows to be true. We know the eternal power and deity of God through His self-revelation in nature, but we refuse to acknowledge it. However, when Paul writes to the Corinthians, he says that the things of God are not known by men. Only as they are revealed by the Spirit of God can God be known.

Knowing God

The concept of knowing in the Bible has a twofold application. On the one hand, the Bible speaks of knowledge or of knowing in the sense of cognitive understanding, being aware of certain truth. On the other hand, the same word is used to refer to a more personal and intimate knowledge. When the Bible says that "Adam knew Eve his wife, and she conceived" (Gen. 4:1), the idea is of two people knowing each other in a relationship of love, of personal intimacy. If we put the two together, we see that Paul is saying that everyone has intellectual knowledge of the existence of God but many have never experienced the sweetness of that personal knowledge that comes when the Holy Spirit opens one's eyes to see it.

The sermon that catapulted Jonathan Edwards into prominence in the eighteenth century was not "Sinners in the Hands of an Angry God" but "A Divine and Supernatural Light." In that sermon Edwards talked about what happens when God brings someone out of darkness and spiritual death. God does that by giving supernatural light. That is the light that the Spirit has shown in your soul and in the deepest chambers of your heart, if indeed you have seen the light.

We use that expression, "seen the light," to speak of someone who professes new faith. The expression is usually used nowadays in a cynical way, but even in the cynicism the truth is being declared, because that is exactly what happens to us when we come to faith in Christ. We see the light, not through the power of our vision but by the condescension of the Spirit of truth. By divine and supernatural light our hearts are changed. In a real sense, when that happens the Morning Star rises in our hearts. Traditionally Venus has been called the morning star because it reflects the light of the sun before the sun has risen. It is the herald, the harbinger, of the dawning day. In biblical application Jesus is the One who ushers in the day that breaks through the darkness in our hearts.

Sola Scriptura

. . . knowing this first, that no prophecy of Scripture is of any private interpretation (v. 20). We find here another similarity to the writings of Paul, who wrote, "All Scripture is given by inspiration of God, and is profitable for doctrine, for reproof, for correction, for instruction in righteousness, that the man of God may be complete, thoroughly equipped for every good work" (2 Tim. 3:16–17); that is, the Scripture is not of human invention. Its origin and authority come from God Himself.

The way in which Peter crafts the same idea here is problematic. His text has proven to be immensely controversial in the history of the church. The central issue of the sixteenth-century Reformation was the question of how we are saved. Although the doctrine of *sola fide* was heart and center of the Reformation, historians have said that the real cause was the formal issue of authority. In the disputations carried out by Luther and the theologians of the church at Rome, it was shown to Luther that his opinions differed from papal encyclicals, as well as from the teaching of the church fathers and from church councils. Luther stubbornly resisted this, saying that councils and popes can err but the Bible cannot. At the Diet of Worms, when Luther was called to recant, he said, "Unless I am convinced by sacred Scripture or by evident reason, I will not recant, because my conscience is held captive by the Word of God, and to act against conscience is neither right nor safe. Here I stand. I can do no other. God help me."

With the Protestant Reformation, a host of things happened with respect to Scripture. The first was the slogan *sola Scriptura*, meaning that the final authority that governs the conscience of the Christian is not found in the decrees of the church or even in the confessions of the church but in Scripture alone. Out of the Reformation also came the radical activity of translating the Bible into the vernacular. Immediately following the Diet of Worms, Luther was kidnapped by his friends, whisked away, and put in hiding, disguised as a knight at the Wartburg Castle where he undertook the task of translating the New Testament into German. Critics in the church said that if the Bible were put into the hands of the people, it would open a floodgate of iniquity because all would interpret the Bible to suit personal preference, thereby warping its meaning. That has certainly happened, but Luther said that despite the dangers of putting Scripture in the hands of the people, the Bible is clear in terms of the things necessary for salvation so that a child can understand it. If giving the Bible into the hands of people opens a floodgate of iniquity, Luther said, so be it.

With the principle of translating the Bible into the vernacular and putting it into the hands of the laity came another precious doctrine of the Reformation—the doctrine of private interpretation. The doctrine of private interpretation set forth by the Reformers stated that every Christian has the right to interpret the Bible. Rome's response to that was set forth in the fourth session of the Council of Trent in the middle of the sixteenth century:

> Furthermore to check unbridled spirits [the Ecumenical Council of Trent] decrees that no one relying on his own judgment shall in matters of faith and morals pertaining to the edification of Christian doctrine, distorting the holy Scriptures in accordance with his own conception, presume to interpret them contrary to that sense which Holy Mother Church, to whom it belongs to judge of their true sense and interpretation has held and holds.

I agree with the first part, that no person in interpreting the Word of God has ever been given the right to distort the Word of God. The principle of private interpretation, which is an integral part of our Christian experience, says that we are given the unspeakable privilege of interpreting the Bible for ourselves. At the same time, we are given the awesome responsibility to interpret it correctly. What I do not agree with is that only the church has the authority to determine the proper interpretation of the Word of God. That was the issue. Luther was interpreting Paul differently than Rome was interpreting Paul, and they rebuked him for having the audacity to read the Bible and to interpret it independently of the church, even though the church had ordained him and knew him as one of the most brilliant linguists and scholars of the biblical language in his day.

When engaged in disputes as to the interpretation of a particular Scripture text, I have often been rebutted with these words: "Well, that's your interpretation." Of course it is my interpretation, since I just stated it as such. My objector means that I interpret it one way and he in another way and that we are all entitled to interpret it however we wish. However, God has never given us the right to be wrong about the Word of God. That is why we guard our interpretation of Scripture carefully, looking at the best commentaries that we can find, studying diligently, and not relying on our naked ability. We consult the giants of church history and the confessions of the church. Even though they do not have binding authority over us, they certainly can inform us and help us out of errors born of our ignorance. Private interpretation always carries with it the heavy burden of accurate interpretation.

Moved by the Spirit

That being said, I do not think that was Peter's point. If we look at the statement in context, it is not the interpretation of the Bible but the authority of the Bible that Peter is talking about. He is saying that prophecy, that is, the declaration of the Word of God, did not arise out of the private insight or judgment of human beings. He immediately says, **for prophecy never came by the will of man** (v. 21). He uses the most forceful word for "never" that appears anywhere in the Bible. He uses "never" in an absolute sense. Rather, Peter says, **holy men of God spoke as they were moved by the Holy Spirit** (v. 21). He did not mean that Scripture came about because people had religious experiences that gave them a sense of ecstasy so that, as their emotions were moved by the presence of the Spirit of God, they gave voice to the emotion and declared what they believed to be the things of God. Peter means that the content of the Word of God does not arise by human will. Its origin and authority are found in God alone.

Peter does not use the word "God-breathed" as Paul does in Timothy, but he uses another metaphor, that of men being moved by the Holy Spirit and, as it were, being borne along by the Holy Spirit. This metaphor goes back to the language of the sea, and it pertains to the movement of a ship on the waters. Without wind, a sailing ship gets stranded. It is unable to go anywhere. The motion of the ship is not found in the inherent power of the ship itself; rather, it moves when the sails are filled with something external to the ship—the blowing wind captured by the sails. The sails cause the ship to be carried across the waves.

When we talk about the inspiration of the Bible, we speak of the superintendence of Scripture by the Holy Spirit. God did not write the book with His own finger. All the books found in the Bible were written by human beings, but these human beings were moved and protected by the revealing authority of the Spirit of God. In the middle of the twentieth century Karl Barth protested the doctrine of the infallibility of Scripture, saying that such a view involves us in bibliolatry, the worship of the Bible. He called the doctrine of inerrancy "biblical Docetism." The heresy of Docetism in the early years of the Christian church claimed that Jesus did not have a body. Greeks could not conceive of the idea that God would join Himself to something physical, so Docetists said the incarnation was only an illusion. Barth applied this to Scripture, saying that if we believe that the Bible contains the actual words of God, then we are guilty of biblical Docetism. The fundamental axiom, he said, is *humanum errare est*, "to err is human," so if we attribute inerrancy to Scripture, we are denying its human character.

We do not need the Holy Spirit for an inerrant grocery list or to get 100 percent on a math test. We have such a proclivity to error that I expect that if anyone wrote a book as big as the Bible, it would be filled with errors. It is precisely because of the proclivity of human beings to make mistakes that the superintendence of the Holy Spirit is necessary.

When the Holy Spirit superintended and moved the human writers, He did not annihilate their humanity. The style of each biblical author comes through in his writings. In the mystery of inspiration, the Holy Spirit so protected the text that He used the very vocabulary and style—the very humanity—that each author brought to the text, but He preserved each author from teaching error, for the author was being used by the Spirit to communicate God's own word. That is why the prophets in the Old Testament could preface their oracles with "Thus says the Lord." The Lord spoke through Jeremiah, Isaiah, Daniel, Ezekiel, Hosea, Joel, Habakkuk, Nahum, Moses, Paul, Peter, Mark, Matthew, and Luke without annihilating their humanity.

I hear all the time that the doctrine of inerrancy is a magical view of inspiration whereby the human writers were reduced to robots or automatons, and how can anyone believe in the dictation theory of inspiration? Nobody I know of holds to the idea that God simply dictated and the authors wrote down every word that He said. Isaiah was not simply a secretary; he was an instrument who received the revelation of God and was carried along by God. This is the point that Peter is making, that none of the Word of God came solely by human power. However, if you reject the writings of those humans, you are rejecting God Himself. That is Peter's estimate of the authority of the written Word of God, which we must heed every day.

29

FALSE PROPHETS

2 Peter 2:1–7

But there were also false prophets among the people, even as there will be false teachers among you, who will secretly bring in destructive heresies, even denying the Lord who bought them, and bring on themselves swift destruction. And many will follow their destructive ways, because of whom the way of truth will be blasphemed. By covetousness they will exploit you with deceptive words; for a long time their judgment has not been idle, and their destruction does not slumber. For if God did not spare the angels who sinned, but cast them down to hell and delivered them into chains of darkness, to be reserved for judgment; and did not spare the ancient world, but saved Noah, one of eight people, a preacher of righteousness, bringing in the flood on the world of the ungodly; and turning the cities of Sodom and Gomorrah into ashes, condemned them to destruction, making them an example to those who afterward would live ungodly; and delivered righteous Lot, who was oppressed by the filthy conduct of the wicked.

The first chapter of 2 Peter ends with an assertion that the word Peter proclaims was not the result of cleverly devised myths or fables but the sober truth from the testimony of eyewitnesses, those who had beheld the glory of Christ with specific reference to the Mount of Transfiguration. Here, Peter speaks against false prophets and teachers.

We are living in perhaps the most anti-intellectual period in the history of Christendom—not anti-academic or anti-scientific but anti-mind. I doubt if there has ever been a time in church history when professing Christians have been less concerned about doctrine than they are in our day. We hear almost daily that doctrine does not matter, that Christianity is a relationship, not a creed. There is not simply indifference toward doctrine but outright hostility, which is exceedingly dangerous and lamentable. We cannot do even a cursory reading of the Word of God without seeing the enormous emphasis accorded to doctrine and that unsound doctrine and false teaching are not merely errors in abstraction but are profoundly destructive to the life of the people of God.

False Prophets

But there were also false prophets among the people, even as there will be false teachers among you, who will secretly bring in destructive heresies, even denying the Lord who bought them, and bring on themselves swift destruction (v. 1). Peter refers back to the Old Testament to the phenomenon of the appearance of false prophets and then says in like manner that just as false prophets invaded the community of Israel, so there will be false prophets in the midst of his readers.

The most destructive threat to the people of God in the Old Testament was not the armies of the Philistines, the Assyrians, or the Amalekites, but the false prophets within their gates. This is poignantly demonstrated in the book of Jeremiah. God gave Jeremiah His word and told him to warn the people that unless they repented, judgment would come upon them and upon all of Judea, Jerusalem, and the temple itself. Jeremiah's famous temple speech occurred when he went to the temple before the priests of the day and said to them, "Thus says the LORD of hosts, the God of Israel: 'Amend your ways and your doings, and I will cause you to dwell in this place. Do not trust in these lying words, saying, "The temple of the LORD, the temple of the LORD, the temple of the LORD are these""" (Jer. 7:3–4). Jeremiah said to the people:

> "Go now to My place which was in Shiloh, where I set My name at the first, and see what I did to it because of the wickedness of My people Israel. And now, because you have done all these works," says the LORD, "and I spoke to you, rising up early and speaking, but you did not hear, and I called you, but you did not answer, therefore I will do to the house which is called by My name, in which you trust, and to this place which I gave to you and your fathers, as I have done to Shiloh." (vv. 12–14)

Shiloh had been the location of the central sanctuary but was desolate by the time of Jeremiah's words. That was the last thing the people of Israel wanted to hear. They could understand that God would judge the Northern Kingdom and let them go into captivity, but it was unthinkable that God would allow the people of Judah and the holy city of Jerusalem to undergo destruction.

My favorite Rembrandt painting is a portrait of a man seated with his hands on a large book, the Bible, and his face betrays a countenance of utter dismay and distress. If you look closely at the painting, where light seems to come suddenly out of nowhere, you will see that the light is produced by the conflagration consuming the city of Jerusalem. The title of the painting is *Jeremiah Laments the Destruction of Jerusalem.*

Day in and day out, Jeremiah pronounced the oracles of God to the people of God, but the people had itching ears. They did not want to hear the Word of God, and into this situation came a flood of false prophets. Every time Jeremiah spoke the truth to the people, many others came along with a completely different message. Their message was, "Don't worry. God is a God of love and peace. Don't listen to this Jeremiah, this prophet of gloom and doom." Every time Jeremiah spoke the word of God, he was contradicted by myriads of false prophets, so he decided to quit, saying, "O LORD, You induced me, and I was persuaded; You are stronger than I, and have prevailed. I am in derision daily; everyone mocks me. . . . Then I said, 'I will not make mention of Him, nor speak anymore in His name'" (Jer. 20:7–9). However, Jeremiah went on to say, "But His word was in my heart like a burning fire shut up in my bones; I was weary of holding it back, and I could not" (v. 9).

Oracles of Jeremiah

If you look carefully at Jeremiah 23, you will read one of the most vivid accounts of the kind of conflict that took place in Old Testament Israel between the true prophet and his rivals, the false prophets. It begins with an oracle of doom: "'Woe to the shepherds who destroy and scatter the sheep of My pasture!' says the LORD" (v. 1). God was saying woe to the shepherd who is not a shepherd, to that one who does not feed His sheep but poisons and scatters them. Jeremiah continues speaking the words of God:

> Therefore thus says the LORD God of Israel against the shepherds who feed My people: "You have scattered My flock, driven them away, and not attended to them. Behold, I will attend to you for the evil of your doings," says the LORD. "But I will gather the remnant of My flock out of all countries where I have

driven them, and bring them back to their folds; and they shall be fruitful and increase. I will set up shepherds over them who will feed them."

> "Behold, the days are coming," says the LORD,
> "That I will raise to David a Branch of righteousness;
> A King shall reign and prosper,
> And execute judgment and righteousness in the earth.
> In His days Judah will be saved,
> And Israel will dwell safely;
> Now this is His name by which He will be called:
> THE LORD OUR RIGHTEOUSNESS." (vv. 5–6)

Later in the chapter we read:

> My heart within me is broken
> Because of the prophets;
> All my bones shake.
> I am like a drunken man,
> And like a man whom wine has overcome,
> Because of the LORD,
> And because of His holy words.
> For the land is full of adulterers;
> For because of a curse the land mourns.
> The pleasant places of the wilderness are dried up.
> Their course of life is evil,
> And their might is not right.
>
> "For both prophet and priest are profane;
> Yes, in My house I have found their wickedness," says the LORD.
> "Therefore their way shall be to them
> Like slippery ways;
> In the darkness they shall be driven on
> And fall in them;
> For I will bring disaster on them,
> The year of their punishment," says the LORD.
> "And I have seen folly in the prophets of Samaria:
> They prophesied by Baal
> And caused My people Israel to err.
> Also I have seen a horrible thing in the prophets of Jerusalem:
> They commit adultery and walk in lies;
> They also strengthen the hands of evildoers,
> So that no one turns back from his wickedness. . . .

Therefore thus says the LORD of hosts concerning the prophets:
> 'Behold, I will feed them with wormwood,
> And make them drink the water of gall;
> For from the prophets of Jerusalem
> Profaneness has gone out into all the land. . . .'"
"Do not listen to the words of the prophets who prophesy to you.
They make you worthless;
They speak a vision of their own heart,
Not from the mouth of the LORD.
They continually say to those who despise Me,
'The LORD has said, "You shall have peace."'" (vv. 9–17)

Elsewhere Jeremiah said that the people cry, "they have healed the hurt of the daughter of My people slightly, saying, 'Peace, peace!' when there is no peace" (Jer. 8:11). He also declared these words of the Lord:

> "I have not sent these prophets, yet they ran.
> I have not spoken to them, yet they prophesied.
> But if they had stood in My counsel,
> And had caused My people to hear My words,
> Then they would have turned them from their evil way
> And from the evil of their doings. . . ."

"I have heard what the prophets have said who prophesy lies in My name, saying, 'I have dreamed, I have dreamed!' How long will this be in the heart of the prophets who prophesy lies? Indeed *they are* prophets of the deceit of their own heart, who try to make My people forget My name by their dreams which everyone tells his neighbor. . . ."
> "The prophet who has a dream, let him tell a dream;
> And he who has My word, let him speak My word faithfully.
> What is the chaff to the wheat?" says the LORD.
> "Is not My word like a fire?" says the LORD,
> "And like a hammer that breaks the rock in pieces?
Therefore behold, I am against the prophets," says the LORD, "who steal My words every one from his neighbor." (Jer. 23:21–30).

God is not just annoyed or mildly displeased about this but furious at the false teachers, because when the truth is distorted, it reaps devastation and destruction in people's lives.

History of Heresy

In the sixteenth century, two famous men picked up their pen to criticize the wanton behavior of the medieval papacy. Desiderius Erasmus of Rotterdam wrote a satire, "The Praise of Folly," in which he attacked the papal propensity for gluttony and immorality. Luther said of Erasmus, "Erasmus attacked the pope in his belly, but I have attacked him in his doctrine." Because when the doctrine goes, the church goes with it.

I repeatedly hear the plea, "Where can I find a church where the truth of Scripture is faithfully proclaimed?" Preachers are giving people what they want to hear. They are scratching their itching ears to entertain them rather than to instruct them in the things of God. Peter said there is nothing new about that. The same tendency plagued Israel throughout the Old Testament. Peter tells his audience that there are false teachers in their midst. He is speaking here about heresy and its destructive capability.

In one of my graduate school courses, "The History of Heresy," we examined heresies from the first century to the mid-twentieth century. All the heresies with which the church has had to fight have been difficult and destructive, yet in every age the appearance of heresy has forced the church to sharpen her definition and confession of the truth. When Arius denied the deity of Christ, the church convened at Nicaea to declare the full deity of our Lord in what became the Nicene Creed. When Eutychus and Nestorius proclaimed their heresies in the fifth century, the church assembled at Chalcedon and gave further definition and precision to our faith in the person of Jesus. The doctrine of imputation is under attack today as powerfully as it was during the sixteenth century. As much as I decry that, I am glad it has come to center stage. More books have been written about justification in the last fifteen years than in the last three hundred years.

If you want a quick course in the history of heresy, you need not go to graduate school. If you spend much time in front of your television watching preachers, you are likely to see and hear virtually every heresy that the church has condemned from the first century to today.

Swift Destruction

So, Peter wrote, "there will be false teachers among you, who will secretly bring in destructive heresies, even denying the Lord who bought them, and bring on themselves swift destruction." I have to wonder about the propriety of this unnecessary qualifier, "destructive." What other kind of heresies are there except for destructive ones? Heresy destroys the truth of God. That second clause, "even denying the Lord who bought them, and bring on themselves swift destruction," has also been the focus of much controversy. It is the text used by those who deny the doctrine of the perseverance of the saints.

Following from that is the doctrine of particular redemption, which teaches that in God's eternal plan of salvation, He designed the atonement of Christ to save His elect, not to save everyone in general. Jesus' propitiation for sin was made only for those who believe. Christ Himself declared about the church that it would be what Augustine called a *corpus permixtum*, a body containing a mixture of tares and wheat. Christ knew that the church for which He died, in terms of its visible manifestation, would include unbelievers, the non-elect. Peter, in a somewhat oblique way here, speaks about those who deny the Lord who bought them. If they had been purchased by Christ, even their denial would not cause them to lose their salvation.

As was typical among the Apostles, Peter is speaking here of those who claim to be Christians but deny the very act of the atonement. There are many in churches today who profess to be Christians yet deny the atonement of Christ. Peter was saying that the heresies plaguing the early church were so severe that they included even a denial of Christ Himself. These were not Christians who had lost their salvation; as John says elsewhere, "They went out from us, but they were not of us; for if they had been of us, they would have continued with us; but they went out that they might be made manifest, that none of them were of us" (1 John 2:19). Jesus said of Judas that he was a devil from the beginning (John 6:70). It is not as if Judas became a believer and then lost his salvation when he committed apostasy. The sin of apostasy, or falling away, is something that a pagan can never do, because a pagan has never made an affirmation of faith in the first place. No true believer can commit apostasy, but apostasy happens in the church every day among those who claim to have faith but then repudiate it, like Demas, who abandoned Paul when Paul was in prison (2 Tim. 4:10).

And many will follow their destructive ways, because of whom the way of truth will be blasphemed (v. 2). In similar terms Paul said of those seeking to be justified by the law, "The name of God is blasphemed among the Gentiles because of you" (Rom. 2:24). Every time there is a scandal in the church—the moral failure of a priest, minister, or teacher—it is delicious fodder for unbelievers and skeptics. They say that Christians are hypocrites, which is an unfair evaluation because Christians do not proclaim the sinlessness of clergy. We do not hold up the sinlessness of the pastor but the sinlessness of Christ. Christianity must, in the final analysis, be evaluated not on the basis of us but on the basis of Him. However, the reality is that because of heretics and immorality within the church, the truth itself is blasphemed.

By covetousness they will exploit you with deceptive words; for a long time their judgment has not been idle, and their destruction does not slumber (v. 3). Peter charges the false prophets and teachers with covetousness. The false prophet uses people to his own advantage. You are supposed to be able to trust your pastor and elders, and when that trust is violated, God promises swift judgment. God may tolerate it for a season, but not forever.

Fallen Angels

In order to illustrate the judgment of God against this kind of sin, Peter brings our attention to three Old Testament examples. He begins with God's judgment on the angels: **For if God did not spare the angels who sinned, but cast them down to hell and delivered them into chains of darkness, to be reserved for judgment** (v. 4). Peter begins with a hypothetical situation, "For if . . . " There are two possibilities for what Peter has in view here. Some believe this refers to the account in Genesis 6 about the sons of God marrying the daughters of men and bringing forth a race of grotesque people. A view widely held in the church is that the Genesis account is about the rape of women by angels. Some use an exhortation issued by the Apostle Paul to support this view. Paul told women to keep their heads covered in church "because of the angels" (1 Cor. 11:10), and some say the purpose for this was to conceal a woman's beauty lest the angels be tempted. That is, of course, not at all what Paul intended.

The Genesis account of the sons of God marrying the daughters of men is not about angels marrying women, as we noted in an earlier study. Just before this text, we are given a lengthy genealogy of the descendants of Seth, who produced one godly person after another. That line of righteous people is identified as "the sons of God," because that appellation refers to those who are obedient to God. Anyone who is obedient to God is called a "son of God." Yes, angels are sometimes called the "sons of God," but so are human beings. In stark contrast we see the descendants of Cain from whom came a rapid expansion of godlessness and wickedness. The two lines remained separate until they intermarried, and the righteous marrying the unrighteous is what produced grotesque offspring.

Women covered their hair for the angels because the angels watch our worship and participate. When we enter into worship, we enter into the presence of God and all the angels—the presence of the general assembly on high. Worship is to be done in a reverent, submissive, honorable way, which is what Paul was saying to the Corinthians.

So, then, to what does Peter's text refer? It refers to the original fall of the angels. When Lucifer and his minions rebelled against God, God cast them out of heaven and gave to them the habitation of hell. That is the penalty they received. God did not spare them but cast them down to hell. The word used here in verse 4 for "hell," *Tartarus*, refers in Homer's poetry to the darkest portion of hell. Later Dante, in his famous *Inferno*, wrote of the various circles of hell. Each circle contains those of increasing degrees of wickedness. In Homer's poetic vision of the underworld and the place of punishment, *Tartarus* is where the most wicked offenders are consigned. Here Peter borrows an image from the Greek poet, even as the Apostle Paul did from time to time. They "delivered them into chains of darkness, to be reserved for judgment." These angels have a reserved seat for the final judgment, and they have to face the judgment of God without a mediator. God gave us a God-man, the only Mediator between us and Him, but He has made no such provision for fallen angels. They are reserved in hell, in chains and darkness, for judgment.

The End of the Ungodly

Second, Peter says that God **did not spare the ancient world, but saved Noah, one of eight people, a preacher of righteousness, bringing in the flood on the world of the ungodly** (v. 5). It boggles the mind to think of the flood, whether it was universal, as I believe, or even local. The deluge that God sent in judgment upon the human race was extreme. Theologians to this day say that the flood has to be a myth because God is too loving to destroy the whole earth, save for eight people. However, God is also holy, and a holy, righteous God would indeed drown everyone in the world except for one family. God said that His Holy Spirit would not strive with men forever (Gen. 6:3). In those days, the world was given to violence; people did what was right in their own sight. What marked the world prior to the flood was the triumph of moral relativism, and finally God destroyed it, sparing only one family—eight people.

The third illustration contains the destruction that fell upon the cities of Sodom and Gomorrah. The citizens of those cities were particularly wicked, the most prominent sin being sexual immorality and homosexual behavior. It is not by accident that even in our day homosexual behavior is often called *sodomy*; it was practiced without restraint in Sodom and Gomorrah. God's judgment was swift on those cities, and in that case there were not eight people spared but only three. **And turning the cities of Sodom and Gomorrah into ashes, condemned them to destruction, making them an example to those who afterward would live ungodly; and delivered righteous Lot, who was oppressed by the filthy conduct of the wicked** (vv. 6–7). Initially it seemed that four would escape—Lot, his wife, and his two daughters—but as they were instructed to flee from Sodom, Lot's wife looked back and was turned into a pillar of salt (Gen. 19:26). This was the fire and brimstone that the Lord Himself sent upon those cities, because his destruction was swift. Forty-five years ago I heard Billy Graham say that if God does not judge America, He is going to have to apologize to Sodom and Gomorrah.

Lot and Abraham had a close relationship, but on one occasion their herdsmen began to fuss with one another. Therefore, Abraham decided that he and Lot should divide the land and separate. Lot's eyes fell upon Sodom with its lush and fertile fields, and he decided to go there. Sodom was a good place to raise cattle, but not children. There are people who have moved to Sanford, Florida, just to be a part of the St. Andrew's community. For them, the church they attend is more important than the job they have. People do select their residence on the basis of a church, which should not surprise us. We must all consider the well-being of our soul as of much greater importance than the profitability of our business.

These three examples from the past Peter sets forth to warn his readers against being seduced by false teachers. False doctrine produces ungodly living. If we are false in our understanding of the truth, how can we possibly be righteous? It is hard enough to be righteous even when we hold to the truth. Holding to sound doctrine is no guarantee that our life will be sound. If we are going to live by the principles of God's Word, we first have to know what those principles are, but that is only part of the battle. It is the easy part. The hard part is having the moral strength to live by those principles.

30

JUDGMENT

2 Peter 2:4–11

For if God did not spare the angels who sinned, but cast them down to hell and delivered them into chains of darkness, to be reserved for judgment; and did not spare the ancient world, but saved Noah, one of eight people, a preacher of righteousness, bringing in the flood on the world of the ungodly; and turning the cities of Sodom and Gomorrah into ashes, condemned them to destruction, making them an example to those who afterward would live ungodly; and delivered righteous Lot, who was oppressed by the filthy conduct of the wicked (for that righteous man, dwelling among them, tormented his righteous soul from day to day by seeing and hearing their lawless deeds)—then the Lord knows how to deliver the godly out of temptations and to reserve the unjust under punishment for the day of judgment, and especially those who walk according to the flesh in the lust of uncleanness and despise authority. They are presumptuous, self-willed. They are not afraid to speak evil of dignitaries, whereas angels, who are greater in power and might, do not bring a reviling accusation against them before the Lord.

T he reason that the New Testament writers are so emphatic in their teaching of sound doctrine is so that our lives may bear the fruit of the gospel. That is why Peter focuses much of his letter on false

teachers who introduce heresies into the church and exploit people with
deceptive words.

In our last study we looked at three examples Peter used from history
to remind his readers how, on the one hand, God does bring judgment
on evildoers, yet, on the other hand, He rescues those who are faithful to
Him. I want to give a word of warning before we look at this text. There is
much in Peter's words here that is politically incorrect in the terms of our
contemporary culture, but Peter, as an Apostle of Christ, is not interested
in accommodating pagan culture. He is desirous to proclaim faithfully what
God has revealed to him.

Cast into Hell

**For if God did not spare the angels who sinned, but cast them
down to hell and delivered them into chains of darkness, to be
reserved for judgment** (v. 4). This is Peter's exhibit A, God's past judgment of the angels. In our last study we looked at a portion of Genesis 6
concerning the intermarriage of the sons of God and the daughters of men.
As we noted, although some commentators tie the Genesis account to Peter's
words here, I believe that the Genesis account pertains to the intermarriage
between the line of Seth and the line of Cain. When the two lines came
together, there was a radical expansion of wickedness in the ancient world
that ultimately led to God's judgment in the flood.

I think that Peter's words reference the fall of the angels with Satan before
men and women were even created. The angels are a higher order of being
than man, but despite their status in the cosmology, God did not hesitate to
punish them, and He sent them to the darkest part of hell. There they have
been sent for a particular duration until an even greater judgment on the
last day. People assume that if there is a hell (many, even some Christians,
do not seem to believe that hell exists), it is a place of equal-opportunity
punishment in which everyone there is consigned to the same degree of judgment. However, the Bible warns us that God's judgment is always according
to justice and that the severity of divine punishment is allocated specifically
according to our sins.

My mentor told me that a sinner in hell would do anything he could to
make the number of his sins in this lifetime one less, yet today we have no
fear of divine judgment, either for ourselves or for our friends and families.
We have been inoculated with a maudlin concept of the universal love of
God so that any idea of everlasting punishment has been removed from our
thinking. Yet we are brought up short by the teaching of our Lord Himself,

who ironically taught more about hell than He did about heaven. There is more instruction about hell from the lips of Jesus than from any other source, and I suspect that is because if anyone but Jesus told us of this dreadful place of punishment, we would dismiss it out of hand.

Jesus told a parable about a rich man and a beggar named Lazarus. Both died, and the rich man went to hell, and from there, he begged for a drop of water to cool his tongue from the torment. When his request was refused, he asked if he could go back and warn his brothers, who were still alive, lest they would be awakened to the same catastrophic disaster that surely awaited them if they did not repent. That request was also denied, and he was told, "They have Moses and the prophets; let them hear them. . . . If they do not hear Moses and the prophets, neither will they be persuaded though one rise from the dead" (Luke 16:29, 31). Every day people die and are plunged into this utter darkness. Peter is warning us that if God did not spare the angels, He will not spare us.

Peter also uses Noah as an example. God **did not spare the ancient world, but saved Noah, one of eight people, a preacher of righteousness, bringing in the flood on the world of the ungodly** (v. 5). Evil proliferated in the ancient world. Violence filled it, and marriage became a merry-go-round. The institution of marriage was designed by God to last a lifetime, but in those days, just as today, it was short-lived. Even worse was the moral relativism; everyone did what was right in his own eyes. People did not care what God commanded or forbade. People did what they wanted to do, and they claimed that no one had a right to take away their autonomy. Jesus warned how the world would be at the time of His ultimate return, saying, "But as the days of Noah were, so also will the coming of the Son of Man be" (Matt. 24:37).

The culture in which we live is best described not as neo-pagan but as neo-barbarian. Our culture is addicted to evil and to the free expression of licentious passions, and that is the way it was in the days of Noah. The people presumed upon the infinite grace of God, and that was fatal, because God destroyed every human being on the face of the earth, except for Noah, his wife, his sons, and their wives.

Peter refers to Noah as "a preacher of righteousness." Scripture tells us that Noah, relatively speaking, was a righteous man in the midst of a fallen and corrupt world and that he was devoted to building the boat as God had commanded. Likely, there were people who mocked him as he worked. "Hey, old man, why are you building this big boat way out here so far away from the sea?" Noah would have responded, "Well, you see, my friend, it's going to rain, and the rain is going to keep on going for forty days and forty nights. Your only hope of rescue is to be inside this ship, repenting of your sins." Yet no one listened. No one had ears to hear. The sermons of this preacher, Noah, went completely unheeded until the whole ungodly world was inundated by the relentless deluge, which was not an accident of nature but a judgment of God. We see here a portrait of judgment, but we also see a portrait of grace. The ark was the instrument God used to save His people from the flood, just as His church is the instrument that God uses to save His people today.

Righteous Lot

Peter's third illustration has to do with the destruction of the cities on the plain. God turned the cities of Sodom and Gomorrah into ashes, making them an example to those who afterward would live ungodly lives, all except for one. God **delivered righteous Lot, who was oppressed by the filthy conduct of the wicked (for that righteous man, dwelling among them, tormented his righteous soul from day to day by seeing and hearing their lawless deeds)** (vv. 7–8). Twice in this text Peter makes reference to Lot as a righteous man, which seems to contradict what we know of him from the Old Testament. Two incidents from Genesis in particular indicate the opposite of righteousness: Lot offered his virgin daughters to satisfy the lusts of those who came to his home, and later he was involved, however unwittingly, in incest, an act perpetrated by his daughters.

In Genesis 18 we read the account of the news that had come to God of the corruption of Sodom and Gomorrah and how God intended to bring destruction upon these centers of sin. In Genesis 19 we read that two angels came to Sodom in the evening while Lot was sitting in the gate, which means that he was in the midst of where court cases were decided. Lot must have been a man of some influence and authority in the city to be numbered among those who "sat at the gate." Lot spoke to the angels and said, "Here now, my lords, please turn in to your servant's house and spend the night, and wash your feet; then you may rise early and go on your way" (Gen. 19:2). The angels declined and said they would spend the night in the open square, but Lot insisted strongly, so finally the angels agreed to enter Lot's house. Lot made them a feast and baked unleavened bread, and they ate. The story continues:

> Now before they lay down, the men of the city, the men of Sodom, both old and young, all the people from every quarter, surrounded the house. And they called to Lot and said to him, "Where are the men who came to you tonight? Bring them out to us that we may know them carnally." (vv. 4–5)

That is one of the grossest, most lurid descriptions of homosexual sin found anywhere in Scripture. These angels, disguised as men, appeared majestic and handsome, and the men in the town, who burned with lust toward men, came and surrounded the house of Lot. It is not hard to understand why Sodom is a synonym for homosexual sin.

When Lot heard this demand from this crowd, he offered them his virgin daughters. On the surface this seems like a horrific thing to do, but Lot, aware of the nature of the clamoring men, knew that they had no interest in women. He offered his daughters merely to protect the angels within his house. The account continues:

> They said, "Stand back!" Then they said, "This one came in to stay here, and he keeps acting as a judge; now we will deal worse with you than with them." So they pressed hard against the man Lot, and came near to break down the door. But the men reached out their hands and pulled Lot into the house with them, and shut the door. And they struck the men who were at the doorway of the house with blindness, both small and great, so that they became weary trying to find the door. (vv. 9–11)

The passion of these men was so intense that even after they were struck blind by the angels of God, they did not leave. They still groped around blindly trying to find a way to gain access into the house to commit their sin. Then the angels said to Lot, "Have you anyone else here? Son-in-law, your sons, your daughters, and whomever you have in the city—take them out of this place! For we will destroy this place, because the outcry against them has grown great before the face of the LORD, and the LORD has sent us to destroy it" (vv. 12–13).

Like the avenging angel that God would later send against the Egyptians on Passover night, these angels were dispatched by God for the purpose of destroying the cities of Sodom and Gomorrah. God's patience had ended.

"So Lot went out and spoke to his sons-in-law, who had married his daughters, and said, 'Get up, get out of this place; for the LORD will destroy this city!' But to his sons-in-law he seemed to be joking" (v. 14). When Lot gave the warning to his family, they laughed at him.

> When the morning dawned, the angels urged Lot to hurry, saying, "Arise, take your wife and your two daughters who are here, lest you be consumed in the punishment of the city." And while he lingered, the men took hold of his hand, his wife's hand, and the hands of his two daughters, the LORD being merciful to him, and they brought him out and set him outside the city. So it came to pass, when they had brought them outside, that he said, "Escape for

your life! Do not look behind you nor stay anywhere in the plain. Escape to the mountains, lest you be destroyed." Then Lot said to them, "Please, no, my lords! Indeed now, your servant has found favor in your sight, and you have increased your mercy which you have shown me by saving my life; but I cannot escape to the mountains, lest some evil overtake me and I die. See now, this city is near enough to flee to, and it is a little one; please let me escape there (is it not a little one?) and my soul shall live." And he said to him, "See, I have favored you concerning this thing also, in that I will not overthrow this city for which you have spoken. Hurry, escape there. For I cannot do anything until you arrive there." Therefore the name of the city was called Zoar. The sun had risen upon the earth when Lot entered Zoar. Then the LORD rained brimstone and fire on Sodom and Gomorrah, from the LORD out of the heavens. (vv. 15–24)

Fire and Brimstone

Preachers who warn about hell and divine judgment are called "fire and brimstone" preachers, and this story is the origin of that label. Brimstone comes from the sulfur and rock salt and bitumen in the rocks of the plains on which these cities were built. Theorists believe that what happened in Sodom and Gomorrah was a strong earthquake, not a volcano, and the combination of the bitumen, sulfur, rock salt, and noxious gasses that released from the earth with the earthquake created an explosion, a massive conflagration that consumed everything in its path, spewing fire and ashes and poison to such a far distance that when Lot's wife disobeyed the warning and turned around, she was covered by the molten ash. In the earlier judgment of the flood, God saved eight people. From the destruction of Sodom and Gomorrah, He saved three—Lot and his two daughters.

> So He overthrew those cities, all the plain, all the inhabitants of the cities, and what grew on the ground. . . . And it came to pass, when God destroyed the cities of the plain, that God remembered Abraham, and sent Lot out of the midst of the overthrow, when He overthrew the cities in which Lot had dwelt. (vv. 25, 29)

Day of Judgment

Peter reminds his people of the judgment of the angels, the judgment of the whole world, and the judgment that befell the cities of Sodom and Gomorrah, and he says that Lot, that righteous man, who dwelt among these wicked people, had his righteous soul tormented simply by watching and listening to the corruption that was all around him. Yet, Peter continues, **the Lord knows how to deliver the godly out of temptations and**

to reserve the unjust under punishment for the day of judgment, and especially those who walk according to the flesh in the lust of uncleanness and despise authority. They are presumptuous, self-willed. They are not afraid to speak evil of dignitaries (vv. 9–10). Peter means that such wicked people are not afraid to speak evil of the higher powers of the angels themselves, **whereas angels, who are greater in power and might, do not bring a reviling accusation against them before the Lord** (v. 11).

In one sense, it gets worse, as we will see. When our culture becomes seared, when we become accustomed to the evil that we live in the midst of—a culture of evil—we, like the pagans, think that God is dead, and we have no fear of Him. There is no fear of God in our country, yet there is nothing I fear more than God, and there is nothing more fearful than the wrath of God. Every one of us has to be prepared to flee from the wrath of God on that day of wrath and to be like Lot, whose soul was torn, whose heart was broken, when he had to watch and listen to everything going on around him. I do not think that Lot was a self-righteous man, that he considered himself somehow superior to the people around him. I think his heart was broken when he saw a culture given over to licentiousness.

Our culture is not unlike that of Sodom and Gomorrah when they were judged. When the Apostle Paul talks about the expansion of sin within fallen humanity, he says that people not only continue doing evil things but also encourage everyone else to be involved as well. If we look at the history of our country over the last several decades, we can clearly see the fight for absolute free reign in sexual behavior, whether heterosexual or homosexual. In the past such things were considered shameful and were covered up, but today adherents march to demand their rights, and the rest of the world is intimidated and calloused.

31

BALAAM REBUKED

2 Peter 2:12–17

But these, like natural brute beasts made to be caught and destroyed, speak evil of the things they do not understand, and will utterly perish in their own corruption, and will receive the wages of unrighteousness, as those who count it pleasure to carouse in the daytime. They are spots and blemishes, carousing in their own deceptions while they feast with you, having eyes full of adultery and that cannot cease from sin, enticing unstable souls. They have a heart trained in covetous practices, and are accursed children. They have forsaken the right way and gone astray, following the way of Balaam the son of Beor, who loved the wages of unrighteousness; but he was rebuked for his iniquity: a dumb donkey speaking with a man's voice restrained the madness of the prophet. These are wells without water, clouds carried by a tempest, for whom is reserved the blackness of darkness forever.

One of the great concerns that Martyn Lloyd-Jones expressed in his lifetime was the way in which the twentieth-century church removed itself from knowledge of the Old Testament and how very few preachers were preaching from it. I am baffled about why there is so little Old Testament preaching. When I was first preaching, I kept a file of my sermons, and after about a year's worth of preaching, I went through that file and discovered that about 75 percent of my sermons were from the Old

Testament. I see the Old Testament—that thick volume that makes up the majority of the Bible—as the autobiography of God Himself. We need to understand more than anything else who God is, and we are shown that marvelously in the pages of the Old Testament.

In our last two studies, we examined the warnings Peter gives to those who propagate heresy. We looked at the judgment of Noah and that of Sodom and Gomorrah, and we saw from the pages of the Old Testament a certain pattern of judgment that God brings upon people in due time. The most famous sermon ever preached in the United States of America was Jonathan Edwards's "Sinners in the Hands of an Angry God." That sermon was an exposition of an Old Testament passage, "Their foot shall slip in due time" (Deut. 32:35). Edwards wanted to warn the people of New England against becoming smug and confident. We, like the people in Edwards's day, have gotten away with our sin for so long that we have begun to assume there is no God, or, if there is, that He will never call us to account. It is dangerous to think that we will outlive the judgment of God.

When we think about God's judgment and what the New Testament says about the wrath of God displayed against sinners, we normally think of that wrath as being reserved for people who live radically immoral and licentious lives. We typically do not consider such wrath and judgment directed at heresy and heretics. We do not make a connection between false doctrine and corrupt living, but the New Testament does just that.

In Romans 1 the Apostle Paul talks about how God reveals Himself clearly through creation to every human being. His revelation is so manifest that everyone in the world knows that there is a God. The great sin of humanity is that while we know that God exists, we refuse to acknowledge what we know to be true. Paul goes on to show the consequences of suppressing and denying that knowledge of God. It results inevitably in the exchanging of the truth of God for a lie, which then, in turn, results in the practice of idolatry.

Brute Beasts

Here, Peter echoes Paul: **But these, like natural brute beasts made to be caught and destroyed, speak evil of the things they do not understand, and will utterly perish in their own corruption** (v. 12). When truth is distorted or denied, when the truth of God is replaced by the falsehoods of heresy, it inevitably and necessarily leads not simply to intellectual error but to gross moral corruption. That is why Peter warned the heretics about the fate of the world as shown in the Old Testament, when everyone did what was right in his own sight and was destroyed by the flood, and when Sodom and Gomorrah were destroyed. Peter links such judgment to the heretics, who were not afraid to accuse and speak evil even of the angels.

When I think of heresy, I think of the three years I spent in seminary listening to it in unvarnished form every day. I sat under professors with advanced degrees who were outspokenly hostile to the things of God and who did everything in their power to undermine whatever faith remained in the hearts of the students under their care. As I endured those three years, I remember thinking, *Do these men not know what awaits them? Have they no fear of God? Their arrogance knows no bounds, and they are not afraid to deny Christ, to deny the Spirit, and to trample the Word of God underfoot.*

This is what Peter was addressing in the early church—heresy did not begin in the twentieth century. Peter likens the heretics to natural brute beasts. Paul says that in repudiating God's revelation, people, professing to be wise, became fools (Rom. 1:22). Heresy is not usually the forte of the washerwoman; it is the occupation of the scholar and the theologian who are puffed up with knowledge and have no fear of God. Peter says that they are like stupid animals who were designed to be captured in the traps of hunters.

Such people, Peter says, speak evil of the things they do not understand and will utterly perish in their own corruption. Not only will they totally perish, but they **will receive the wages of unrighteousness, as those who count it pleasure to carouse in the daytime. They are spots and blemishes, carousing in their own deceptions while they feast with you** (v. 13). It was Paul who said, "The wages of sin is death" (Rom. 6:23). Unrighteousness earns something for us; sin merits something. I hesitate to use the word *merit*, because the more accurate term is *demerit*. Either way, the point is that we must pay for our crimes against God, which is what Peter is saying to his readers. If you do not repent of these things, you will receive the wages of unrighteousness, and the wages of unrighteousness are death. That is what sin earns. Peter likens the heretics to those who count it pleasure to carouse in the daytime. He is saying that heretics are not like people who are a bit ashamed of their nighttime behavior. Rather, they are so arrogant and bold that they do their carousing in the middle of the day and make no attempt to hide it from the eyes of the world.

It is interesting to note that Peter's words "spots" and "blemishes" are used in a positive form for our Lord and for His body, the church. Our Lord was the Lamb without blemish, and although His church right now still has its blemishes and bad spots, in heaven the church, Christ's bride, will be presented spotless before the Father. Peter's application of these words to the heretics stands in stark contrast. He does not simply say that the heretics are marked by spots, but that they are spots themselves. Their entire being is defined in terms of their blemishes.

Imagine if God were to look at us and see nothing but blemishes. In fact, that is all He would see were we not covered by the cloak of the righteousness of Christ. That is why we should never despise that transfer, that imputation of righteousness, that was given to us freely by God when we put our trust in Christ. Because of that, the Father sees His Son, without spot or blemish, when He looks at us. However, when He looks at the heretic, all He sees are spots and blemishes.

Heretics carouse in their own deceptions. Such deceptions have not been imposed upon them from the outside; they are self-generated. Heretics frolic in these deceptions even "while they feast with you." Peter is talking about heretics inside the church. The great danger in the church are the tares sitting right beside the wheat. In view in Peter's words is the early church's love feast. In addition to the celebration of the Lord's Supper, the church used to come together for a large feast, and in the midst of such celebrations, the heretics were having a ball.

. . . having eyes full of adultery and that cannot cease from sin, enticing unstable souls. They have a heart trained in covetous practices, and are accursed children (v. 14). Their eyes are always looking around for another victim. They are predators. They think only about more opportunities for corruption, and they cannot stop. They cannot cease from sin, and they entice unstable souls. The word Peter uses for "trained" was typically used for the sort of rigorous exercise that gymnasts in antiquity underwent to prepare themselves for competition. These heretics have undergone rigorous training, but it is not training in godliness. It is training in covetousness. Their hearts are trained in greed, for what they want to possess. Their hearts are trained with jealousy and envy toward those who have something that they themselves may lack, and they are "accursed children." They are not the children of God's blessing but of God's curse.

Peter is not describing pagans here but apostates. One cannot apostatize apart from having made a profession of faith, but such profession was false to begin with. These are people who joined the church for every reason except for the right one. They were never true believers. They are unbelievers in the midst of believers, and they will sooner or later depart from the presence of the church. As John tells us, "They went out from us, but they were not of us; for if they had been of us, they would have continued with us; but they went out that they might be made manifest, that none of them were of us" (1 John 2:19).

Balaam Rebuked

Peter goes on to speak of them in this way: **They have forsaken the right way and gone astray, following the way of Balaam the son of Beor, who loved the wages of unrighteousness; but he was rebuked for his iniquity: a dumb donkey speaking with a man's voice restrained the madness of the prophet** (vv. 15–16). They know the right way; they have been exposed to the teachings of the gospel; they know what the truth is—they have heard it proclaimed repeatedly—but they have forsaken it and gone a different way. Paul writes, "There is none righteous, no, not one; there is none who understands; there is none who seeks after God" (Rom. 3:10–11). Every one of us has gone out of the way; we have strayed from the path that God has set for righteousness, and Peter says the heretics have forsaken the right way.

Peter offers this example from the Old Testament: they have followed the way of Balaam the son of Beor, who loved the wages of unrighteousness but was rebuked for his iniquity. A donkey speaking with a man's voice restrained the madness of the prophet.

> Then the children of Israel moved, and camped in the plains of Moab on the side of the Jordan across from Jericho. Now Balak the son of Zippor saw all that Israel had done to the Amorites. And Moab was exceedingly afraid of the people because they were many, and Moab was sick with dread because of the children of Israel. So Moab said to the elders of Midian, "Now this company will lick up everything around us, as an ox licks up the grass of the field." (Num. 22:1–4)

Balak, king of Moab in those days, saw a clear and present danger in the threat of the armies of Israel at his gates. He knew that they had annihilated the Amorites, and the Moabites were next. He sent for a pagan prophet, Balaam, because he wanted Balaam to pronounce a curse upon the armies of Israel. The king sent for Balaam via messengers carrying a large sum of money to pay for the prophet's services. God intervened and spoke to Balaam, saying, "You shall not go with them; you shall not curse the people, for they are blessed" (v. 12).

Balaam was scared, so he spoke to the messengers sent by the king and said, "Go back to your land, for the LORD has refused to give me permission to go with you" (v. 13). So the messengers returned, but the king sent them back once again with the message that if Balaam would come, the king would honor Balaam greatly. Balaam said to the messengers, "Though Balak were to give me his house full of silver and gold, I could not go beyond the word of the LORD my God, to do less or more" (v. 18). However, with God's somewhat strange and conditional permission, Balaam rose to go with the princes of Moab. Balaam was enticed by the offer of the fee and of prestige, so he set out on his donkey, which he had ridden for many years.

Suddenly the Angel of the Lord stood with a sword in front of the donkey, which the donkey could see but Balaam could not. The donkey stopped, and Balaam began cursing the donkey and told him to keep moving. The donkey turned aside and went into a field, and Balaam struck the donkey to turn her back onto the road.

> Then the Angel of the LORD stood in a narrow path between the vineyards, with a wall on this side and a wall on that side. And when the donkey saw the Angel of the LORD, she pushed herself against the wall and crushed Balaam's foot against the wall; so he struck her again. Then the Angel of the LORD went further, and stood in a narrow place where there was no way to turn either to the right hand or to the left. And when the donkey saw the Angel of the LORD, she lay down under Balaam; so Balaam's anger was aroused, and he struck the donkey with his staff. Then the LORD opened the mouth of the donkey, and she said to Balaam, "What have I done to you, that you have struck me these three times?" And Balaam said to the donkey, "Because you have abused me. I wish there were a sword in my hand, for now I would kill you!" So the donkey said to Balaam, "Am I not your donkey on which you have ridden, ever since I became yours, to this day? Was I ever disposed to do this to you?" And he said, "No." Then the LORD opened Balaam's eyes, and he saw the Angel of the LORD standing in the way with His drawn sword in His hand; and he bowed his head and fell flat on his face. (vv. 24–31)

Balaam's Prophecies

Only by divine coercion did Balaam obey God, and then he gave four prophecies, the exact prophecies that the king of Moab did not want to hear. The first prophecy was this:

> Who can count the dust of Jacob,
>   Or number one-fourth of Israel?
>   Let me die the death of the righteous,
>   And let my end be like his! (Num. 23:10)

The king was ready to kill Balaam, who defended himself, saying that he could say only what God had put in his mouth. Then he said:

> God is not a man, that He should lie,
>> Nor a son of man, that He should repent.
>> Has He said, and will He not do?
>> Or has He spoken, and will He not make it good?
> Behold, I have received a command to bless;
>> He has blessed, and I cannot reverse it. (vv. 19–20)

Then Balaam issued another prophecy:

> How lovely are your tents, O Jacob!
>> Your dwellings, O Israel! . . .
> Blessed is he who blesses you,
>> And cursed is he who curses you. (24:5, 9)

Yet it is Balaam's fourth prophecy that is so magnificent:

> The utterance of Balaam the son of Beor,
>> And the utterance of the man whose eyes are opened;
> The utterance of him who hears the words of God,
>> And has the knowledge of the Most High,
>> Who sees the vision of the Almighty,
>> Who falls down, with eyes wide open:
>
> I see Him, but not now;
>> I behold Him, but not near;
>> A Star shall come out of Jacob;
>> A Scepter shall rise out of Israel,
>> And batter the brow of Moab,
>> And destroy all the sons of tumult. (vv. 15–17)

This prophecy, of course, referred specifically to the Bright and Morning Star, who would rise in Bethlehem in fulfillment of the prophecy of this evil prophet of unrighteousness, who spoke the blessing of God in spite of himself and was finally slain by the sword. So, Peter says, these heretics follow the way of Balaam, who loved the wages of unrighteousness. He concludes this section with these words: **These are wells without water, clouds carried by a tempest, for whom is reserved the blackness of darkness forever** (v. 17).

Wells without Water

The film *Sahara*, made in 1942, is the story of a tank commander who survived the Battle of Tobruk. He started out across the desert to the south, after being given the message that the German panzer divisions under Erwin Rommel controlled the north, the east, and the west. The only safe passage was to the south. Much of the drama of the movie focuses on the painful trek across the Sahara Desert with very limited water resources. They knew of an oasis that contained a well, and if they could get to the well before their gasoline ran out, they could survive. After they had traveled about seventy miles through the desert, they came to the well, and when they looked down into the well there was only sand. Similarly, Peter speaks of heretics as being wells without water. Their teaching is sand that will give life to no one.

His second metaphor is clouds carried by a tempest. When people pray for rain in such terrain, they become excited when they see the clouds gather on the horizon. Nothing is more disappointing than to see a strong east wind come and blow the clouds away before rain falls and brings relief to the land. This, Peter says, is what heretics are like. These are the people "for whom is reserved the blackness of darkness forever." In the Upper Room Discourse, Jesus told His disciples, "Let not your heart be troubled; you believe in God, believe also in Me. In My Father's house are many mansions; if it were not so, I would have told you" (John 14:1–2). Every believer has a reservation in heaven, whereas every heretic has a reservation in hell. That is what Peter says.

We need to realize that heresy is serious and that false doctrine is destructive. We must avoid the popular thinking that doctrine is unnecessary. When people say, "All I need is Jesus," they are failing to see that there are a multitude of heretical views of Jesus. We need to know the truth about Jesus, about God, and about the Holy Spirit. We need to know the truth about our own spiritual condition. These heretics had brilliant minds, but they were spiritually dead, and they did not know it.

God forbid that we should be like that.

32

ENTANGLED AND OVERCOME

2 Peter 2:18–22

For when they speak great swelling words of emptiness, they allure through the lusts of the flesh, through lewdness, the ones who have actually escaped from those who live in error. While they promise them liberty, they themselves are slaves of corruption; for by whom a person is overcome, by him also he is brought into bondage. For if, after they have escaped the pollutions of the world through the knowledge of the Lord and Savior Jesus Christ, they are again entangled in them and overcome, the latter end is worse for them than the beginning. For it would have been better for them not to have known the way of righteousness, than having known it, to turn from the holy commandment delivered to them. But it has happened to them according to the true proverb: "A dog returns to his own vomit," and, "a sow, having washed, to her wallowing in the mire."

In our last study we completed our review of the metaphors Peter used to describe the heretics and false teachers who were threatening the church. We also noted the dire warnings found in that section of the text, which are sobering to think about, and Peter continues his revelation of God's judgment in the section before us now.

Empty Words

When they speak great swelling words of emptiness, they allure through the lusts of the flesh, through lewdness, the ones who have actually escaped from those who live in error (v. 18). Other translations simply say that "they are those who deliver empty words." Words are vitally important to our lives. We hear words of promise that we rely on and act upon because we trust them. We hear words of slander or of hostile accusations that wound us deeply. There are organizations that exist solely for the purpose of assessing the damage done to the human psyche by the spoken word. We learn principally through words, both spoken and written. Scripture itself is called "God's Word." Not only do we have the written Word of God in sacred Scripture, but the Son of God Himself is called the Word, the eternal Word, who became flesh and dwelt among us (John 1:14).

Years ago I preached at a small church one Sunday morning. Sometime later a man who had been in the congregation that day approached me and said, "The day you preached at that church, I was wrestling with a decision about whether to go into the ministry. After the service, I stopped and greeted you and asked you a question. After we spoke, I went home, but your words haunted me all afternoon, and I didn't get any relief until I made the decision then and there to give my life full-time to Christian ministry." You might think that I was pleased to hear that I had had that kind of salutary impact on this man's life. On the contrary, I was terrified, and I thought, *How many times have I uttered words that I didn't remember the next day that perhaps wounded people for years to come?* How often we speak without thinking. The thoughtless words we utter can be used of the Lord for good, but they can also inflict great damage.

This is Peter's concern here. He is concerned about the words of heretics and false prophets, which is why he says that "they are great swelling words of emptiness." They are words without content, meaningless words that cannot be trusted.

In graduate school I learned through a course on heresy that throughout church history heretics have been known for taking the words of Scripture and twisting them, reformulating them, and using them in a way that the Bible never intended. Heretics take the words of creeds and drain out their historic meaning and substitute the original words with their own content, and by this they deceive many people.

In the third century, the Gnostics developed some heretical understandings of the nature of God and most importantly of the nature of Christ. They developed a concept called *monarchical modalism*. The idea is simply that God is one, but His being is so pervasive that He generates His own being from the core of Himself. The further these generations go out from Himself, the less perfect and pure they are with respect to deity. Monarchical modalism is a kind of pantheism where everything is god but not at the same level. They saw God as being like the center in a pond into which you throw a pebble, and then ripples come away from the center in concentric circles, and the further away the ripples get from the center, the weaker the motion of the current.

A favorite way of illustrating their doctrine of God was to use the rays that come out from the center of the sun. They distinguished between the sun, which was the core, and the rays of the sun. When the sun shines, those rays travel 93 million miles through space, and by the time they come to us, they are not as hot as the actual sun. If they were, they would kill us. The farther they move from the center, the weaker they are. However, although the sun rays are not exactly the same as the sun, they are of the sun; they are a kind of extension of the sun.

In the third century, a false teacher named Sabellius saw Jesus in this way. He said that Christ is the same essence as God but less than God. The word that Sabellius used to describe this relationship between God the Father and God the Son was *homoousios*, which means literally "of the same essence." This word was crucial to the modalistic heresy of Sabellius. At Antioch in A.D. 267, the church condemned Sabellius as a heretic and repudiated the word *homoousios* and substituted for it the word *homoiousios*, which means "a like essence." That one-letter difference changes the word from "same essence" to "a like essence." The church was trying to say that Christ, as the second person of the Trinity, is not so far removed from the essence of God that He cannot be understood as God; rather; He is just like God. With the rejection of the term *homoousios*, Sabellius and his followers were condemned.

In the fourth century the church faced the most critical heretical crisis in her history up until that time. It originated with the heretic Arius, whom we looked at in an earlier study. By way of review, Arius believed that Jesus and the Father are one, in the sense of sharing the same purpose; he did not believe that Jesus and the Father share the same essence. The dispute that arose was so intense that it became necessary for the emperor to call a council together to study the matter. The Council of Nicaea produced the Nicene Creed.

The Nicene Creed declared that the only word we can use to communicate the full deity of Christ is *homoousios* rather than *homoiousios*. The word that the church condemned in A.D. 267 it embraced in A.D. 325. The church reversed its view at this point because the threat of Sabellianism had vanished, but the danger of Arianism had become severe. To say that the Father, the Son, and the Holy Spirit are one in essence but three in person is a dramatic affirmation of the formula of the Trinity.

A few years ago, a crisis emerged as the result of the publication of a document called *Evangelicals and Catholics Together*. The document came about after representatives from the evangelical world joined with representatives from the Roman Catholic community to take a stand against the relativism and secularism that have invaded our culture. The crisis arose because they declared unity of faith in the gospel of Jesus Christ. Someone pointed out that the statement of unity provoked a strong, negative reaction among many (including me). An architect of the document pointed out that evangelicals and Catholics each mean different things by the words they use to affirm faith. A friend of mine responded sharply to that, saying, "If you know you don't mean the same thing by the words that you are using, how can you foist this off to the Christian world as an agreement?" It was fundamentally dishonest, but the use of studied ambiguity is common. When people attempting to unite come up against areas about which they disagree, they start using language that can be interpreted in more than one way, which is an intentional ambiguity. All that is left are enormous, swelling, empty words. We need to watch out for that.

Slaves of Corruption

The false teachers accosting the church in Peter's day were not satisfied merely to distort the ideas of the gospel; they used their distortion as license for immorality. Moreover, those who were involved in the immorality not only tried to justify their actions with words but also encouraged others to join them in their sin. **While they promise them liberty, they themselves are slaves of corruption; for by whom a person is overcome, by him also he is brought into bondage** (v. 19). They allured, through the lusts of the flesh, people who had recently been exposed to the way of righteousness and had come into the church from out of their godless lifestyle. The false teachers were giving them license to go back to the things they had left with a promise of liberty.

Many sins are justified in the name of freedom. The social historians of America say that the revolution in 1960s America had more impact on our culture and way of life than the Revolution of the eighteenth century. The American Revolution was fought by people who were trying to preserve their way of life. Conversely, the French Revolution was a bloody upheaval intended to overcome the established way of life in France and to bring in a new culture. The so-called bloodless revolution of the 1960s was that kind of revolution—a revolt against the traditional culture of America. All the cultural changes came to pass in the name of liberty.

The Free Speech Movement began with the words of Mario Savio on the steps of a building at the University of California at Berkeley. Much of this movement was less about affirmation of free speech than was about freedom of vulgarity without restraint. However, the Free Speech Movement was a mild thing compared to what followed. Sexual liberation came on its heels, and all the taboos were removed so that people were free to participate in sexual activity with no restraints.

It was no accident that then came the abortion movement and women's liberation. Obviously there were ways that women were exploited in the earlier culture, and certainly chauvinism was a sin of previous generations. However, no movement in our history has created more damage to the social fabric of America than women's liberation. It has not liberated women, nor has it liberated the country. This was followed by gay liberation. All these liberation movements promised freedom but have brought much pain to many people.

When you declare your emancipation from the law of God, you are not free; you become a slave, which is Peter's point in verse 19. To that Peter adds, **For if, after they have escaped the pollutions of the world through the knowledge of the Lord and Savior Jesus Christ, they are again entangled in them and overcome, the latter end is worse for them than the beginning** (v. 20). Similarly, Jesus said that after demons are driven out of someone, if the Spirit of God is not put in the demon's place, many more will come in, leaving one worse off than he was in the beginning (Matt. 12:43–45; Luke 11:24–26). Peter is talking about people who had come out of that barbarian culture and made a profession of faith, but their profession was not genuine. It never took root. The Word fell upon stones and thorns rather than on good soil. They were willing victims of the false teachers, who said that believers are free from the law of God and can do whatever they please. However, if you are accountable to no one, you are free only to be enslaved.

For it would have been better for them not to have known the way of righteousness, than having known it, to turn from the holy commandment delivered to them (v. 21). The contrast Peter gives here is between empty words and holy words, from enslaving words and liberating words. **But it has happened to them according to the true proverb:**

"A dog returns to his own vomit," and, "a sow, having washed, to her wallowing in the mire" (v. 22). These are crude metaphors, but we need only remember that Peter began by calling these people "brute beasts" (v. 12). Dogs were not household pets among the Jews; they were despised scavengers. They were the lowest form of wildlife, and Peter does not hesitate to describe the heretics as being like them. Jews also despised swine, and Peter likens the false teachers to those animals as well. The filth of a pigsty is almost indescribable. Farmers hose off the mud-caked pigs, but no sooner is their skin clean and pinkly shining than they run back to the mud for another roll. The mud is a pig's natural environment. That is the nature of the brutes who lead the sheep of Christ astray. They entice people to leave the truth of God for a greater liberty, and the freedom they find ends in vomit and mud.

Truth divides because it is important, and it is important because the consequences are eternal. Peter is not asking people to hate the false prophets. He is asking them to flee from them and to protect the flock from their influence. That is a task the church has to do in every generation.

33

THE PROMISE OF HIS COMING

2 Peter 3:1–9

Beloved, I now write to you this second epistle (in both of which I stir up your pure minds by way of reminder), that you may be mindful of the words which were spoken before by the holy prophets, and of the commandment of us, the apostles of the Lord and Savior, knowing this first: that scoffers will come in the last days, walking according to their own lusts, and saying, "Where is the promise of His coming? For since the fathers fell asleep, all things continue as they were from the beginning of creation." For this they willfully forget: that by the word of God the heavens were of old, and the earth standing out of water and in the water, by which the world that then existed perished, being flooded with water. But the heavens and the earth which are now preserved by the same word, are reserved for fire until the day of judgment and perdition of ungodly men. But, beloved, do not forget this one thing, that with the Lord one day is as a thousand years, and a thousand years as one day. The Lord is not slack concerning His promise, as some count slackness, but is longsuffering toward us, not willing that any should perish but that all should come to repentance.

A s a Reformed theologian, I have lectured on the doctrines of grace countless times. The five points of Calvinism, represented in the acrostic TULIP, were never set forth by Calvin but were a result of the remonstration of a group in later centuries that protested against elements of Reformed doctrine. The *U* in TULIP represents the doctrine of unconditional election, which teaches that God determined to elect some for salvation out of the fallen mass of humanity, none of whom deserved such privilege, and to pass over the rest, leaving them to their own devices. In the sovereign decree of election, God did not choose people based on any foreseen action or merit on their part but only as He sovereignly decreed.

Those who believe that the doctrine of unconditional election is unbiblical cite 2 Peter 3:9 as their proof text: "The Lord is not slack concerning His promise, as some count slackness, but is longsuffering toward us, not willing that any should perish but that all should come to repentance." When we encounter a verse like this, we have to consider its meaning in the context in which it appears in sacred Scripture, which is why in this study we are considering a large portion of the epistle. We need to understand at least the immediate context in which Peter declares that God is not willing that any should perish but that all should come to repentance.

Beloved, I now write to you this second epistle (in both of which I stir up your pure minds by way of reminder), that you may be mindful of the words which were spoken before by the holy prophets, and of the commandment of us, the apostles of the Lord and Savior (vv. 1–2). Some believe that verse 1 begins a third epistle of Peter's, but that is a technical question that we do not need to be concerned about here. Peter has written these letters to focus his readers' minds, not on new ideas but on the words that they had already heard, in the first instance, from the Old Testament prophets, whom he describes here as "holy prophets."

Throughout this epistle Peter has been warning against destructive heresies, and now he is reminding his readers to keep their eyes on the words that came through the holy prophets. Earlier Peter said that the writings of the Old Testament prophets were not of their own initiative but from God Himself, and with the same sweep of the pen he mentions the commandments that come from him and the rest of the Apostles. It is clear that by the time the New Testament was written, the teachings of the Apostles were considered on par with the teachings of the prophets, so that together the Old Testament prophets and the New Testament Apostles make up the foundation of the church. Both the Old Testament prophet and the New Testament Apostle were agents of divine revelation, so that whatever they taught carries with it the authority of the God who inspired them.

Scoffers

Peter's readers are to avoid the teachings of heretics but to pay close attention to the words of the prophets and Apostles, **knowing this first: that scoffers will come in the last days, walking according to their own lusts** (v. 3). Peter has already given a catalogue of the lusts that come from the false prophets and scoffers. In their scoffing, in their ridiculing of the teaching of the Apostles and the prophets, they are going to say this: **"Where is the promise of His coming? For since the fathers fell asleep, all things continue as they were from the beginning of creation"** (v. 4). In higher critical attacks on the veracity and trustworthiness of the New Testament Scriptures, they focus on the doctrine of *parousia delay*. As we noted earlier, parousia-delay theology basically has its roots in eighteenth-century Enlightenment criticism, and it got its heaviest momentum in the nineteenth century through European Liberalism.

We think, first of all, of Albert Schweitzer, who believed that Jesus was a remarkably wonderful, loving human being who nevertheless suffered from delusions of grandeur. Schweitzer said that when Jesus began His earthly ministry, He thought that the initiation of that ministry would provoke God to bring the kingdom, which was why Jesus went out announcing that the kingdom of God was at hand. When the kingdom did not come right away, Jesus sent out the seventy, hoping that would induce God to bring about the kingdom, but that also ended in failure. Toward the end of His life, Schweitzer said, Jesus began to accept the grim possibility that the only way the Father would be moved to bring about His eschatological kingdom was if Christ were to suffer. So, Jesus set His face like a flint toward Jerusalem, and in the last hours of His agony, He prayed that there might be some other way. He had hope to the end that the Father would send the kingdom in the last hour of His suffering. As He was on the cross, He realized that a last-minute deliverance was not going to happen, so He screamed in pathos, "My God, My God, why have You forsaken Me?" That was Schweitzer's view.

Scholars of the same period said that Jesus' disillusionment presented a difficult problem for the early church. Not only had Jesus expected the immediate coming of His kingdom, but He had made bold pronouncements about His own return at the end of the age. He said, "Assuredly, I say to you that there are some standing here who will not taste death till they see the kingdom of God present with power" (Mark 9:1; cf. Matt. 16:28; Luke

9:27). On another occasion He said, "Assuredly, I say to you, you will not have gone through the cities of Israel before the Son of Man comes" (Matt. 10:23). The most poignant and controversial of His prophecies is found in the Olivet Discourse, when He said, "Assuredly, I say to you, this generation will by no means pass away till all these things take place" (Matt. 24:34; Mark 13:30; cf. Luke 21:32). Because of those statements, New Testament experts said that those in the early church believed that Jesus was coming back during their generation (a generation to the Jews was approximately forty years), but when it appeared that this was not going to happen, they adjusted their theology to accommodate this disappointment, this delay of the *parousia*, and wrote a new eschatology based upon the lack of fulfillment of the original one.

Part of the delay theology is found in Peter's talking about a day in the Lord's sight being as a thousand years (v. 8). Jesus did say that a generation would not pass away, but a generation of forty years multiplied by a thousand years per day allows a long time for the fulfillment of that prophecy. Perhaps that is what Peter was saying here.

Another possible view is that there was no *parousia* delay in the New Testament, and everything Jesus said He would do within the space of one generation, He did do. A judgment did come upon Israel in A.D. 70 with the destruction of the temple and of Jerusalem.

I am simply setting forth the context in which Peter gives us this problematic text, that God is not willing that any should perish but that all should come to repentance. So, in the first instance the context has to do with false prophets who were mocking the early Christian church, saying, "Where is the promise of His coming? For since the fathers fell asleep, all things continue as they were from the beginning of creation." We cannot rule out that Peter's reference to the fathers who fell asleep is to the Old Testament patriarchs, but that would not have much sense for this particular issue. More likely, Peter was referencing the early church fathers who walked with Jesus, the early martyrs, some of whom had already died. Many had died by the time Peter wrote this epistle, and they had died without seeing the promises fulfilled.

The Danger of Forgetting

The challenge, the scoffing ridicule and mockery, was that all things continue as they were from the beginning of creation. Nothing had changed. It was as if the Messiah had never come in the first place. The skeptics of our society say that if the church were erased from our nation, life would be no different, but I do not believe that, for the very reason that Peter brings forth here. He said that when scoffers talk about such things, they willfully forget something: **that by the word of God the heavens were of old, and the earth standing out of water and in the water, by which the world that then existed perished, being flooded with water. But the heavens and the earth which are now preserved by the same word, are reserved for fire until the day of judgment and perdition of ungodly men** (vv. 5–7).

People tend to have selective memories. They remember what they want to remember but forget what they want to forget. It is not simply the words of the prophets and the Apostles that the scoffers forget but the power of God over creation. Pagans despise intelligent design more than any other concept because it challenges their autonomy. They cannot bear the idea that this world and everything in it were brought into being not just by some vague, amorphous, intelligent design but by the eternal, immutable God Himself.

He brought the universe into being by His word. God said, "Let there be . . . ," which is a divine imperative. God is the only being who has the ability to bring something out of nothing by the sheer power of His command. Peter says they had forgotten that. By the word of God the waters were separated from dry land. By the word of God it rained forty days and forty nights. The created order was subject to a deluge sent by God because He would no longer strive with human evil, because everyone was doing what was right in his own eyes. By God's word the worlds were made, by His word the world was covered with water, and by His word the heavens and earth are being preserved.

The Hebrew word *bara*, translated "to create," indicates a sustained action. What God creates by the power of His word, He sustains by the power of that same word. The universe did not just start by His word, but it is preserved moment to moment by the power of His word, and by that same word, it is being preserved until the day of judgment.

The Longsuffering God

Some have a willful forgetting, but to the saints Peter says, **Beloved, do not forget this one thing, that with the Lord one day is as a thousand years, and a thousand years as one day. The Lord is not slack concerning His promise, as some count slackness, but is longsuffering toward us, not willing that any should perish but that all should come to repentance** (vv. 8–9). The fact that all these things have not yet come to pass is not because God is slack. It is not because His word has become of no effect. It is not because He is a God of false promises.

Rather, God is longsuffering toward us. The kingdom had not been fully realized when these words were written because God is unwilling that any should perish.

When Peter says that God is not willing that any should perish, there are two ambiguities to consider. First is with respect to the meaning of the term "willing." In the New Testament there are two distinct Greek words that can be translated by the English word *willing*. It would be helpful to be able to discern the meaning simply by looking at the Greek and seeing which word is used, but it is not that easy, because each of the words has several nuances. The Bible uses the term *will* with respect to God in several ways. Of the three most frequent ways, the first is what we call His "sovereign will" or "decretive will"; that is, whatever God wills must necessarily come to pass. When God willed the universe into creation, He did not wish it; He sovereignly decreed it, and it had to come into being.

The second way in which the Bible speaks of the will of God is in a perceptive sense, that is, in what God commands His followers to do. It is God's will that you have no other gods before Him. That is His perceptive will, His law. It is not a sovereign will that must necessarily come to pass, because every human being by nature breaks that will. We can violate the perceptive word of God, and we do violate it every time we sin.

The third use of the term *will* in the New Testament has to do with the basic disposition of God toward fallen humanity. We can call that the "will of disposition." The Bible tells us, for example, that God does not delight in the death of the wicked or in the punishment of evildoers. He still decrees their punishment, but His doing so is almost like a just judge sentencing his son to prison. He would not do so with glee or delight.

Of these three major usages of the term *will*, we have to ask which one is in view in Peter's text. I think at face value the text is teaching something about God's sovereign, efficacious, decretive will. We have to read this to mean that God sovereignly, efficaciously is not willing that any should perish but that all should come to repentance. The critics of election say that we cannot hold that God sovereignly wills to save some and not others since the text says that He sovereignly wills to save everybody. This does pose some ambiguity as to what the term "willing" refers to here.

The real question concerns the word "any"—"God is not willing that *any* should perish." The assumption that people read into the text is that "any" refers to everyone or any person. If that is the case, then Peter would be saying that God sovereignly is not willing that anyone should perish. Sometimes when an objection is raised to a position, the argument brought forth proves more than the objectors want it to prove. The Arminian objection to the Reformed view of this text is that if God is not willing that anyone should perish, then it proves universalism. It would prove that everyone is saved and that no one perishes, but how can that be squared with everything else the Bible teaches to the contrary?

If we are going to understand this text in its context, we have to consider the antecedent of the word "any." There is no mystery to that; it is abundantly clear in the text itself. God is "longsuffering toward us, not willing that any should perish"—the antecedent of "any" is "us." The only question left to answer is the identity of the "us." That, again, is not difficult. Peter is clearly distinguishing the believer from the unbeliever, the scoffer, and the false prophet. In order to correctly grasp the context of "us" in 1 and 2 Peter, we need only look to whom these epistles are addressed—Peter is writing to the elect. Therefore, the "any" and the "us" are the elect. No passage in all Scripture more strongly defends unconditional election than this one. God sovereignly decrees that none of His elect will perish and that all whom He has chosen will come to Him. They will repent. They will come in faith to Him, because election is not in the abstract. Election is unto faith, repentance, and salvation.

If the kingdom had been finished a hundred years ago, none of us would have made it in. God is not going to consummate that kingdom unless or until every last one of His elect is brought into it. There is no problem here concerning God's sovereignty, but there is a testimony to the grace and mercy of it.

34

THE DAY OF THE LORD

2 Peter 3:10–18

But the day of the Lord will come as a thief in the night, in which the heavens will pass away with a great noise, and the elements will melt with fervent heat; both the earth and the works that are in it will be burned up. Therefore, since all these things will be dissolved, what manner of persons ought you to be in holy conduct and godliness, looking for and hastening the coming of the day of God, because of which the heavens will be dissolved, being on fire, and the elements will melt with fervent heat? Nevertheless we, according to His promise, look for new heavens and a new earth in which righteousness dwells. Therefore, beloved, looking forward to these things, be diligent to be found by Him in peace, without spot and blameless; and consider that the longsuffering of our Lord is salvation—as also our beloved brother Paul, according to the wisdom given to him, has written to you, as also in all his epistles, speaking in them of these things, in which are some things hard to understand, which untaught and unstable people twist to their own destruction, as they do also the rest of the Scriptures. You therefore, beloved, since you know this beforehand, beware lest you also fall from your own steadfastness, being led away with the error of the wicked; but grow in the grace and knowledge of our Lord and Savior Jesus Christ. To Him be the glory both now and forever. Amen.

When I approach the teaching of a New Testament text that deals with future things, with what we call "eschatology," I intensify my plea that the Holy Spirit would help in the understanding of it. Trying to understand all the details of what is set forth in the New and Old Testaments about future things taxes us beyond perhaps any other dimension of biblical understanding.

In our last study we noted that Peter spoke of those who would scoff, saying, "Where is the promise of His coming?" (v. 4). He had in mind those who make fun of the seeming delay of the promises of Christ's coming again and of the consummation of His kingdom. Peter gave instructions to us in that section concerning God's forbearance, and now he turns to the consummation of it: **But the day of the Lord will come as a thief in the night, in which the heavens will pass away with a great noise, and the elements will melt with fervent heat; both the earth and the works that are in it will be burned up** (v. 10).

Day of Visitation

Every Jew of the first century was somewhat familiar with the phrase "the day of the Lord." The expression is deeply rooted in the Old Testament, particularly in the teaching of the prophets. There seems to have been an unfolding progression of understanding throughout the Old Testament about the day of the Lord. The day of the Lord would be the day when the brilliance of His glory would shine so intensely that the entire world would see His majesty and God would vindicate Himself in victory and vindicate His people.

As Israel was brought into conflict with her neighboring nations, the phrase became part of that future prophecy, as we find, for example, in Isaiah. Not only would there be a vindication of God's wondrous majesty, but also there would be a strong element of judgment against the nations that raged against His people. However, when Israel's godliness began to deteriorate, the picture of the future day of the Lord became darker, to the point that when the prophet Amos spoke of the day of the Lord, he said, "Woe to you who desire the day of the LORD! For what good is the day of the LORD to you? It will be darkness, and not light" (Amos 5:18). Increasingly, the concept of the day of the Lord became identified with God's final judgment, which would be a time of supreme blessedness for the faithful but of uttermost doom for those who resist Him and His kingdom.

Closely linked to this idea of the day of the Lord was the concept of the "day of divine visitation." There were two sides to the day of divine visitation.

One side of the day was good news, when God would visit His people and bring redemption. The other side, the dark side, involved judgment. The Greek word most commonly used in the New Testament for "judgment" is *krisis*, from which we get the English word *crisis*. In Jesus' understanding of the significance of His coming into the world, He announced His coming in terms of crisis: "He came to His own, and His own did not receive Him. But as many as received Him, to them He gave the right to become children of God, to those who believe in His name" (John 1:11–12).

There is a third concept, which is linked to these other two, and that is the concept of the bishop, which we noted earlier. The designation comes from the Greek word *episkopos*, a term used in the Greek military for the overseeing general. The Latin term conveys the idea of a supervisor or a superintendent. Supervisors in the industrial world are called to watch what is happening, to make sure that a job is done properly. This idea of the bishop is linked with the idea of the day of the Lord, the day of God's visitation.

To this point in history, the supreme day of visitation was that of the birth of Jesus, but the birth of Jesus brought a crisis that hangs over the world until the final manifestation of the day of the Lord. As Paul warned the people in Athens, God has established a day in which He will judge the world, that that day has already been set on God's calendar (Acts 17:31). We do not know what that day is, but God has established it, and He will come to bring His final judgment on the world.

Like a Thief in the Night

Peter says that this day of the Lord will come "as a thief in the night." The metaphor of the thief who breaks in was used also by Jesus and Paul. The point of the metaphor is that the day of the Lord will come when we least expect it. The thrust of this portion of the text was a call to the first-century church to be vigilant and to be ready. Peter does not assign a date, which is why we cannot be sure whether he was talking about the judgment that loomed over Israel in the fall of Jerusalem in A.D. 70 or about the final judgment. I believe that Peter had in mind the final judgment. Either way, the figure used is that of an unwelcome guest, and more importantly, an unexpected intrusion.

The New Testament tells us that this day will come like a thief comes—unannounced and unexpected. The church is called to be vigilant, always ready for the consummation of the kingdom of God. In our day, a rash of eschatological expectation has taken hold to a significant degree, perhaps because of the creation of the state of Israel in 1948 or because of the Jews' regaining control of Jerusalem in 1967. At that time, some theologians were reading the Bible in one hand and the newspaper in the other. We have seen a massive renewal of interest in eschatology, evidenced by such things as the vast sales of the *Left Behind* series of books.

I have seen numerous predictions of the exact day and hour when Jesus was supposedly going to return. People use all sorts of events and prophetic messages to venture a guess, yet every one of those predictions has failed to come to pass. Because of the unprecedented turmoil that the church was experiencing during the sixteenth century, Martin Luther became persuaded that the coming of the kingdom in its fullness would occur in his day. Jonathan Edwards came to the same conclusion in the middle of the eighteenth century. I have tremendous respect for both Luther and Edwards, but on that issue I know they were wrong.

I am sure, however, that the day is closer now than it was when Luther and Edwards lived. It might happen today or tomorrow, or it may take another ten thousand years. At the risk of sounding cynical, I really do not care about the exact date. I know that God is going to keep His word, and I know that He has set a date. All we need to know is what we are supposed to do in the meantime, which is to avoid getting caught as by a thief in the night. We are called to be vigilant and diligent and to look forward. We will be grateful if He comes tomorrow, but if we die before He comes, we will be at no disadvantage to those who are still alive at His coming. We do not need to be overly concerned about the Lord's timetable other than to obey the principles of vision.

The Coming Fire

Therefore, since all these things will be dissolved, what manner of persons ought you to be in holy conduct and godliness, looking for and hastening the coming of the day of God, because of which the heavens will be dissolved, being on fire, and the elements will melt with fervent heat? (vv. 11–12). The description here is of a cataclysmic conflagration in which the world will be destroyed by fire. If we look at the rest of the prophecies of the coming of Christ, we read of the moon turning to dripping blood and the heavens rolling up like a scroll (Joel 2:31; cf. Acts 2:20). What are we to make of that? The basic principle of biblical interpretation is to interpret Scripture with Scripture. One of the most difficult things about interpreting future prophecies is that they are couched in highly symbolic, imaginative language. This seems to give license to people who want to find literal interpretations in every human event.

I was on a television program once with Hal Lindsey, the author of the book *The Late, Great Planet Earth*. He spoke excitedly to the program host about goings-on in the Middle East. He pointed to some prophetic passages in the Old Testament and said, "These prophecies are going to take place literally, so we must not interpret them figuratively or symbolically." He went on to talk about theologians who water down the Bible by taking away the literal meanings and substitute them with something less. He referenced a prophecy about the earth's being consumed by giant grasshoppers and said that Sikorsky helicopters are the fulfillment of that prophecy. I said, "Mr. Lindsey, if you want to be literal, shouldn't we be looking for grasshoppers instead of helicopters?" We have to be careful with how we handle the Word of God.

When the prophetic utterances of future conflagration took place, all kinds of images of astronomical perturbations were used. When an Old Testament prophet said that the moon is going to turn to dripping blood, he did not mean that someday blood would drip through the sky from the surface of the moon. He was likening the coming judgment to a cosmic upheaval in God's hands. I suspect, however, that Peter was looking for some kind of conflagration that will radically alter the character of this planet.

I do not believe that the Bible teaches a literal end to the world. God judged the world with water in the great deluge during the days of Noah, and He promised never again to destroy the world with water. Destruction by fire is prophesied, and I would not be surprised if God has not stored up a cataclysmic event in the future that involves unprecedented measures of heat that will melt some of the elements, but it is not going to be the end of the world. God has no design to annihilate this present world. His plan is to redeem it.

We are not to understand Peter's words here to mean that God is going to burn up the universe and throw it away. There will be an end to the world as we know it, because we find in this text the same language that we find at the end of Revelation of new heavens and a new earth. However, God is not going to annihilate the old in order to create the new. Instead He is going to redeem the old, shaping it into what He wants it to be.

The whole of creation groans together even now. The impact of sin upon this world does not just affect us, but it also affects the animals, the plants—the whole planet. The planet is reduced to a state of groaning, waiting for this final day when God will make all things new. I am speculating at this point, but when I read these images of fire, I think not so much of fire that annihilates as of the fires of a crucible that produce the final product, removing slag, impurities, and dross. How and when God is going to do it, I have no idea, but I am confident that He is going to do it.

Looking Forward

Peter comes to a conclusion, asking what manner of persons ought we to be. We ought to be people who are marked by holy conduct and godliness, looking for the coming of the day of God, and hastening it. Some think "hastening" means that, by our efforts, particularly in world missions, we can shorten the days. We are certainly encouraged to exert such effort, but I guarantee that all the labor in our hands is not able to change the day that God has appointed from the foundation of the world. I do not know why Peter says this or what he means by it. **Nevertheless we, according to His promise, look for new heavens and a new earth in which righteousness dwells** (v. 13). God is not willing that any of His people will perish; as we noted in our last study, the "we" Peter speaks of are believers.

I hope God does not delay too much longer, because this earth is getting worse. In the 1960s I read an essay from a secular historian who discussed man's margin of error. He wrote about a calculus of violence that could be measured back to pre-Christian days and showed that the first twenty-five years of the twentieth century were the most violent in recorded history. There was more violence and war in the first twenty-five years of the twentieth century than in any full century before that—and this was before World War II. The historian went on to say that as we become increasingly sophisticated in our capacity for violence, we reduce the margin of error so that one pressing of a button can destroy the planet.

By 1945 the United States of America was the first nation in history to have the uncontested ability to rule the world, because it was the only nation that possessed an atomic bomb. No nation on this planet could have resisted the imperialism of the United States in 1945. The only time that a nation had such an opportunity to rule the world but walked away from it was 1945, which is why those living then were the great generation. However, the bomb we had in 1945 was a toy compared to what is stored in the arsenals of the nations today. I thank God that, for the last several decades, nobody has used those weapons, yet when in the history of the world have men invented weapons of destruction that sooner or later they did not use? I am not optimistic. The only possible reason I can give as to why there has been no atomic episode since 1945 is the restraining power of the providence of God. We have no margins left for ourselves. Our only hope is in His restraint over the madness of this world. Nevertheless, we look for new heavens and a new earth according to His promise. In the darkest days, when the margins diminish, we always have in front of us the promise of God, and there is nothing more certain than that.

Therefore, beloved, looking forward to these things, be diligent to be found by Him in peace, without spot and blameless (v. 14). The two most important words with respect to the last things of which the Bible speaks are *vigilance* and *diligence*. We should be watching, but not from some mountaintop, disengaged from the work of the kingdom of God. While we are watching, waiting, and being vigilant, we are called to be diligent concerning our sanctification.

And consider that the longsuffering of our Lord is salvation—as also our beloved brother Paul, according to the wisdom given to him, has written to you, as also in all his epistles, speaking in them of these things, in which are some things hard to understand, which untaught and unstable people twist to their own destruction, as they do also the rest of the Scriptures (vv. 15–16). We have noticed throughout our entire study the number of parallels between the teaching in Peter's epistles and the teaching in Paul's. Here Peter acknowledges Paul as his beloved brother, despite their various points of dispute along the way. We note here also that even Peter struggled with some of what Paul wrote; when we struggle with it, we know therefore that we are in good company.

Peter comes back to the theme of the false prophets, probably the Gnostics, which is found throughout the epistle. The Gnostics were trying to use the epistles of Paul for their own ends. In their distortions of Paul's teaching, they worked their own destruction. This is an important text for those who have sought to understand the early church's view of the New Testament documents. It is clear that Peter, at least, looked upon Paul's epistles as being on par with the Old Testament Scripture. We have the testimony of one Apostle to the authority of another.

You therefore, beloved, since you know this beforehand, beware lest you also fall from your own steadfastness, being led away with the error of the wicked (v. 17). In college I majored in philosophy. I was rebuked for that by those who saw it as a threat to my salvation. They would quote, "Beware lest anyone cheat you through philosophy and empty deceit, according to the tradition of men" (Col. 2:8). I would reply, "How can we beware of something that we are not first aware of?" So Peter says that we are to beware lest we weaken in our resolve, our commitment, and find ourselves led away by error. Even the most dedicated of Christians can get into trouble if they get itchy ears. They can be led away by the sophisticated rhetoric of the gnostics of our day.

Grow in Grace

But grow in the grace and knowledge of our Lord and Savior Jesus Christ. To Him be the glory both now and forever. Amen (v. 18). I have a recurring dream in which I am about to flunk a school course because I failed to attend the class. The point of the dream seems to be that I have failed to do something that I should have done, so I am disqualified. I have yet to see anyone who has earned a diploma from the school of Christ. When we become disciples of Christ, we enter His school for the duration. Our pilgrimage of growth in the knowledge and grace of God will not be over until we get to heaven. Every day we should be seeking to learn new things about God and His kingdom.

In that admonition three things are said about Jesus: (1) He is the Lord; (2) He is the Savior; and (3) He is the Messiah, the Christ.

Peter concludes with doxology, which is the proper place to conclude our study of this portion of Scripture: "To Him be the glory." The final petition of the Lord's Prayer reaches a crescendo with the conclusion, "For Yours is the kingdom and the power and the glory forever. Amen" (Matt. 6:13). We are impotent in spiritual things. All glory is God's, and He will not share it with any man. That should be the capstone of every prayer we pray. "Lord, help me not to forget who You are and who I am. It is Your kingdom, not mine; it is Your power, not mine; and it is Your glory." However, Peter does not end his epistle with "Yours is the kingdom, the power, and the glory." He says simply, "To Him be the glory," which says it all.

I look forward in the new heavens and the new earth to viewing the unveiled glory of God, to seeing Him as He is, to having the vision of blessedness for which my soul was created in the first place—and for which your soul was made. Augustine had it right when he said, "Almighty God, You have made us for yourself, and our hearts are restless till they find their rest in you." As creatures of the living God, we will never experience the fullness of our humanity until we behold His glory. We are going to behold it the first day we are there, and it will be unabated the second day and the third day and long past the time when we ever talk about days or months or weeks or years. We will see His glory forever and ever, and there will be nothing in the new heavens and the new earth to hide or diminish His glory. Amen. It is so.

INDEX OF NAMES

About Ligonier Ministries

Ligonier Ministries, founded in 1971 by Dr. R. C. Sproul, is an international teaching ministry that strives to help people grow in their knowledge of God and His holiness.

"We believe that when the Bible is taught clearly, God is seen in all of His majesty and holiness—hearts are conquered, minds are renewed, and communities are transformed," Dr. Sproul says.

From its base near Orlando, Florida, Ligonier carries out its mission in various ways:

- By producing and broadcasting solid, in-depth teaching resources.
- By publishing and promoting books true to the historic Christian faith.
- By publishing *Tabletalk*, a monthly theological/devotional magazine.
- By publishing *The Reformation Study Bible*.
- By training and equipping young adults, laypeople, and pastors through the Ligonier Academy of Biblical and Theological Studies.
- By creating and releasing recordings of beautiful music.
- By producing and promoting conferences.

For more information, please visit www.ligonier.org.

PUFFIN BOOKS

JAMES AND THE GIANT PEACH

Roald Dahl was born in 1916 in Wales of Norwegian parents. He was educated in England before starting work for the Shell Oil Company in Africa. He began writing after a 'monumental bash on the head' sustained as an RAF fighter pilot during the Second World War. Roald Dahl is one of the most successful and well-known of all children's writers. His books, which are read by children the world over, include *James and the Giant Peach*, *Charlie and the Chocolate Factory*, *The Magic Finger*, *Charlie and the Great Glass Elevator*, *Fantastic Mr Fox*, *Matilda*, *The Twits*, *The BFG* and *The Witches*, winner of the 1983 Whitbread Award. Roald Dahl died in 1990 at the age of seventy-four.

Quentin Blake was born in the suburbs of London in 1932. He read English at Cambridge, and did a postgraduate certificate in education at London University. From 1949 he worked as a cartoonist for many magazines, most notably *The Spectator* and *Punch*. He moved into children's book illustration where his inimitable style has won him enormous acclaim. Alongside this he has pursued a teaching career: he was head of the illustration department at the Royal College of Art and is now a visiting Professor. Quentin Blake was awarded the OBE in 1988.

ROALD DAHL

James and the Giant Peach

Illustrated by
QUENTIN BLAKE

PUFFIN BOOKS

PUFFIN BOOKS

Published by the Penguin Group
Penguin Books Ltd, 27 Wrights Lane, London W8 5TZ, England
Penguin Putnam Inc., 375 Hudson Street, New York,
New York 10014, USA
Penguin Books Australia Ltd, Ringwood, Victoria, Australia
Penguin Books Canada Ltd, 10 Alcorn Avenue, Toronto, Ontario,
Canada M4V 3B2
Penguin Books (NZ) Ltd, 182–190 Wairau Road, Auckland 10,
New Zealand

Penguin Books Ltd, Registered Offices: Harmondsworth, Middlesex,
England

First published in the USA 1961
First published in Great Britain by George Allen & Unwin 1967
Published in Puffin Books 1973
Reissued in this edition 1995
13 15 17 19 20 18 16 14 12

Text copyright © Roald Dahl Nominee Ltd, 1961
Illustrations copyright © Quentin Blake, 1995
All rights reserved

The moral right of the illustrator has been asserted

Made and printed in England by Clays Ltd, St Ives plc

British Library Cataloguing in Publication Data
A CIP catalogue record for this book is available from the British Library

ISBN 0–140–37156–7

This book
is for Olivia and Tessa

One

Until he was four years old, James Henry Trotter had a happy life. He lived peacefully with his mother and father in a beautiful house beside the sea. There were always plenty of other children for him to play with, and there was the sandy beach for him to run about on, and the ocean to paddle in. It was the perfect life for a small boy.

Then, one day, James's mother and father went to London to do some shopping, and there a terrible thing happened. Both of them suddenly got eaten up (in full daylight, mind you, and on a crowded street) by an enormous angry rhinoceros which had escaped from the London Zoo.

Now this, as you can well imagine, was a rather nasty experience for two such gentle parents. But in the long run it was far nastier for James than it was for them. *Their* troubles were all over in a jiffy. They were dead and gone in thirty-five seconds flat. Poor James, on the other hand, was still very much alive, and all at once he found himself alone and frightened in a vast unfriendly world. The lovely house by the seaside had to be sold immediately, and the little boy, carrying nothing but a small suitcase containing a pair of pyjamas and a toothbrush, was sent away to live with his two aunts.

Their names were Aunt Sponge and Aunt Spiker, and I am sorry to say that they were both really horrible people. They were selfish and lazy and cruel, and right from the beginning they started beating poor James for almost no reason at all. They never called him by his real name, but always referred to him as 'you disgusting little beast' or 'you filthy nuisance' or 'you miserable creature', and they certainly never gave him any toys to play with or any picture books to look at. His room was as bare as a prison cell.

They lived – Aunt Sponge, Aunt Spiker, and now James as well – in a queer ramshackle house on the top of a high hill in the south of England. The hill was so high that from almost anywhere in the garden James could look down and see for miles and miles across a marvellous landscape of

woods and fields; and on a very clear day, if he looked in the right direction, he could see a tiny grey dot far away on the horizon, which was the house that he used to live in with his beloved mother and father. And just beyond that, he could see the ocean itself – a long thin streak of blackish-blue, like a line of ink, beneath the rim of the sky.

But James was never allowed to go down off the top of that hill. Neither Aunt Sponge nor Aunt Spiker could ever be bothered to take him out herself, not even for a small walk or a picnic, and he certainly wasn't permitted to go alone. 'The nasty little beast will only get into mischief if he goes out of the garden,' Aunt Spiker had said. And

terrible punishments were promised him, such as being locked up in the cellar with the rats for a week, if he even so much as dared to climb over the fence.

The garden, which covered the whole of the top of the hill, was large and desolate, and the only tree in the entire place (apart from a clump of dirty old laurel bushes at the far end) was an ancient peach tree that never gave any peaches. There was no swing, no seesaw, no sand pit, and no other children were ever invited to come up the hill to play with poor James. There wasn't so much as a dog or a cat around to keep him company. And as time went on, he became sadder and sadder, and more and more lonely, and he used to spend hours every day standing at the bottom of the

garden, gazing wistfully at the lovely but forbidden world of woods and fields and ocean that was spread out below him like a magic carpet.

Two

After James Henry Trotter had been living with his aunts for three whole years there came a morning when something rather peculiar happened to him. And this thing, which as I say was only *rather* peculiar, soon caused a second thing to happen which was *very* peculiar. And then the *very* peculiar thing, in its own turn, caused a really *fantastically* peculiar thing to occur.

It all started on a blazing hot day in the middle of summer. Aunt Sponge, Aunt Spiker and James were all out in the garden. James had been put to work, as usual. This time he was chopping wood for the kitchen stove. Aunt Sponge and Aunt Spiker were sitting comfortably in deck-chairs near by, sipping tall glasses of fizzy lemonade and watching him to see that he didn't stop work for one moment.

Aunt Sponge was enormously fat and very short. She had small piggy eyes, a sunken mouth, and one of those white flabby faces that looked exactly as though it had been boiled. She was like a great white soggy overboiled cabbage. Aunt Spiker, on the other hand, was lean and tall and bony, and she wore steel-rimmed spectacles that fixed on to the end of her nose with a clip. She had a screeching voice and long wet narrow lips, and whenever she got angry or excited, little flecks of spit would come shooting out of her mouth as she talked. And there they sat, these two ghastly hags, sipping their drinks, and every now and again screaming at James to chop faster and faster. They also talked about themselves, each one saying how beautiful she thought she was. Aunt

12

Sponge had a long-handled mirror on her lap, and she kept picking it up and gazing at her own hideous face.

'*I look and smell,*' Aunt Sponge declared, '*as lovely as a rose!*
Just feast your eyes upon my face, observe my shapely nose!
Behold my heavenly silky locks!
And if I take off both my socks
You'll see my dainty toes.'
'*But don't forget,*' Aunt Spiker cried, '*how much your tummy shows!*'

Aunt Sponge went red. Aunt Spiker said, 'My sweet, you cannot win,
Behold MY gorgeous curvy shape, my teeth, my charming grin!
Oh, beauteous me! How I adore
My radiant looks! And please ignore
The pimple on my chin.'
'*My dear old trout!*' *Aunt Sponge cried out, 'You're only bones and skin!*'

'*Such loveliness as I possess can only truly shine*
In Hollywood!' *Aunt Sponge declared: 'Oh, wouldn't that be fine!*
I'd capture all the nations' hearts!
They'd give me all the leading parts!
The stars would all resign!'
'*I think you'd make,*' *Aunt Spiker said, 'a lovely Frankenstein.*'

Poor James was still slaving away at the chopping-block. The heat was terrible. He was sweating all over. His arm was aching. The chopper was a large blunt thing far too heavy for a small boy to use. And as he worked, James began thinking about all the other children in the world and what they might be doing at this moment. Some would be riding tricycles in their gardens. Some would be walking in cool woods and picking bunches of wild flowers. And all the little friends whom he used to know would be down by the seaside, playing in the wet sand and splashing around in the water . . .

Great tears began oozing out of James's eyes and

rolling down his cheeks. He stopped working and leaned against the chopping-block, overwhelmed by his own unhappiness.

'What's the matter with you?' Aunt Spiker screeched, glaring at him over the top of her steel spectacles.

James began to cry.

'Stop that immediately and get on with your work, you nasty little beast!' Aunt Sponge ordered.

'Oh, Auntie Sponge!' James cried out. 'And Auntie Spiker! Couldn't we all – *please* – just for once – go down to the seaside on the bus? It isn't very far – and I feel so hot and awful and lonely . . .'

'Why, you lazy good-for-nothing brute!' Aunt Spiker shouted.

'Beat him!' cried Aunt Sponge.

'I certainly will!' Aunt Spiker snapped. She glared at James, and James looked back at her with large frightened eyes. 'I shall beat you later on in the day when I don't feel so hot,' she said. 'And now get out of my sight, you disgusting little worm, and give me some peace!'

James turned and ran. He ran off as fast as he could to the far end of the garden and hid himself behind that clump of dirty old laurel bushes that we mentioned earlier on. Then he covered his face with his hands and began to cry and cry.

Three

It was at this point that the first thing of all, the *rather* peculiar thing that led to so many other *much* more peculiar things, happened to him.

For suddenly, just behind him, James heard a rustling of leaves, and he turned round and saw an old man in a funny dark-green suit emerging from the bushes. He was a very small old man, but he had a huge bald head and a face that was covered all over with bristly black whiskers. He stopped when he was about three yards away, and he stood there leaning on his stick and staring hard at James.

When he spoke, his voice was very slow and creaky. 'Come closer to me, little boy,' he said, beckoning to James with a finger. 'Come right up close to me and I will show you something *wonderful*.'

James was too frightened to move.

The old man hobbled a step or two nearer, and then he put a hand into the pocket of his jacket and took out a small white paper bag.

'You see this?' he whispered, waving the bag gently to and fro in front of James's face. 'You know what this is, my dear? You know what's inside this little bag?'

Then he came nearer still, leaning forward and pushing his face so close to James that James could feel breath blowing on his cheeks. The breath

smelled musty and stale and slightly mildewed, like air in an old cellar.

'Take a look, my dear,' he said, opening the bag and tilting it towards James. Inside it, James could see a mass of tiny green things that looked like little stones or crystals, each one about the size of a grain of rice. They were extraordinarily beautiful, and there was a strange brightness about them, a sort of luminous quality that made them glow and sparkle in the most wonderful way.

'Listen to them!' the old man whispered. 'Listen to them move!'

James stared into the bag, and sure enough there was a faint rustling sound coming up from inside it, and then he noticed that all the thousands of little green things were slowly, very very slowly stirring about and moving over each other as though they were alive.

'There's more power and magic in those things in there than in all the rest of the world put together,' the old man said softly.

'But – but – what *are* they?' James murmured, finding his voice at last. 'Where do they come from?'

'Ah-ha,' the old man whispered. 'You'd never guess that!' He was crouching a little now and pushing his face still closer and closer to James until the tip of his long nose was actually touching the skin on James's forehead. Then suddenly he jumped back and began waving his stick madly in the air. 'Crocodile tongues!' he cried. 'One thousand long slimy crocodile tongues boiled up in the skull of a dead witch for twenty days and nights with the eyeballs of a lizard! Add the fingers of a young monkey, the gizzard of a pig, the beak of a green parrot, the juice of a porcupine, and three spoonfuls of sugar. Stew for another week, and then let the moon do the rest!'

All at once, he pushed the white paper bag into James's hands, and said, 'Here! You take it! It's yours!'

Four

James Henry Trotter stood there clutching the bag and staring at the old man.

'And now,' the old man said, 'all you've got to do is this. Take a large jug of water, and pour all the little green things into it. Then, very slowly, one by one, add ten hairs from your own head. That sets them off! It gets them going! In a couple of minutes the water will begin to froth and bubble furiously, and as soon as that happens you must quickly drink it all down, the whole jugful, in one gulp. And then, my dear, you will feel it churning and boiling in your stomach, and steam will start coming out of your mouth, and immediately after that, *marvellous* things will start happening to you, *fabulous*, *unbelievable* things – and you will never be miserable again in your life. Because you *are* miserable, aren't you? You needn't tell me! I know *all* about it! Now, off you go and do exactly as I say. And don't whisper a word of this to those two horrible aunts of yours! Not a word! And don't let those green things in there get away from you either! Because if they do escape, then they will be working their magic upon somebody else instead of upon *you*! And that isn't what you want at all, is it, my dear? *Whoever they meet first, be it bug, insect, animal, or tree, that will be the one who gets the full power of their magic!* So hold the bag tight! Don't tear the paper! Off you go! Hurry up! Don't wait! Now's the time! Hurry!'

With that, the old man turned away and disappeared into the bushes.

Five

The next moment, James was running back towards the house as fast as he could go. He would do it all in the kitchen, he told himself – if only he could get in there without Aunt Sponge and Aunt Spiker seeing him. He was terribly excited. He flew through the long grass and the stinging-nettles, not caring whether he got stung or not on his bare knees, and in the distance he could see Aunt Sponge and Aunt Spiker sitting in their chairs with their backs towards him. He swerved away from them so as to go round the other side of the house, but then suddenly, just as he was passing underneath the old peach tree that stood in the middle of the garden, his foot slipped and he fell flat on his face in the grass. The paper bag burst open as it hit the ground and the thousands of tiny green things were scattered in all directions.

James immediately picked himself up on to his

hands and knees and started searching around for his precious treasures. *But what was this?* They were all sinking into the soil! He could actually see them wriggling and twisting as they burrowed their way downward into the hard earth, and at once he reached out a hand to pick some of them up before it was too late, but they disappeared right under his fingers. He went after some others, and the same thing happened! He began scrabbling around frantically in an effort to catch hold of those that were left, but they were too quick for him. Each time the tips of his fingers were just about to touch them, they vanished into the earth! And soon, in the space of only a few seconds, every single one of them had gone!

James felt like crying. He would never get them back now – they were lost, lost, lost for ever.

But where had they gone to? And why in the world had they been so eager to push down into the earth like that? What were they after? There was nothing down *there*. Nothing except the roots of the old peach tree . . . and a whole lot of earthworms and centipedes and insects living in the soil.

But what was it that the old man had said? *Whoever they meet first, be it bug, insect, animal, or tree, that will be the one who gets the full power of their magic!*

Good heavens, thought James. What is going to happen in that case if they do meet an earthworm? Or a centipede? Or a spider? And what if they do go into the roots of the peach tree?

'Get up at once, you lazy little beast!' a voice was suddenly shouting in James's ear. James glanced up and saw Aunt Spiker standing over him, grim and tall and bony, glaring at him through her steel-rimmed spectacles. 'Get back over there immediately and finish chopping up those logs!' she ordered.

Aunt Sponge, fat and pulpy as a jellyfish, came waddling up behind her sister to see what was going on. 'Why don't we just lower the boy down the well in a bucket and leave him there for the night?' she suggested. 'That ought to teach him not to laze around like this the whole day long.'

'That's a very good wheeze, my dear Sponge. But let's make him finish chopping up the wood first. Be off with you at once, you hideous brat, and do some work!'

Slowly, sadly, poor James got up off the ground and went back to the woodpile. Oh, if only he hadn't slipped and fallen and dropped that precious bag. All hope of a happier life had gone completely now. Today and tomorrow and the next day and all the other days as well would be nothing but punishment and pain, unhappiness and despair.

He picked up the chopper and was just about to start chopping away again when he heard a shout behind him that made him stop and turn.

Six

'Sponge! Sponge! Come here at once and look at this!'

'At what?'

'It's a peach!' Aunt Spiker was shouting.

'A what?'

'A peach! Right up there on the highest branch!
Can't you see it?'

'I think you must be mistaken, my dear Spiker.
That miserable tree *never* has any peaches on it.'

'There's one on it now, Sponge! You look for
yourself!'

'You're teasing me, Spiker. You're making my

mouth water on purpose when there's nothing to put into it. Why, that tree's never even had a *blossom* on it, let alone a peach. Right up on the highest branch, you say? I can't see a thing. Very funny . . . Ha, ha . . . *Good gracious* me! Well, *I'll be blowed!* There really *is* a peach up there!'

'A nice big one, too!' Aunt Spiker said.

'A beauty, a beauty!' Aunt Sponge cried out.

At this point, James slowly put down his chopper and turned and looked across at the two women who were standing underneath the peach tree.

Something is about to happen, he told himself. *Something peculiar is about to happen any moment.* He hadn't the faintest idea what it might be, but he could feel it in his bones that something was going to happen soon. He could feel it in the air around him . . . in the sudden stillness that had fallen upon the garden . . .

James tiptoed a little closer to the tree. The aunts were not talking now. They were just standing there, staring at the peach. There was not a sound anywhere, not even a breath of wind, and overhead the sun blazed down upon them out of a deep blue sky.

'It looks ripe to me,' Aunt Spiker said, breaking the silence.

'Then why don't we eat it?' Aunt Sponge suggested, licking her thick lips. 'We can have half each. Hey, you! James! Come over here at once and climb this tree!'

James came running over.

'I want you to pick that peach up there on the

highest branch,' Aunt Sponge went on. Can you see it?'

'Yes, Auntie Sponge, I can see it!'

'And don't you dare eat any of it yourself. Your Aunt Spiker and I are going to have it between us right here and now, half each. Get on with you! Up you go!'

James crossed over to the tree trunk.

'Stop!' Aunt Spiker said quickly. 'Hold everything!' She was staring up into the branches with her mouth wide open and her eyes bulging as though she had seen a ghost. '*Look!*' she said. '*Look,* Sponge, *look!*'

'What's the matter with you?' Aunt Sponge demanded.

'It's *growing*!' Aunt Spiker cried. 'It's getting bigger and bigger!'

'What is?'

'The peach, of course!'

'You're joking!'

'Well, look for yourself!'

'But my dear Spiker, that's perfectly ridiculous. That's impossible. That's – that's – that's – Now, wait *just* a minute – No – No – that can't be right – No – Yes – Great Scott! The thing really *is* growing!'

'It's nearly twice as big already!' Aunt Spiker shouted.

'It can't be true!'

'It is true!'

'It must be a miracle!'

'Watch it! Watch it!'

'I am watching it!'

'Great Heavens alive!' Aunt Spiker yelled. 'I can actually see the thing bulging and swelling before my very eyes!'

Seven

The two women and the small boy stood absolutely still on the grass underneath the tree, gazing up at this extraordinary fruit. James's little face was glowing with excitement, his eyes were as big and bright as two stars. He could see the peach swelling larger and larger as clearly as if it were a balloon being blown up.

In half a minute, it was the size of a melon!

In another half-minute, it was *twice* as big again!

'Just *look* at it growing!' Aunt Spiker cried.

'Will it ever stop!' Aunt Sponge shouted, waving her fat arms and starting to dance around in circles.

And now it was so big it looked like an enormous butter-coloured pumpkin dangling from the top of the tree.

'Get away from that tree trunk, you stupid boy!' Aunt Spiker yelled. 'The slightest shake and I'm sure it'll fall off! It must weigh twenty or thirty pounds at least!'

The branch that the peach was growing upon was beginning to bend over further and further because of the weight.

'Stand back!' Aunt Sponge shouted. 'It's coming down! The branch is going to break!'

But the branch didn't break. It simply bent over more and more as the peach got heavier and heavier.

And still it went on growing.

In another minute, this mammoth fruit was as large and round and fat as Aunt Sponge herself, and probably just as heavy.

'It *has* to stop now!' Aunt Spiker yelled. 'It can't go on forever!'

But it didn't stop.

Soon it was the size of a small car, and reached halfway to the ground.

Both aunts were now hopping round and round the tree, clapping their hands and shouting all sorts of silly things in their excitement.

'Hallelujah!' Aunt Spiker shouted. 'What a peach! What a peach!'

'Terrifico!' Aunt Sponge cried out, 'Magnifico! Splendifico! And what a meal!'

'It's still growing.'

'I know! I know!'

As for James, he was so spellbound by the whole thing that he could only stand and stare and murmur quietly to himself, 'Oh, isn't it beautiful. It's the most beautiful thing I've ever seen.'

'Shut up, you little twerp!' Aunt Spiker snapped, happening to overhear him. 'It's none of your business!'

'That's right,' Aunt Sponge declared. 'It's got nothing to do with you whatsoever! Keep out of it.'

'Look!' Aunt Spiker shouted. 'It's growing faster than ever now! It's speeding up!'

'I see it, Spiker! I do! I do!'

Bigger and bigger grew the peach, bigger and bigger and bigger.

Then at last, when it had become nearly as tall as the tree that it was growing on, as tall and wide, in fact, as a small house, the bottom part of it gently touched the ground – and there it rested.

'It can't fall off now!' Aunt Sponge shouted.

'It's stopped growing!' Aunt Spiker cried.

'No, it hasn't!'

'Yes, it has!'

'It's slowing down, Spiker, it's slowing down! But it hasn't stopped yet! You watch it!'

There was a pause.

'It has now!'

'I believe you're right.'

'Do you think it's safe to touch it?'

'I don't know. We'd better be careful.'

Aunt Sponge and Aunt Spiker began walking slowly round the peach, inspecting it very cautiously from all sides. They were like a couple of hunters who had just shot an elephant and were not quite sure whether it was dead or alive. And the massive round fruit towered over them so high that they looked like midgets from another world beside it.

The skin of the peach was very beautiful – a rich buttery yellow with patches of brilliant pink and red. Aunt Sponge advanced cautiously and touched it with the tip of one finger. 'It's ripe!' she cried. 'It's just perfect! Now, look here, Spiker. Why don't we go and get a shovel right away and dig out a great big chunk of it for you and me to eat?'

'No,' Aunt Spiker said. 'Not yet.'

'Why ever not?'

'Because I say so.'

'But I can't *wait* to eat some!' Aunt Sponge cried out. She was watering at the mouth now and a thin trickle of spit was running down one side of her chin.

'My dear Sponge,' Aunt Spiker said slowly, winking at her sister and smiling a sly, thin-lipped smile. 'There's a pile of money to be made out of this if only we can handle it right. You wait and see.'

Eight

The news that a peach almost as big as a house had suddenly appeared in someone's garden spread like wildfire across the countryside, and the next day a stream of people came scrambling up the steep hill to gaze upon this marvel.

Quickly, Aunt Sponge and Aunt Spiker called in carpenters and had them build a strong fence round the peach to save it from the crowd; and at the same time, these two crafty women stationed themselves at the front gate with a large bunch of tickets

and started charging everyone for coming in.

'Roll up! Roll up!' Aunt Spiker yelled. 'Only one shilling to see the giant peach!'

'Half price for children under six weeks old!' Aunt Sponge shouted.

'One at a time, please! Don't push! Don't push! You're all going to get in!'

'Hey, you! Come back, there! You haven't paid!'

By lunchtime, the whole place was a seething mass of men, women, and children all pushing and shoving to get a glimpse of this miraculous fruit. Helicopters were landing like wasps all over the hill, and out of them poured swarms of newspaper reporters, cameramen, and men from the television companies.

'It'll cost you double to bring in a camera!' Aunt Spiker shouted.

'All right! All right!' they answered. 'We don't care!' And the money came rolling into the pockets of the two greedy aunts.

But while all this excitement was going on outside, poor James was forced to stay locked in his bedroom, peeping through the bars of his window at the crowds below.

'The disgusting little brute will only get in everyone's way if we let him wander about,' Aunt Spiker had said early that morning.

'Oh, *please!*' he had begged. 'I haven't met any other children for years and years and there are going to be lots of them down there for me to play with. And perhaps I could help you with the tickets.'

'Shut up!' Aunt Sponge had snapped. 'Your Aunt Spiker and I are about to become millionaires, and the last thing we want is the likes of you messing things up and getting in the way.'

Later, when the evening of the first day came and the people had all gone home, the aunts unlocked James's door and ordered him to go outside and pick up all the banana skins and orange peel and bits of paper that the crowd had left behind.

'Could I please have something to eat first?' he asked. 'I haven't had a thing all day.'

'No!' they shouted, kicking him out of the door. 'We're too busy to make food! We are counting our money!'

'But it's dark!' cried James.

'Get out!' they yelled. 'And stay out until you've cleaned up all the mess!' The door slammed. The key turned in the lock.

Nine

Hungry and trembling, James stood alone out in the open, wondering what to do. The night was all around him now, and high overhead a wild white moon was riding in the sky. There was not a sound, not a movement anywhere.

Most people – and especially small children – are often quite scared of being out of doors alone in the moonlight. Everything is so deadly quiet, and

the shadows are so long and black, and they keep turning into strange shapes that seem to move as you look at them, and the slightest little snap of a twig makes you jump.

James felt exactly like that now. He stared straight ahead with large frightened eyes, hardly daring to breathe. Not far away, in the middle of the garden, he could see the giant peach towering over everything else. Surely it was even bigger tonight than ever before? And what a dazzling sight it was! The moonlight was shining and glinting on its great curving sides, turning them to crystal and silver. It looked like a tremendous silver ball lying there in the grass, silent, mysterious, and wonderful.

And then all at once, little shivers of excitement started running over the skin on James's back.

Something else, he told himself, *something stranger than ever this time, is about to happen to me again soon.* He was sure of it. He could feel it coming.

He looked around him, wondering what on earth it was going to be. The garden lay soft and silver in the moonlight. The grass was wet with dew and a million dewdrops were sparkling and twinkling like diamonds around his feet. And now suddenly, the whole place, the whole garden seemed to be *alive* with magic.

Almost without knowing what he was doing, as though drawn by some powerful magnet, James Henry Trotter started walking slowly towards the giant peach. He climbed over the fence that surrounded it, and stood directly beneath it, staring up at its great bulging sides. He put out a hand and touched it gently with the tip of one finger. It felt soft and warm and slightly furry, like the skin of a baby mouse. He moved a step closer and rubbed his cheek lightly against the soft skin. And then suddenly, while he was doing this, he happened to notice that right beside him and below him, close to the ground, there was a hole in the side of the peach.

Ten

It was quite a large hole, the sort of thing an animal about the size of a fox might have made.

James knelt down in front of it, and poked his head and shoulders inside.

He crawled in.

He kept on crawling.

This isn't a hole, he thought excitedly. *It's a tunnel!*

The tunnel was damp and murky, and all around him there was the curious bittersweet smell of fresh peach. The floor was soggy under his knees, the walls were wet and sticky, and peach juice was dripping from the ceiling. James opened his mouth and caught some of it on his tongue. It tasted delicious.

He was crawling uphill now, as though the tunnel were leading straight towards the very centre of the gigantic fruit. Every few seconds he paused and took a bite out of the wall. The peach flesh was sweet and juicy, and marvellously refreshing.

He crawled on for several more yards, and then suddenly – *bang* – the top of his head bumped into something extremely hard blocking his way. He glanced up. In front of him there was a solid wall that seemed at first as though it were made of wood. He touched it with his fingers. It certainly felt like wood, except that it was very jagged and full of deep grooves.

'Good heavens!' he said. 'I know what this is! I've come to the stone in the middle of the peach!'

Then he noticed that there was a small door cut into the face of the peach stone. He gave a push. It swung open. He crawled through it, and before he had time to glance up and see where he was, he

heard a voice saying. '*Look* who's here!' And another one said, 'We've been *waiting* for you!'

James stopped and stared at the speakers, his face white with horror.

He started to stand up, but his knees were shaking so much he had to sit down again on the floor. He glanced behind him, thinking he could bolt back into the tunnel the way he had come, but the doorway had disappeared. There was now only a solid brown wall behind him.

Eleven

James's large frightened eyes travelled slowly round the room.

The creatures, some sitting on chairs, others reclining on a sofa, were all watching him intently.

Creatures?

Or were they insects?

An insect is usually something rather small, is it not? A grasshopper, for example, is an insect.

So what would you call it if you saw a grasshopper as large as a dog? As large as a *large* dog. You could hardly call *that* an insect, could you?

There was an Old-Green-Grasshopper as large as a large dog sitting directly across the room from James now.

And next to the Old-Green-Grasshopper, there was an enormous Spider.

And next to the Spider, there was a giant Lady-bird with nine black spots on her scarlet shell.

Each of these three was squatting upon a magnificent chair.

On a sofa near by, reclining comfortably in curled-up positions, there were a Centipede and an Earthworm.

On the floor over in the far corner, there was something thick and white that looked as though it might be a Silkworm. But it was sleeping soundly and nobody was paying any attention to it.

Every one of these 'creatures' was at least as big as James himself, and in the strange greenish light that shone down from somewhere in the ceiling, they were absolutely terrifying to behold.

'I'm hungry!' the Spider announced suddenly, staring hard at James.

'*I'm* famished!' the Old-Green-Grasshopper said.

'So am *I*!' the Ladybird cried.

The Centipede sat up a little straighter on the sofa. '*Everyone's* famished!' he said. 'We need food!'

Four pairs of round black glassy eyes were all fixed upon James.

The Centipede made a wriggling movement with his body as though he were about to glide off the sofa – but he didn't.

There was a long pause – and a long silence.

The Spider (who happened to be a female spider) opened her mouth and ran a long black tongue delicately over her lips. 'Aren't *you* hungry?' she asked suddenly, leaning forward and addressing herself to James.

Poor James was backed up against the far wall, shivering with fright and much too terrified to answer.

'What's the matter with you?' the Old-Green-Grasshopper asked. 'You look positively ill!'

'He looks as though he's going to faint any second,' the Centipede said.

'Oh, my goodness, the poor thing!' the Ladybird cried. 'I do believe he thinks it's *him* that we are wanting to eat!'

There was a roar of laughter from all sides.

'Oh dear, oh dear!' they said. 'What an awful thought!'

'You mustn't be frightened,' the Ladybird said kindly. 'We wouldn't *dream* of hurting you. You are one of *us* now, didn't you know that? You are one of the crew. We're all in the same boat.'

'We've been waiting for you all day long,' the Old-Green-Grasshopper said. 'We thought you were never going to turn up. I'm glad you made it.'

'So cheer up, my boy, cheer up!' the Centipede said. 'And meanwhile I wish you'd come over here and give me a hand with these boots. It takes me *hours* to get them all off by myself.'

Twelve

James decided that this was most certainly not a time to be disagreeable, so he crossed the room to where the Centipede was sitting and knelt down beside him.

'Thank you so much,' the Centipede said. 'You are very kind.'

'You have a lot of boots,' James murmured.

'I have a lot of legs,' the Centipede answered proudly. 'And a lot of feet. One hundred, to be exact.'

'*There* he goes again!' the Earthworm cried, speaking for the first time. 'He simply cannot stop telling lies about his legs! He doesn't have anything *like* a hundred of them! He's only got forty-two! The trouble is that most people don't bother to count them. They just take his word. And anyway, there is nothing *marvellous*, you know, Centipede, about having a lot of legs.'

'Poor fellow,' the Centipede said, whispering in James's ear. 'He's blind. He can't see how splendid I look.'

'In my opinion,' the Earthworm said, 'the *really*

marvellous thing is to have no legs at all and to be
able to walk just the same.'

'You call that *walking!*' cried the Centipede.
'You're a *slitherer*, that's all you are! You just *slither*
along!'

'I glide,' said the Earthworm primly.

'You are a slimy beast,' answered the Centipede.

PUFFIN BOOKS

JAMES AND THE GIANT PEACH

Roald Dahl was born in 1916 in Wales of Norwegian parents. He was educated in England before starting work for the Shell Oil Company in Africa. He began writing after a 'monumental bash on the head' sustained as an RAF fighter pilot during the Second World War. Roald Dahl is one of the most successful and well-known of all children's writers. His books, which are read by children the world over, include *James and the Giant Peach*, *Charlie and the Chocolate Factory*, *The Magic Finger*, *Charlie and the Great Glass Elevator*, *Fantastic Mr Fox*, *Matilda*, *The Twits*, *The BFG* and *The Witches*, winner of the 1983 Whitbread Award. Roald Dahl died in 1990 at the age of seventy-four.

Quentin Blake was born in the suburbs of London in 1932. He read English at Cambridge, and did a postgraduate certificate in education at London University. From 1949 he worked as a cartoonist for many magazines, most notably *The Spectator* and *Punch*. He moved into children's book illustration where his inimitable style has won him enormous acclaim. Alongside this he has pursued a teaching career: he was head of the illustration department at the Royal College of Art and is now a visiting Professor. Quentin Blake was awarded the OBE in 1988.